The Building of

Liverpool Cathedral

Carnegie Publishing, 1991

Though born across the water in Birkenhead, Peter Kennerley has spent most of his life in Liverpool.
He went to school at the Liverpool Institute High School for Boys, in the shadow of the Cathedral Tower, before reading English at Liverpool University. He studied for his postgraduate teaching certificate in a building in Abercromby Square, next door to the old Bishop's Palace.
His lifelong interest in children's books and making good material easily available to children led to his opening the first school bookshop in the country, editing *School Bookshop News*, a magazine for teachers for four years, and being a founder director of The School Bookshop Association. In 1977, he received the Eleanor Farjeon Award for services to children's books and his service to education was marked by the award of the M.B.E. in 1986.
He took early retirement from Liverpool Polytechnic in 1989 to become Cathedral Education Officer and a year later was invited to be the Cathedral *Custos*, with a wide and varied range of duties.

Peter Lynan was a former head chorister at Liverpool Cathedral before becoming Organ Scholar to study with Ian Tracey. He won a scholarship to St. Edmund Hall, Oxford. In 1990 he gave recitals in Liverpool and St. Paul's Cathedrals.

The Building of Liverpool Cathedral

by Peter Kennerley

with a foreword by the Right Reverend David Sheppard, Bishop of Liverpool, and a postscript by the Very Reverend Derrick Walters, Dean of Liverpool.

Published by Carnegie Publishing Ltd., 18 Maynard Street, Preston, Lancashire, PR1 2AL.
Typeset in 10½/12 Times and Caslon, and designed by Carnegie Publishing Ltd.
Printed and bound in the UK by the Bath Press, Bath.

British Library Cataloguing-in-Publication Data
A CIP catalogue record for this book is available from the British Library

ISBN 0 948789 71 9 (Casebound)
ISBN 0 948789 72 7 (Softback)

The Building of Liverpool Cathedral

by Peter Kennerley

Liverpool Cathedral Custos and Education Officer

Picture research by Peter Lynan

Organ Scholar, St. Edmund Hall, Oxford

with a foreword by the Rt. Rev. David Sheppard

Bishop of Liverpool

and a postscript by the Very Rev. Derrick Walters

Dean of Liverpool

Carnegie Publishing, 1991

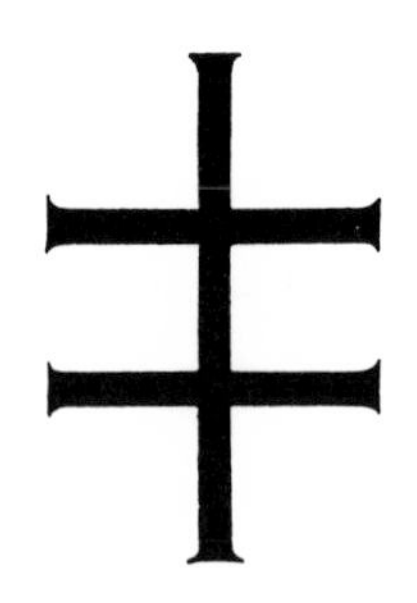

In memory of my parents

Samuel and Gladys Kennerley

who did not live to see the completion of this book

Contents

Foreword

by the Bishop of Liverpool the Right Reverend David Sheppard

Liverpool's Anglican Cathedral is an awesome place: I felt that more keenly than any visitor when I was installed as the new Bishop in the still uncompleted Cathedral in 1975. After all the processions had entered, I knocked and was admitted and then walked through the vast central space 'alone and unattended'. Its soaring arches lifted the heart up and made one small human being very conscious of his dependence on the living God.

In the succeeding years I have entered into the vigorous life of the Cathedral and been part of its great occasions, joyful and sad as they have been. Peter Kennerley writes with love for the place and from within its robust history which is still being made.

His account places the seventy years' building of the Cathedral firmly in the developing history of Liverpool. There have always been at least two Liverpools, Enterprise City, booming in the 1900s, when the plan for a great Cathedral was launched, reviving in confidence today; and Hurt City, which was always there, and which remains part of the reality today.

The 1900s were also some of the worst years of sectarian division and rivalry between Protestants and Catholics. One of the greatest causes for thankfulness in more recent years has been the partnership and trust between the Churches; this is epitomised in our great Two Cathedral Services at Pentecost every other year, when a great Ecumenical act of witness begins with a service in one Cathedral and is completed in the other following a walk along Hope Street, which links the two buildings. That is a great witness to the way in which the two Cathedrals and the Christians of the different Churches of Merseyside and region seek to serve the needs of the city together.

David Liverpool
August 1991

Prelude

Liverpool Cathedral is one of the great church buildings of the world. Unlike many of its medieval counterparts, the process of its construction has been fully recorded in photographs, letters, newspaper articles, reports of meetings, and in the conversations of many of the people who built it. Most of my professional life has been spent as a teacher conscious of the potency of story to listener and reader alike. I am not an historian by training, but I wanted to tell an interesting story.

My first intentions were to tell the story of the fabric, the building itself, but before I had made much progress I knew that I had to try to tell the story of the Cathedral community: the people who planned and built it, the people who work and worship in it. Because Liverpool is a twentieth-century cathedral, it has been possible for me to feel very close to many of the characters in the story. I remember all four Deans, and I have spoken with three of them within the last six months. I have read the letters of the Bishop who inspired the diocese to start building the Cathedral; I have spoken with members of his family and have been given access to family photographs. I went to school in the shadow of the partially completed building. I have spoken with a stonemason who worked on the Cathedral for 49 years: I have many of his tools and I spoke at his funeral in his Cathedral. I am now a member of the Cathedral staff; I am part of that community whose story I am trying to tell.

Only now am I beginning to uncover the riches of the Cathedral archive. This book can be seen only as an inadequate prelude to more detailed studies.

Though Liverpool Cathedral cannot boast that it is the last resting place of the bones of some Anglo-Saxon saint, or that the stonework of the Chancel reveals the ravages of Reformation or Civil War, it is justifiably proud of its rich archive record. I have deliberately made considerable use of letters, reports, sermons, newspaper accounts, and, particularly, of the hundreds of archive photographs.

The book is an attempt to tell the story of the Cathedral from its planning at the beginning of the century to its active role in the life of the city and diocese as we approach the twenty-first century. Essentially it is a book about people: Francis James Chavasse, the Bishop who inspired the building project; Giles Gilbert Scott, appointed architect at the age of twenty-two; Owen Pittaway, Clerk of Works with forty-six years of service on the site; and John Rowbottom, stonemason, whose hands cut and fixed the red sandstone.

Peter Kennerley, 1991

CHAPTER
— *One* —

'The time has arrived'

JUST as the light of a fine summer evening began to fade, the wheels of a hansom cab joggled their way over the cobbles of Manchester Street. To the casual passer-by the cab seemed empty, but there in the well-worn leather of the seats sat the small figure of a man. At first glance he may have seemed only a boy but a prominent head and slightly curved back were those of a man in his mid-fifties. As the cab moved briskly through the deserted street towards the Old Haymarket, the massive bulk of a superbly proportioned classical building stood out against the evening sky, the windows ablaze and the stonework warmed by the final rays of the setting sun. The figure in the cab moved as if seeing the building for the first time. As the cab turned right along St. John's Lane the classical splendour of the whole scene was revealed as he saw to his left the elegance of museum, library and art gallery set against the sloping, terraced gardens, the site of the old St. John's Church and the municipal splendour of St. George's Hall.

Francis James Chavasse, the second Bishop of Liverpool, was returning to the Bishop's Palace in Abercromby Square after preaching in a church on the outskirts of the growing city. He was a new bishop with a great enterprise in his mind for on the following day, Monday 17th June 1901, it was his task to persuade the men of influence in the diocese that Liverpool needed to embark without delay on the planning and building of a cathedral.

The vista which had opened to him between William Brown Street and St. John's Lane inspired and troubled him. On the one hand it spoke of the civic pride of one of the great cities of the Empire; on the other hand the civic pride reminded him painfully that nowhere on the skyline was there a great building to be a visible witness to the presence of God in the middle of this city. The events of the evening focused his mind on the crucial importance of what was to happen the following day in the magnificence of the Council Chamber of the Town Hall. The view of St. George's Hall was a challenge, and a reminder of failure. Less than fifteen years ago there had been plans for a splendid domed cathedral on the site of the old church at the western end of St. George's Hall. Those plans had failed and the Bishop's Throne remained in its cramped and temporary

The cathedral which Liverpool did not build. In 1885 an Act of Parliament authorised the building of a cathedral near St. George's Hall (seen here on the left of the picture), and a competition for designs was held, but neither the site nor Sir William Emerson's plans met with the approval of the people of Liverpool and the scheme was abandoned. Not only would the proposed cathedral have clashed terribly in style with the classicism of the surrounding buildings, but the site would have been extremely cramped. When the second competition was held in 1903, however, Emerson was reputedly quite optimistic that his design would be re-adopted.

home in St. Peter's Church, hemmed in by the commerce of Church Street. The Bishop's thoughts must have been turned towards memories of his predecessor, John Charles Ryle, first Bishop of Liverpool, and as he moved up the hill and away from the river he must have thought about the history of the sprawling city of Liverpool.

Chavasse might well have thought of another journey: that made by Ryle summoned in haste to London on a February day in 1880 by the Prime Minister, Benjamin Disraeli. At the age of sixty-four, Ryle had journeyed to London without any idea as to the purpose of his visit. He had recently been nominated to the Deanery of Salisbury but had not yet made the move from his parish of Stradbrook in Suffolk. The Prime Minister's message to him was short; he offered the elderly evangelical clergyman – six feet four inches tall, weighing seventeen stone, a great sportsman in his youth – the bishopric of Liverpool. 'Well, you strike me all of a heap. I don't know what to say,' he had replied when told that he had to make an immediate decision. He decided, and returned to break the news to his wife: 'I am Bishop of Liverpool.'

His feelings on 1st July 1880 when he took up office must have been as divided as those of his successor twenty-one years later. The challenge was immense and it was a city of such contrasts. As Bishop Chavasse drove up the hill to the Palace he did not need statistics to tell him about the task which had faced his predecessor. Abercromby and Faulkner Squares, Rodney Street, Canning Street, Gambier Terrace spoke of wealth and elegance, but they were shadowed by the vast range of buildings stretching from the new University buildings in Brownlow Hill right across to the Convent of Notre Dame in Mount Pleasant – the Workhouse, home, if you could call it that, to five thousand people.

Liverpool was a city of wealth: second city of the land, handling a greater tonnage of cargo than the Port of London. The wealthy traders and shipowners had built their elegant town houses in wide tree-lined roads and beautifully proportioned squares. Neither Bishop needed to be reminded that so much of Liverpool's wealth was based on the privateer and the slave trade. Though the rich might live in comfort and prosperity overlooking Joseph Paxton's Princes Park or the riverside residences of Grassendale and Cressington, thousands of young, old, sick and destitute lived rough, sleeping out in the streets. The slum conditions in the courts and cellars were as bad as could be found anywhere in Europe. The hungry 'forties brought wave after wave of starving Irish who had paid sixpence to huddle on the deck of a boat carrying them and the clothes they stood up in, from the starvation of the potato famines to the abject poverty of the Liverpool slum with its attendant cholera, dysentery and malnutrition.

But the good men of Liverpool had raised £100,000 to endow the new bishopric which was carved out of the extensive Bishopric of Chester, and hopes were high that the first bishop would lead the campaign for the building of a great cathedral to take its place on the city skyline with the

Left: *St. Peter's Church in Church Street became the pro-cathedral and functioned as such until 1910; all that is left is a brass consecration cross in the pavement. The building on the right now houses a branch of Marks and Spencer. There was strong opposition to the demolition of the church and selling of the site.*

Below: *The interior of the pro-cathedral. Clearly, it was totally inadequate for use as a cathedral, being far too small to seat large congregations.*

important civic buildings.

The new Bishop had his own order of priorities. He knew the richness and diversity of his extensive diocese and he knew how stretched were the resources of the existing parishes after the massive population increases of the century. All the people needed the services of the clergy and the Church 'should never rest until there is neither a street, nor a lane, nor a house, nor a garret, nor a cellar, nor a family, which is not regularly looked after'. Though every diocese needed a cathedral as its mother church the 'first and foremost business as Bishop of a new diocese was to provide for the preaching of the Gospel to souls'. Sir William Forwood, Lord Mayor at the time of Ryle's enthronement, was eager for a cathedral on the site of the old St. John's Church, near to St. George's Hall. A design was prepared by Sir William Emerson, but after three years the scheme failed through lack of enthusiasm. The failure of the plan weighed heavily on the mind of the second bishop on that night in June 1901.

His predecessor had probably been right to use the Church's limited financial resources out in the parishes, but further delay now in embarking on the building of a cathedral would surely be wrong. The services at St. Peter's Church were well-ordered, but the building was narrow and cramped and lacking in the size and splendour needed in the design for a cathedral in a thriving, prosperous city. However firm his faith in the project, he must have been daunted that, apart from Truro, no other cathedral had been built in England on a new site for six hundred years. He, Francis James Chavasse, had to inspire his diocese into undertaking this great work. Unlike his predecessor, he was not an imposing figure physically - complications after an attack of measles had led to curvature of the spine - but he became a small figure recognised throughout his diocese and held in high affection.

As the new Bishop he had several heartening conversations with distinguished men from his diocese. Sir William Forwood, central to the original plan, had agreed to help again, though on rather strange terms: no committee and no mention of a specific site, and the agreement to campaign for funds for six weeks. The Bishop had been amused by the terms of this offer; to raise enough to build a great cathedral would take a lifetime. But maybe he remembered the story of five loaves and two fishes. Sir William was a tall, commanding figure with greying hair and beard; a man of standing in the community; a man who would not take kindly to failure.

Together with Sir Alfred Jones, Sir William had driven out to Knowsley to put their need before the Earl of Derby. They did not come away disappointed. His lordship received them kindly, headed their subscription list with a donation of £10,000 and showed his willingness to put his influence behind the new cathedral scheme. The journey out to Knowsley must have been salutary. The new cathedral was to be the cathedral of that whole widespread diocese, not just the city of Liverpool itself, a fact readily acknowledged by the new Bishop. Cathedral was in the air; the new lord mayor was behind the scheme and the new Bishop seemed to have a magnetic quality which inspired the confidence of his people. Liverpool might have failed once, but it was not going to fail again.

Though Sir William Forwood was not making mention of a site for the cathedral in his fund-raising work, a number of minds were studying maps and viewing several possible

Bishop Chavasse preaching from the pulpit of St. Peter's Church. Will Morgan's depiction of the Bishop is an excellent representation of the man.

sites. At a meeting early in December 1900 five possible sites were considered: St. James's Cemetery; Commutation Row; Monument Place; Abercromby Square; and St. George's Dock. Later in the same month, people were considering the St. Peter's site, Monument Place and St. James's Cemetery. In the view of many people, the first cathedral plans had not been successful because the site near St. George's Hall had not inspired confidence. Any building there would inevitably have been somewhat overshadowed by the sheer bulk of the great classical building. The site normally referred to as Monument Place had a lot of support. It was the triangle of ground where London Road and Islington merge, and had great potential as a site provided that a number of existing buildings could be demolished; to build there would be very costly. The other contender for people's consideration was St. James's Mount, an imposing ridge on the river side of a large quarry, now a municipal cemetery.

Partly for sentimental reasons, some in the diocese favoured the building of the cathedral on the site of St. Peter's Church, but that site was cramped and would have cost in the region of £150,000 – about the same as the Monument Place site. Sir William Forwood was strongly in support of the St. James's Mount site, and wrote enthusiastically to the Bishop in May 1901:

> Money keeps coming in and if we only decide in favour of St. James's Mount site – it will roll in – we now reach £116,000 – the Mount would cost us £20,000. I wish you would go and look at it. Walk over it, then round the cemetery and through the cemetery – look at it from the south east corner of the cemetery; it is simply an ideal site from an architectural point of view. Then it would be so quiet, free from all noises and yet within a quarter of a mile radius it has a large church-going population and it is within cab drive from all the stations and close to main lines of trams. The surroundings of Monument Place are very low – within one hundred yards we have the abattoir and within the same distance in the other Blandford Street, the street of very evil repute. Tramways run on either side every minute – it is flanked on the South by six public houses and on the North by seven.

Meetings of clergy and laity had discussed the issues at length and a number of positive proposals had been made, but to awaken the diocese there was a need for a great public meeting to launch the new scheme. The fine newly completed Council Chamber of the Town Hall was chosen as the venue for the meeting, and on Monday 17th June 1901 at 3.00 p.m. it was filled to overflowing for one of the most important meetings ever to be held there. The significance of the date had not been overlooked by the Lord Mayor as he welcomed people to the meeting. They were meeting on St. Alban's Day; six hundred years previously the first British martyr had died for his faith, though the Church for which he stood had grown and spread.

The Earl of Derby took the Chair. His long speech made clear his own strong support for the cathedral scheme, and he stressed the importance of rapid progress over the whole matter. Though he made an influential speech, Lord Derby knew that it was to the Bishop that the diocese looked on this great occasion, and that it was his words which would decide the future. So in the Victorian splendour of the Council Chamber, the diminutive figure of the Right Reverend Francis James Chavasse rose to address the representatives of his diocese. Even much later, at the end of his life, he had an extraordinarily impressive voice, and on that hot summer day in Liverpool he was humbly aware that the meeting was waiting for his words:

> My Lord, my Lord Mayor, and Gentlemen: I never rose up to face a meeting with a greater feeling of responsibility and awe than I rise up to move this resolution which has been placed in my hands. The resolution is this – 'That this public meeting of the Diocese of Liverpool is of opinion that the time has arrived when active steps should be taken to provide a Cathedral for the Diocese'. My Lord, that is an epoch-making resolution. It means a new era for the Diocese, a new witness for God in this great commercial city, and a new source of strength for the Church of England . . . The Church of England has since the Reformation built only one Cathedral, and that in the remote and poor Diocese of Truro. It speaks well I think for the sagacity, for the faith, for the courage, and for the noble self-sacrifice of Cornishmen that they have set the whole of England such an example in this respect. We have before us here in Liverpool a greater scheme than that of Truro. We are about, by God's help, to build a Cathedral in Liverpool, in a diocese four times the size of that of Truro, in the midst of a great commercial city . . .

The Right Reverend Francis James Chavasse in 1901. Although Chavasse had been a prominent figure in Oxford, first as Rector of St. Peter-le-Bailey and then as Principal of Wycliffe Hall, he had to establish himself in Liverpool as a man capable of leading a troubled diocese into the twentieth century. He was never reconciled with some of the extreme Anglo-Catholics in Liverpool.

The Bishop knew that he would have to leave a few very clearly stated points in the minds of the people. Aspirations had to be crystalised if they were to lead forward to positive action. He put the main lines of argument in front of the meeting:

> Might I be allowed to remind you briefly why the Cathedral is needed? First, it will be a visible witness for God in the midst of the great city . . . Why not something to speak for God in this great city as St. George's Hall speaks for our great municipality? Secondly, a Cathedral is needed for diocesan and popular services. Thrice in the course of my brief residence among you we have felt the need for such a building as a Cathedral.

The Bishop thought back to the impossibility of conducting properly the service to mark the death of Queen Victoria in the cramped temporary cathedral building in Church Street.

> Thirdly, we need a Cathedral which will express and deepen the spiritual longings and aspirations of many among us.

The people of Liverpool deserved and needed a building with the majestic qualities of a St. Paul's Cathedral or a Westminster Abbey. Chavasse had the very highest ideals for the new Cathedral.

The oldest existing photograph of the Cathedral site, from the corner of Rodney Street and Duke Street. To the left is the Oratory, the mortuary chapel for the cemetery. This photograph was taken before work started on the site in 1903, possibly as early as 1901.

> It must in the first place be worthy of Liverpool. We must give to God not that which costs us nothing, but the very best that Liverpool and the Diocese of Liverpool can afford. We must build for posterity, we must take a leaf out of the book of our noble forefathers, who have handed down to us those great Cathedrals which are among the greatest heritages of the English nation. We must leave to those who come after us at least the beginning, if not the completion of a Cathedral equal to any that has come down to us. Secondly the Cathedral must be a Cathedral of the whole Diocese . . . Lastly, it must be the offering of all classes. The other day I had the happiness of sending to the bank a cheque for £1,000 and five shillings in postage stamps, the one sent by a most distinguished resident of this city, and the other by 'a poor working man', as he called himself, who did not sign his name.

From the interrupting surge of applause from the audience, the Bishop must have known for sure the rightness of his case, and he warmed to the obvious affection of all of his people:

> I trust that when this Cathedral is built it will be built not only by the thousands and tens of thousands contributed by the rich, but also by the pence of our poor, and that through the length and breadth of this great Diocese the Sunday School children and the poor working people will be able to look up to it and say 'we helped to build it', for nothing, I believe, will so much help to draw to our Church of England those whom we sometimes call 'the lapsed masses', as making them feel that they have an interest in the concern, and that the Church belongs to them, and that they belong to the Church.

The warmth of the reception made it quite clear that the Bishop's proposals were carried without hesitation by the whole meeting.

Wise minds who had remembered the humiliating failure of the first cathedral plan recognised that there was only one possible stumbling block, and that was the question of the site. Arguments had raged in the press, and there was at least one gentleman present brandishing a lengthy

The view from Hope Street across the end of the cemetery. The chaplain's house and the mortuary chapel can be seen to left and right, with the houses of St. James's Road in the centre. Many later photographs taken from this position chart the progress of the building.

petition against the proposal to adopt the St. James's Mount site. Strategies were well-formulated; the Honourable Arthur Stanley MP rose to his feet to put the resolution that the St. James's Mount site be accepted, and it was eventually approved by an overwhelming majority.

Up to this day, the Bishop had wisely worked with the support of a very small committee, but now the time was right to draw together a much larger and more comprehensive committee whose combined wisdom and expertise could carry the project forward into the practical business of building. Such a committee was proposed by the Venerable Archdeacon Taylor. Sir William Forwood was proud to announce that in response to his financial appeals he already had promises amounting to £134,868; the money was beginning to flow, and it looked as though the long-running battle of the sites was over.

It was a tired but an exhilarated Bishop who was driven back up to the Palace that afternoon. If he then stood looking through one of its elegant Georgian first-floor windows across the grass and trees of the square he must, in his mind's eye, have imagined tower and spire springing above the rooftops of the opposite corner of the square. Did he walk after dinner and gaze across the chasm of the old graveyard and try to imagine what was soon to rise there? Chavasse had accepted the bishopric with considerable misgiving. In a letter to a close friend he had admitted, 'A man with my feeble body, average ability and temperament can hardly be intended by God to such a diocese. God is blessing Wycliffe [Hall], and ought I to leave it at present? Can I not do more good by training bishops than by becoming one . . .?'

Liverpool was a difficult diocese and the new Bishop faced opposition from both extremes of churchmanship. Two Anglo-Catholic parishes which defied his ruling on Incense and Reservation were never visited by him. However, the integrity of his decisions was beyond question and this saintly man worked unstintingly for the next 22 years for the building of the great Cathedral Church whose completion he would never see.

Choosing an architect

CHAPTER
— *Two* —

FEW architects ever have the opportunity of designing a cathedral, and a small advertisement which appeared in the London papers early in 1902 must have stirred up quite a flurry of excitement in the architectural world: 'Competitions. Proposed Cathedral for the Diocese of Liverpool. To Architects. The Committee for the Erection of the intended Cathedral, being desirous of obtaining Designs for a Cathedral in the Gothic Style of Architecture, invite the attention of Architects to the consideration of the following proposals'. The advertisement went on to invite the submission of portfolios of work for the consideration of the Committee. By June 30th 1902, 102 portfolios of work had been submitted, some from the most famous architects of the day.

The mind of one young man was fired by the challenge, though he could hardly have hoped that his previous design work would give the Committee any confidence in his abilities. Mr. Giles Gilbert Scott, at the age of 21, had designed and seen through to completion nothing more substantial than a pipe rack.

Though he himself was an unknown and untried novice, the name Scott was one of the most famous names in the country in the field of ecclesiastical architecture. His grandfather was Sir Gilbert Scott, famous for his restoration of medieval cathedrals, as well as for his original work as designer of St. Pancras Station, the Albert Memorial, and the Foreign Office. His father was George Gilbert Scott, and his uncle John Oldrid Scott. As a boy, Giles Gilbert and his brother Adrian had made many cycle trips, which he called 'church crawls', visiting some of the masterpieces of church architecture on the Kent–Sussex border. Both the young Scotts were eventually articled to Temple Moore, who had himself been articled to their father.

For a young man so steeped in the architecture of England, the prospect of designing a great twentieth-century cathedral must have been exhilarating, and he understood the huge importance of the undertaking:

> When a Cathedral is to be built of such vast proportions as that contemplated for the city of Liverpool, we have an event which is epoch making in the history of English architecture. Liverpool is about to build a great church the likes of which, in point of size, has not been equalled by any Cathedral Church in the United Kingdom.

G. F. Bodley and Giles Gilbert Scott. Bodley, one of the two assessors in the competition, was one of the foremost Gothic experts in the world. Although Giles was untried, he rose from a famous architectural family.

This part of the story is best told in Scott's own words, recorded thirty years later for the readers of *The Daily Herald*:

> It fired my imagination. So I asked my chief if I might enter. He said I might, and added that it would be good practice for me. He was quite kind about it, but his manner clearly showed that he thought my enthusiasm considerably outweighed my talent. However I set to work.
>
> Nine months may seem a long time in which to prepare a design. But I not only had to get my 'inspiration', I had besides to prepare nine drawings, each measuring 6 feet by 4 feet, and showing every detail drawn to a small scale. When you remember that I had only my spare time to work in, you will realise that it meant very hard work.
>
> I was at it all hours - late into the night, early in the morning. And to be quite truthful, I am afraid often during office hours my mind wandered to my precious design when it should have been thinking of the work in hand.

Without warning, Scott's enthusiasm for his project suddenly faded and he lost all confidence in the design. Liverpool came very close indeed to losing a great building.

One early summer evening in 1902, an event occurred which was to change the future skyline of the city of Liverpool. The Scott family was visited for dinner by Giles's cousin, Henry Cooper, then a medical student. He asked about the progress of the Cathedral designs. 'Oh! I've chucked it,' Scott replied, 'it couldn't possibly stand a chance.' After dinner the two young men retired to Scott's room and he showed Cooper the unfinished drawings. His response was unequivocal. 'Don't be a fool. Finish it. You've done the biggest part, so you might as well finish it. If it fails it does not matter. But for goodness sake send it in.'

That bit of encouragement was all that was needed to rekindle the enthusiasm and confidence, but a whole month of working time had been lost. Work was re-started with vigour, but he soon realised that it would be a physical impossibility for him to finish all the details of the drawings himself. Fortunately, his younger brother was also an architect, and he was persuaded into drawing some of the insignificant bits. 'In the end even my mother took a hand and helped to draw in the lines representing the stone joints - quite a simple but tedious job which had to be done and for which I never would have had the time.'

All the portfolios of work submitted to the Committee were examined by two eminent architectural assessors, Mr. G. F. Bodley and Mr. R. Norman Shaw, and they were to recommend to the Committee those architects who might be invited to submit specific designs for a cathedral on St. James's Mount in the second round of the competition. After careful deliberation, they were able to recommend that five architects be invited to submit full designs, and Giles Gilbert Scott was one of them.

The minutes of numerous committees do not make the foundations for an exciting story, but the work undertaken by the various Cathedral Committees was essential for the smooth running of the project, and much happened which went unseen by the general public.

On 9th February 1903, the Committee paid £10,000 to the Corporation of Liverpool for the purchase of St. James's Mount. They also had to buy the leases on a number of houses on the Mount which had to be demolished before building could begin. Early in the eighteenth century the site had been known as Quarry Hill, and the area had been quarried until 1825 when the good building stone was exhausted. Most of the Mount was made ground, and in 1767 the top had been levelled, houses built, and the rest laid out as 'a pleasure ground'. When St. James's Church was built in 1774, the area became known as St. James's Walk, while the old worked-out quarry became a cemetery - a burial ground for 58,000 people.

As the old quarry had long been worked out, the Committee had to look elsewhere for suitable stone. They had decided upon a local red sandstone, and tests were carried out on samples from several sites. Although stone from more than one place was used in the final building, the vast majority was cut from Woolton Quarry, some five miles from the Cathedral; the owner of the quarry, the Marquis of Salisbury, later presented the quarry to the Committee, thus ensuring an adequate supply of stone for the whole

The design which won the competition in 1903. The view is that from St. James's Road. As can be seen, the first plan bears little resemblance to the final building, for, having won the competition, Scott started all over again with his designs. When compared with what was actually built, this design appears fussy in its external features, without the clean, strong lines of the final plan. There is a chapel to the east of the Chancel (extreme right of plan), in the traditional position of many older Lady Chapels. This original deisgn had a proportionately larger Nave than the final design, with five bays as opposed to the three actually built. This allowed the creation of a massive central space, with a single tower.

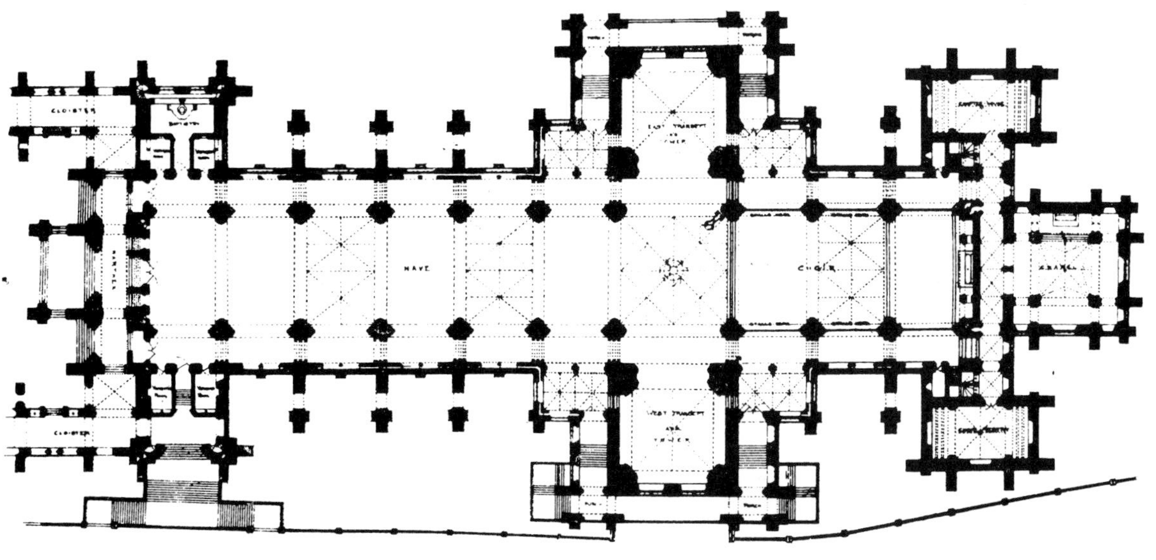
CLOISTER
NAVE
WEST TRANSEPT AND TOWER
CLOISTER
CHOIR

building. All the early stone was transported to the Cathedral site by teams of six heavy horses pulling low timber carts.

Over the winter of 1902–1903, the six architects talented enough to proceed to the second phase of the competition were hard at work. We know something of what Scott was attempting to achieve in his design from a short comment which accompanied his drawings: 'The general effect aimed at has been dignified serenity and largeness of scale . . . The effect of mass obtained with Gothic forms has been my chief object'.

Many of the members of the Cathedral Committee were men of considerable standing in the city, and Bodley and Norman Shaw became aware of certain pressures being brought to bear upon them. Both men, highly esteemed in their profession, were more than a match for the Committee, but some of Norman Shaw's letters reveal a certain amused tetchiness about their treatment:

> My dear Bodley,
>
> You have had a letter from Mr. Gladstone! I don't like it; it looks like an attempt to boycott us and make us say what he wishes.
>
> I really don't know what these silly people mean . . . If there is to be any fighting, it must be between Sir William Forwood and Mr. Gladstone and the rest of their committee. I hope there will be; I should like to see some blood.

The Committee consisted of powerful men used to their own way, but Bodley and Shaw had their own ideas. They travelled up from London on 4th May 1903 and planned to spend the whole of the following morning examining the drawings 'by ourselves'. On the morning of 7th May, they met the Committee at the Walker Art Gallery and informed them that they recommended Design No. 1. The Committee asked them to submit a written report, and adjourned the meeting until 15th May. The architect was not mentioned by name, but the similarity to Scott's first-round design was so strong that they would all have recognised the architect.

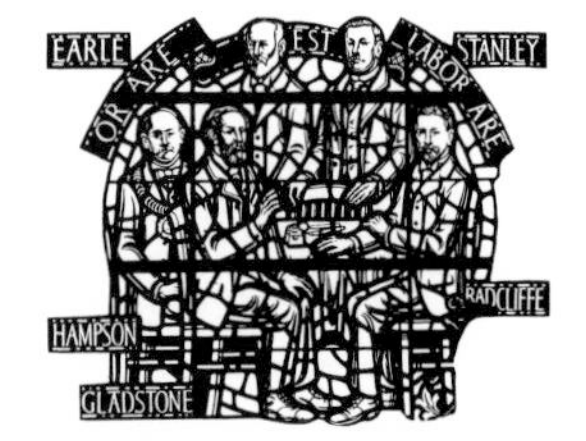

No-one will ever know all the thoughts of the Committee members when they met again, though we do know that Mr. Bradbury, the Committee's surveyor, declared that in Design No. 1 'only a thousand persons could hear or see the preacher'. Sir Frederick Radcliffe tried to save the day with his practical proposal:

> That immediate steps be taken to ascertain whether an arrangement can be made with Mr. Bodley to act as a consulting architect and the author of the Design marked No. 1 to act as architect to the Cathedral Committee . . . the designs marked No. 1 to be adapted with such modifications as may be agreed upon by the Committee after conferring with the architect.

This amendment was defeated and the meeting adjourned. As far as Sir William Forwood was concerned, the matter was closed and he wrote personally to Mr. Bodley that same day to give him the information:

> The Executive Committee met today, when your report was read, after which we proceeded to examine Plan No. 1 in detail, and were surprised to find that the seat room at the crossing was so small and quite inadequate for the accommodation of a large congregation.
>
> You will perhaps remember we set great store upon this point, as we considered it should be the distinguishing feature of a twentieth century cathedral, and we stipulated in our conditions that a congregation of about 3,000 should be provided for. We could not find space to seat more than 1,200.
>
> In other designs it was evident that the authors had made an effort to meet our wishes, though they had not been entirely successful; probably, in their effort they had to sacrifice proportion and other desirable features.
>
> The Committee felt that they could not erect a Cathedral which would afford only the accommodation of a parish church and therefore decided not to accept any of the plans.
>
> We shall meet in a fortnight to consider our next step.
>
> The Committee very highly appreciate the great assistance they have received from you and Mr. Norman Shaw, and they trust that the new departure they now take with much regret and great reluctance may be conducive to the success of our scheme.

Forwood wrote the briefest of rejections to Scott the following day, 'I regret to inform you that the Executive Committee find themselves unable to recommend the acceptance of your design for the new Cathedral'.

At least one member of the Committee was seriously concerned at the outcome of the deliberations. Giles Scott was a Roman Catholic who was designing a cathedral for a strongly Protestant diocese, and Radcliffe had been aware of the possible denominational conflicts which might be roused by either the choice or the rejection of a design from a Roman Catholic. He wrote to Bishop Chavasse on 18th May:

> I begged the Executive to face the difficulty then, pointing out how much greater it would be if he were successful. So long as the religious difficulty was not put plainly I felt the more in honour bound to take No. 1 which I entirely believe to be the best design. I hope you do not think we undervalued the religious difficulty. We are fortunately able to say it was not discussed. I say fortunately because I have already been attacked on the supposition that we had thrown over a masterpiece because of the religion of its author after admitting him to compete.

When the press took up the competition saga, some people must have thought that the whole project might founder. *The Builders' Journal* of May 1903 was forthright in its condemnation of the matter: 'the Liverpool practice, in effect, induces architects who would otherwise not compete to enter a competition, and then leaves the building committee free to act as though no skilled assessor had been appointed'.

This criticism was mild in comparison with the frenzied attack in *Truth*:

> Architects of position are not likely to trouble themselves further with the work of a Committee of dunderhead amateurs which proceeds in so eccentric and skimble-skamble a fashion. The building of Liverpool Cathedral is, *a priori*, a hideous waste of money, and the egregious Committee need not be so feverishly anxious to provide for a large congregation, considering the notorious fact that not a church in the city is ever more than half full, and most of them are nearly empty at all the services.

The Roman Catholic journal *The Tablet* took just the line that Radcliffe had feared, and increased Catholic and Protestant tensions in the city:

> If a Catholic is to be debarred from employment in the building of a Protestant Cathedral, the invitation to competitors should notify this restriction. It should be frankly stated at the outset that no Catholics need apply . . . The reason given for the rejection of the design appears, if I may say so with great respect, to be inadequate . . .

When the Committee met again on 26th May, they had been in receipt of several letters from Norman Shaw expressing his considerable displeasure at the way in which the assessors' recommendations had been handled. The alleged accommodation problem was completely erroneous, as there was

> no difficulty in getting about 3,000 people all within reasonable distance of the Pulpit and none behind pillars, or in out of the way places . . . About the quality and promise of the design we have no shadow of doubt and when at the last meeting I ventured to suggest that Mr. Bodley should be associated as your advisor, I really began to hope that all difficulties were resolved, but as things turned out I was sadly wrong.

There were forces at work within the Committee which did not want Giles Gilbert Scott, and proposals went to Bodley to ask whether he would be the architect; whether he would act together with Mr. Nicholson; whether he would act with another young architect of his own choosing. He was ready to agree to what had been Radcliffe's amendment: that he would be willing to associate himself with Scott. After deliberations about which we can know little, there was a unanimous resolution:

> That Mr. G. F. Bodley RA and Mr. Giles Gilbert Scott be approached with a view to their appointment as joint architects, and that the Design marked No. 1 be selected subject to such alterations and modifications as may be advised by the Architects and approved by the Committee and also subject to the signing of an approved Agreement.

The proposal satisfied even the irascible Norman Shaw, who wrote:

> Beyond doubt you have two quite exceptional men to deal with. Scott's work is no 'fluke', it is manifestly the work of a most gifted man, of course it is somehow or other in his blood and appears when the opportunity offers. Bodley is beyond all doubt the most accomplished and refined architect in Europe and if between them they cannot do you

Scott's second design, completed in 1904. The view in the drawing is from Hope Street; the plan below is seen here from the other side. A new feature is the rectangular Chapter House which can be seen at the left (the liturgical east) end of the building. The foundations were begun for this Chapter House, and they remain today, larger and more massive than needed for the smaller, octagonal Chapter House which was actually built. Note the larger, revised Lady Chapel, and the 'Invalids' Slope', an extremely early disabled access from St. James's Road.

a superb Cathedral, in every way worthy of Liverpool (and that is saying a good deal) I don't know what you are to do or where you are to look.

The first news that Scott's designs had won the competition came to

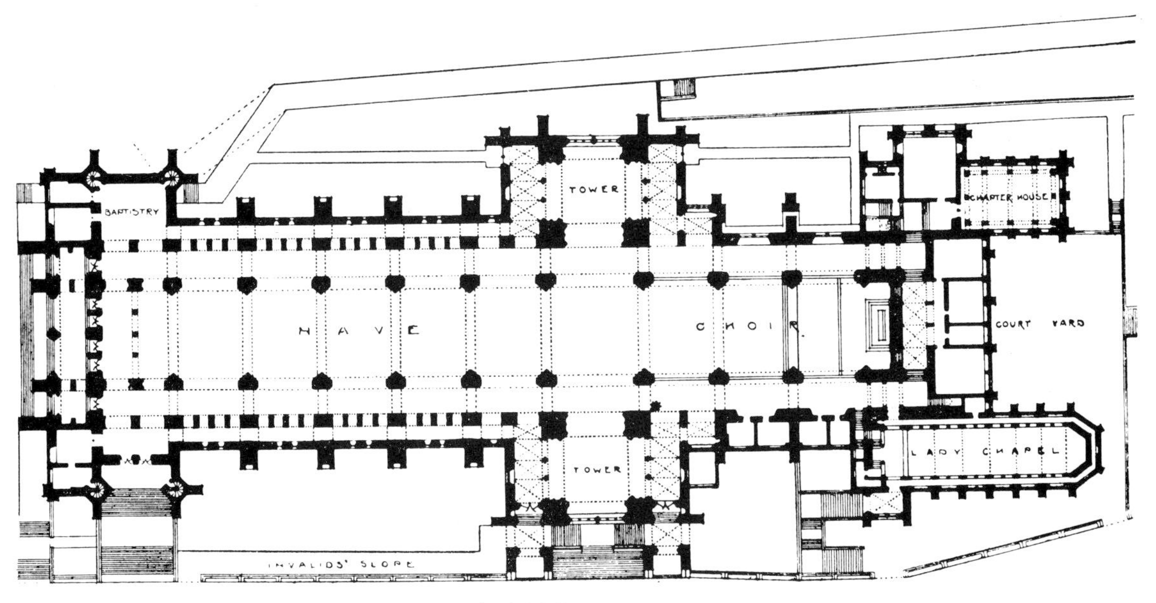

him, brought by Mr. Bradbury, while he was at work: 'When he told me who he was and the news he brought, I was stunned with amazement. For a few minutes I could not speak and when I could I have no idea what I said. I was overwhelmed.'

The Committee seemed more than satisfied with their young architect, who had been described to them as 'very pleasant, agreeable, enthusiastic, tall and looks considerably older than he actually is'.

The original plans and drawings submitted for the competition are in existence, together with artists' impressions of the completed building, and a large model of the east end. The original building differs markedly from the building we see today, because throughout the period of his work on the Cathedral, Scott constantly changed and refined his ideas.

By the beginning of 1904, more and more people were becoming aware of the great Cathedral scheme. Plans were set in motion for the formal laying of the foundation stone; builders were appointed; committees were hard at work trying to settle details. At the end of 1903, after some preliminary work by the firm of William Thornton, the first of the building contracts had been given to the Wavertree firm of William Morrison, the firm which was eventually to undertake the construction of the whole building.

The first half of 1904 was a time of tremendous activity. For a time there was some uncertainty as to whether or not the King was going to perform the ceremony of the laying of the foundation stone. The Cathedral Committee and the authorities of the city were determined that the ceremony was to be a memorable occasion, and plans were made to build a vast open-air amphitheatre 'to accommodate 7,000 if the King comes or 4,000 otherwise'. King Edward VII announced his willingness to perform

Preparations for the first Liverpool Cathedral service, the laying of the foundation stone in July 1904. The vast amphitheatre was planned to accommodate 7,000 people. Little material was wasted: most of the timbering was later re-used in the building process.

Final preparations for the laying of the foundation stone. In the foreground, left to right, are T. Shelmerdine, Robert Gladstone, Arthur Stanley, Frederick Radcliffe, Sir William Forwood, Bishop Chavasse, Archdeacon Madden and J. Alderson-Smith.

the ceremony and, from the contemporary records, Tuesday 19th July 1904 was one of the greatest royal visits ever made to Liverpool. It was declared a public holiday, and the weather was hot and fine.

The Committee realised that the wide interest caused by the laying of the stone would attract large crowds, and that thousands of people trailing round on a building site would hardly be appropriate. A semi-circular amphitheatre of raised wooden benches was constructed - not quite as elegant as the dress of the ladies and gentlemen who were to attend in all their finery. Thousands of people journeyed into the town to line the processional route in the hopes of seeing the King and Queen.

Their Majesties travelled to Liverpool by train, arriving at Lime Street Station at 1.30, and proceeded by carriage to the Town Hall where they had lunch in the banqueting room. Fifty people were invited to lunch, among them Mr. Frederick Moreton Radcliffe, a lawyer, whose name was to be linked with the Cathedral project for the rest of his life. He was a member of the Committee from 1901 until 1953. The horseshoe-shaped table was laden with silver and glass, and festooned with flowers and foliage, and a small orchestra played throughout the meal.

While the dignitaries were lunching at the Town Hall, the final preparations were being made up on the Mount. Most of the ticket-holders took their seats well over an hour before the start of the ceremony, and were entertained by the Band of the Grenadier Guards. Mr. Ralph Baker, the Secretary of the Liverpool Church Choir Association, had received over 4,000 applications from choristers wishing to sing at the great occasion. From that number, a choir of 1,000 voices was selected and trained, in area groups, by Mr. Frederick Burstall, the Cathedral organist, before coming together for the final rehearsal. They assembled in the Liverpool Institute in Mount Street, where they put on their robes - black cassocks, clean white surplices, black skull caps with a red button on the top, purchased for 6½d from Lewis's - and no-one was permitted to parade in brown shoes or boots. The thousand robed figures marched to take up their positions headed by the trumpeters of the High Sheriff. Lining St. James's Road were 1,000 children from the Sunday Schools of the diocese, forty boys from the Jewish Lads Brigade, and 250 each from the Church Lads Brigade and Boys Brigade. The choir procession was followed by over 430 robed clergy. The crowd then waited expectantly for the arrival of the royal party.

The arrival of the King and Queen was signalled by a fanfare of trumpets which was immediately drowned by a spontaneous burst of cheering from the vast crowd. The royal standard was raised, their Majesties mounted the rostrum and the national anthem was sung. Speeches of welcome were made by Lord Derby and Sir William Forwood, and then the King replied, expressing his pleasure at being involved in the great venture in Liverpool. Soon after 4 o'clock the service

King Edward VII and Queen Alexandra during the service. The glass jar to be sealed in below the stone can still be clearly seen. This foundation stone is still the largest single stone used in the construction of the Cathedral: 'the biggest brick', as one visitor recently put it.

itself began. Bishop Chavasse read the opening sentences and the prayers. The Archbishop of York presided at the next phase: the singing of *All people that on earth do dwell*. Then followed the laying of the stone by His Majesty, with trowel and mallet of gold and ivory. After further prayers and a fanfare of trumpets, everyone sang *O God, our help in ages past*, and the Bishop of Chester led the final prayers before the Archbishop pronounced the blessing. The whole congregation remained standing while the choir sang the *Hallelujah Chorus* from *Messiah*.

For one day, the building site on St. James's Mount had become a great public spectacle, at the centre of which was a block of red sandstone, destined to be the largest single stone in the whole building. It had come from the quarry at Runcorn, the gift of the Mothers' Meetings of the diocese, and it weighed 5 tons 15 cwts. Generations of visitors have read the two inscriptions: 'To the glory of God this Foundation Stone was laid by King Edward the Seventh on the 19th day of July, 1904', and 'Other foundation can no man lay than that which is laid, which is Jesus Christ'. What later visitors were not to see was the glass jar carefully placed in a cavity below the stone. Inside were placed copies of the Liverpool *Mercury*, *Courier*, *Post*, and *Times*, a 1901 report containing a list of the General Committee, a copy of the Cathedral Act of Parliament, and the Foundation Stone edition of the Cathedral Committee's Handbook, containing the history of the movement, a list of offerings, and the form of service.

The people departed, but memories remained, many of them recalled sixty years later:

> I was four and a half years old at the time and remember going along Parliament Street and seeing the tramcars decorated with flags secured to the trolleys.
>
> I was a Maid of Honour to the Red Rose Queen, who presented Her Majesty Queen Alexandra with a magnificent bouquet of Red Roses . . . I almost forgot to curtsey.
>
> We were placed outside the arena to witness the arrival and departure of the Royal Party, which we did, and to hear what singing drifted out from the service. The day was hot and sultry and for more than two hours we were in a sheep pen enclosure on dry sandy ground in the roasting sunshine. It was a mercy that the weather held until the service was over, but the climax came when a heavy thunder storm broke as the crowd was dispersing. I still feel grateful to the shop keeper in Myrtle Street whose friendly door way sheltered me from the drenching rain.

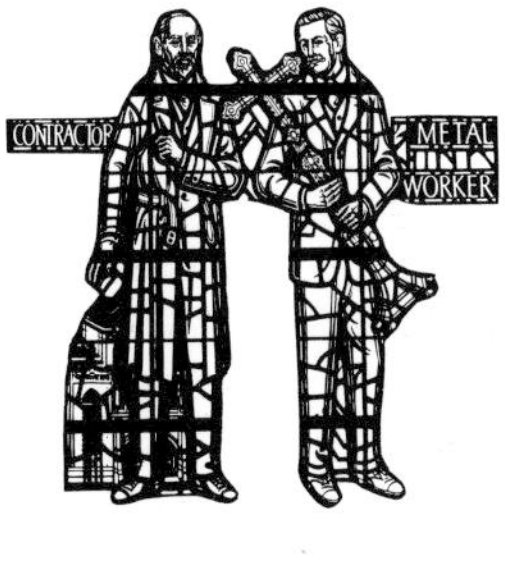

Quickly the building site returned to normal. The seating was dismantled and much of it used during the later building processes. The foundation stone itself, to prevent accidental damage, was encased in what looked like a little wooden hut. Liverpool people had a day to be remembered, and the serious and massive task of actually building the Cathedral began.

Laying foundations

CHAPTER
- Three -

THE events of the summer of 1904 had focused great public interest on the new building site on St. James's Mount. Bands and choirs and civic and church dignatories had made the foundation stone ceremony a great public occasion, but from then on the real labour of laying brick and stone began. Work commenced on the foundations for the Lady Chapel, Vestries, Choir, Transepts and Chapter House. It was not easy ground to work, for although solid rock was near to the surface on the south side, the foundations had to go down forty feet in places overlooking the cemetery. Gradually the shape of the future building could be seen as the lower courses of brick and stone were laid.

In 1903 it had been decided to concentrate efforts on the Lady Chapel, so that at least one small section of the building would be completed as quickly as possible. Late in 1904, the Committee received an offer from Mr. Arthur Earle, on behalf of the Earle and Langton families, of £25,000 for the building of the Lady Chapel 'as a thank offering to God for the many material advantages we have derived from our long association with Liverpool and as a memorial to members of our families who have passed away'. In November, the Building Committee requested the architects to submit the plans for the Chapel within three months.

On 17th July 1906, a crowd of some 2,000 spectators gathered at the building site to witness the laying of another foundation stone – that for the Chapter House. £10,000 towards the cost of that part of the building was contributed by the Freemasons of West Lancashire in memory of the first Earl of Lathom, who had been their Provincial Grand Master. The ceremony took place on a platform which resembled a mason's square, and the stone was to be laid by the Duke of Connaught. When he had approved the stone, he said, 'I find this stone to be plumb, level, and square, and I declare it to be duly prepared and truly laid, and that the craftsmen have worked well'. On a table close to the stone were three gold vessels containing corn, wine and oil. They were handed in turn to the Duke, who said:

> I scatter corn on this stone as an emblem of plenty and abundance. May the blessings of morality and virtue flourish within this building,

An early view of excavation work for the foundations. Much of the timber had been used to construct the amphitheatre in 1904 and would be used many times again. Despite the mechanical cranes, the labour-intensive nature of the work is obvious; like their medieval predecessors, the Cathedral workmen used pick, shovel and muscle.

> producing fruit a hundred fold. I pour wine upon this stone, the emblem of joy and gladness. I sprinkle oil upon this stone, the emblem of peace and unanimity. May prosperity, happiness, and goodwill ever prevail amongst those assembled in this building, to the glory of the Most High, until time shall be no more.

The laying of foundation stones stirs considerable public interest, but the building of a great cathedral is a long, slow and very expensive process. A steady flow of money is essential, and though generous benefactors might willingly contribute large sums towards a magnificent memorial window, the Cathedral had to attract regular funds for digging foundations, and laying the millions of bricks which were later to be covered by stone and never seen again. The efforts of Sir William Forwood and a strong Executive Committee were successful in establishing a steady flow of funds from many sources.

In his little book *The Liverpool Cathedral – the story of its foundation*, Sir William gives an account of his successful 'begging' amongst the wealthy businessmen of Liverpool:

> It is little use asking a man who seldom enters a church to give for church purposes, but an appeal to do something for his native city may be successful. Never unduly press your claim; leave it for another day. Always accept a refusal pleasantly, although it may come to you at the top of four or five flights of office stairs, and never accept 'No' for a final answer. Some of the largest sub-scriptions to the Cathedral have come after several emphatic 'No's.

Sir William was even successful in persuading a Jewish man to contribute £1,000. 'Yes,' he at once replied, 'I have put all my money on the Synagogue, but I should like to hedge a little by giving £1,000 for the Cathedral.'

Everyone realised that in order to build the largest cathedral in Britain a steady supply of money would be required over many years. As was the Bishop's wish, money came in from literally thousands of people from across the diocese – church groups, Sunday Schools and individuals, as well as industry, commerce and generous donations and bequests. The sheer scale of the project can be appreciated when it is realised that in the first sixty years over £2½ million were donated to the project. Although one single family donated over £250,000 – for the building of the tower – local collectors from the Cathedral Builders went around gathering small sums weekly or monthly from hundreds of individual people, many of them far from well-off; for, whilst several benefactors gave huge sums, the number of individual donors was very large indeed. And despite the scale of the fund-raising activities, people appear to have given to the Cathedral as well as to the town's other charities, and the Cathedral scheme does not seem to have left other good causes short of money.

But how on earth could such expenditure be justified, in a town like Liverpool of all places? Some eyebrows must have been raised at the huge

Above: *The earliest photograph of the Lady Chapel, dating from about 1905. The foundations in the right foreground are still being dug but concreting has begun on the left-hand side.*

Right: *Order out of chaos – a slightly later photograph of the same scene, with the emerging ground plan clearly visible. The massive scale of the work, including layer upon layer of brick, is obvious. Note the hand-operated crane in the centre of the photograph.*

Left: *The 'shed' in the centre of this early photograph is the timber cladding that was used to protect the foundation stone from damage. These workmen are standing below the floor level of the Cathedral in what is now part of the Crypt occupied by the Maintenance Department. December, 1905.*

Below: *Early work on the Chancel. Blocks of stone from the quarry are piled in the foreground. Many banker masons worked in the line of open-fronted sheds parallel to the crane tracks.*

sums of money being spent on a cathedral that stood cheek by jowl with some of the worst housing and most deprived social conditions in the country. Many old photographs show the Cathedral growing inexorably above squalid courts and alleys, houses without water or sanitation and children without shoes. Yet the Cathedral was rising, not as a product of Liverpool's lack of concern for the poor in its midst, as some may have thought, but as a symbol of faith and hope for a brighter and better future.

All the early building work on the site was, of course, directed downwards in the digging of the foundations for the east end of the building. It was not an easy site to work because of considerable variations in the depth of the rock. The operation was labour-intensive, with groups of workers excavating with pick and shovel, and great iron buckets of debris being filled and lifted to the surface by small cranes. The excavations were heavily timbered before the concrete of the foundations went in.

The Committee had engaged two architects to oversee the building of Scott's overall design. Some of the members of that Committee did not seem to wish to leave crucial decisions in the hands of the two professionals, and one suspects that the widely-experienced Bodley was not pleased to receive such comments as these from Robert Gladstone:

> In considering the revised design for the Cathedral, you will no doubt bear in mind that there are very many people who would prefer to have the two towers at the north end, and a large central tower over the crossing as at Canterbury, Durham, York, Lincoln and others. We have still to raise a very large sum of money, and, I fear this will not be easily done if the design has not general approval.
>
> I assure you many people dislike the present Elevation, including the budding transepts, who would, I am sure, be pleased, and would open their purses, if the alterations which I have mentioned can be made . . . A large wheel window over the Porch in the north front, like Notre Dame in Paris. A large pointed window (like the east window of Carlisle) at the other end of the transepts.

In a later letter, however, detailed suggestions begin to sound rather more like orders:

> The stairs connected with the gallery at the end of the Morning Chapel are too narrow (barely 4 ft.) . . . The Heating apparatus should consist of large low-pressure hot-water pipes, as in the offices of the Royal Insurance Co. and the White Star Co. in Liverpool. No hot air . . . A clock with chimes and a loud hour bell should be placed in one of the towers, and a complete peal of 12 (or more) bells in the other. The details of the towers do not show any clock faces . . . It seems to me that the aisles on each side of the nave are too narrow – only 12 feet 6 inches – and will be out of proportion to the space of the nave arches and of the nave itself.

Taken in 1907, this photograph shows some of the building work on one of the side walls of the Lady Chapel up to gallery level. This section of stonework can be seen in photographs of the completed Chapel (see, for example, page 48). The rough timber scaffolding poles and rope lashings are clearly visible.

Scott was even more roughly handled in more than one letter from Arthur Earle:

> I trust you fully realise the immense trouble, annoyance and confusion caused by the constant change of front. I most assuredly supposed that when the plan of the windows in the Chapel were sent down and approved of, they had been thought out by Mr. Bodley and yourself and finally fixed, and after going through a good deal of work, to find the whole thing is altered is, to say the least, annoying. Of course the remark is at once made, which you will agree is only reasonable 'Does not Mr. Scott know his own mind, or does Mr. Bodley alter all because he was not consulted about the first drawings, and if this is so, why did Mr. Bodley sign the first drawings?' I quite realise that architects have inspirations but when it comes to altering a plan entirely it is a very serious question.

Even after the successful completion of the Lady Chapel, Arthur Earle's comments in a letter to Bishop Chavasse do show more than a little arrogance: 'I advocate a much more stringent hand being kept upon our young and somewhat foolish architect'.

As far as most people were concerned, the partnership of the young and the old architects was working well, but only recently the full extent of their disagreement has come to light. Frederick Radcliffe became a life-

The steam-driven frame saws which worked constantly every day cutting the large blocks of stone straight from the quarry before they went to be finished by the banker masons. The saws did not have teeth but steel blades that moved backwards and forwards in the cut, lubricated by jets of water. The saws cut at the rate of around six inches an hour, producing a low rumble and a characteristic 'chink, chink' sound familiar to local people for many years.

long friend of Scott, and in a number of letters he expressed his considerable frustration at what was happening. We must try to imagine Sir William Forwood and his Committee busily engaged in raising money throughout the diocese; William Morrison and Son, builders, under the direction of Mr. Greene, Clerk of Works, excavating the eastern foundations; and the brilliant but inexperienced young architect at work on his plans in London. Scott's genius had won the competition, but in the early years he was uncomfortably yoked with the vastly experienced, but elderly, Mr. Bodley. They were appointed joint architects, and all plans had to carry both signatures before the Clerk of Works could proceed. They may have been joint architects in name, but the majority of work was done by Scott alone, though Bodley constantly made minor changes. Scott was worried: 'The Cathedral at one time had a narrow escape of disaster, it became a mongrel and I began to lose interest'.

To walk around the completed Cathedral with a discerning eye is to understand the enormous volume of work undertaken by the young architect. Liverpool Cathedral dominated the whole of his life. Having only just finished the design for the first round of the competition in 1902, he had to set to work on the plan which won the competition in 1903 – and having won the competition, he produced a further set of plans in 1904. It was not the architect's job to produce a few inspiring but vague drawings which other people translated into plans from which the builders could work. Every detail, down to the hinges and door handles, was the responsibility of the architect.

Bodley's status with regard to Liverpool Cathedral changed slightly when he agreed to design the cathedral for Washington, and he became the consultant architect – though his and Scott's signatures still had to be on every drawing. Scott's letter to Radcliffe in April of 1907 reveals that the tensions were becoming even greater, and the future of the enterprise was in jeopardy.

> I want your advice . . . about the present arrangement with the 'master of detail'. This new place he has taken near Oxford and the fact that he has two Cathedrals to do besides Liverpool [Washington and San Francisco] has made the working partnership agreement more of a farce than ever, and to tell the truth my patience with the existing state of affairs is about exhausted . . . Mr. B. is of course pleased to have a sorry fool who is willing to work for him and allow him to haul in the money, nothing could be nicer for him . . . and the Committee see the drawings on the site signed by both of us and say 'this arrangement is working satisfactorily' . . . the only consolation I have is that no one can accuse me of grasping propensities at least no one who knows what goes on behind the scenes . . . Of course every bit of designing down to the minutest detail I am doing also but this I don't complain about as I am keen on this work and am willing to do it. I am in fact carrying on this Cathedral by myself entirely and have done so almost from the beginning and now after several years I have had enough, and no one can say I have lacked patience . . . I feel I must do something drastic as appeals to fairness have failed with Mr. B.

The autumn of 1907 was a time of great pressure. There were more disagreements between the architects over the Lady Chapel windows and the builders were pressing for final drawings of other sections of the building. Though the eminent architect was always keen to undertake the interesting detailing work, he seemed wholly unwilling to undertake the other necessary, but tedious, aspects. Over four years, Scott made forty site visits: Bodley made four. The young architect wrote over eight hundred letters and undertook frequent meetings with a whole regiment of people involved in the building of the Cathedral. The vast majority of the work was done by Scott, but the two men were both receiving the same remuneration, and Scott declared that he could have made a better living as an architect's assistant. We shall probably never know the whole story, but after weeks of working long hours over the plans, Scott once again encountered disagreements with Bodley and, in a state of weary exasperation, sat down and wrote his letter of resignation to Sir William Forwood.

Before action could be taken on the matter, however, the elderly Mr. Bodley suddenly died, and Giles Gilbert Scott became the sole architect, and started work again with renewed vigour.

The physical realisation of the vision of the Bishop, the plans of the architect, and the hopes of the whole diocese, lay in the hands of the craftsmen, and their story begins not on St. James's Mount, but five miles away at Woolton Quarry. The stone in the quarry was in layers or beds three to four feet thick. There were also natural fissures, or 'backs', in the stone, and it was these fissures that assisted the opening-up of the beds. A series of 'shot holes' was bored vertically into the stone to a depth of several feet. Early in the century, these holes were bored slowly by 'jumping' up and down on a heavy crowbar, though by the 1920s powerful pneumatic drills made the work easier and quicker. About three pounds of black powder was used in each hole as explosive, and 'stemmed' with sand and clay. A slow fuse was used to fire the charges and, if these were placed well, quite large blocks of stone were produced. Much of the stone near the surface was not of sufficiently high quality to be used as masonry, but it did not go to waste: most of the poor quality stone was crushed on the site to be used as aggregate in the concrete of the foundations, and the sand was used in the concrete and cement.

The finest building stone was to be found in the lower beds, and it was taken by striking wedges into the 'backs'. Explosives were not used, so there was little waste as a result of shattering, and blocks of two or three tons in weight were removed. In the early days, the carts drawn by six heavy horses were a regular sight in the village, and one little girl was always intrigued when they stopped at the public house half way up the hill so that the horses could refresh themselves at the horse trough, and the men from the barrels of beer.

From medieval times, skilled stonemasons have often moved about during their working lives, from one great building to another. In 1907 there was a young man living in the Oxfordshire village of Taynton, near Burford; an area famous for producing good stone. He had been brought up by his aunt and uncle and, as was often the case, the young man was apprenticed to the same trade as the head of the house, and served an apprenticeship of seven years as a stonemason. He had moved from job to job with his uncle, until he read the news that a great cathedral was to be built in Liverpool; a cathedral which could provide a lifetime of employment for a good craftsman. Although confident that he was making the right decision, it must have been with some trepidation that the young man arrived at the site one morning and announced himself as Owen Pittaway, stonemason.

When the wagons from Woolton arrived at the site, the blocks of stone were stacked carefully at the west end near the stone saws. These saws did not have teeth, but the steel blades were drawn backwards and forwards over the stone, lubricated with jets of water, and cut at the rate of six inches an hour. The chink-chink of those saws was the constant sound on the Mount for over seventy years. The final working of all the stones was under the mallet and chisel of a great team of masons. When young Owen Pittaway began his career at Liverpool there was a massive demand for a

This photograph of the quarry at Woolton shows the bedding planes of the rock with particular clarity. Also obvious is the systematic way in which the good stone was quarried. Though little of the old quarry can be seen today, the name Quarry Street and the number of sandstone buildings in Woolton are evidence of the importance of Woolton Quarry in the past. The best stone was to be found in the lower beds and is hardwearing as long as it does not include pebbles. Some inferior stone was used at the newer west end, leading to some erosion problems (some finials even fell down recently) which are not encountered on earlier parts of the Cathedral.

steady flow of stones, and he worked each day with his mallets and chisels. When a stone was completed, he carved his own mason's mark on to a face of the stone which would not be seen once it was set into position. Gradually Mr. Pittaway's skills as a craftsman began to show themselves, and he was promoted to the highly responsible position of setter-out. It

Right: *The start of everything. Massive blocks of sandstone at Woolton Quarry. The best beds yielded very large blocks of good quality stone.*

Below: *The workers at Woolton Quarry in 1901.*

was the job of the setter-out to convert the plans of the architect into a series of zinc templates that were then used by the masons to produce a stone perfectly accurate in shape and size. Though the material used for the templates has changed, the method of working has remained the same for hundreds of years. The banker mason worked with mallet and chisels and the aid of the template to produce the constantly-needed supply of stone. It was highly skilled work, though a complete novice worked at the craft for five minutes on 10th December 1913. Making a private visit to the site, Her Majesty Queen Alexandra approached Mr. W. H. Selsby and asked to borrow his mallet and chisel. The Queen handed him her fur muff and umbrella, and while he steadied her hand she worked at the stone, so that when she finished she was able to say, 'Now I have helped to build Liverpool Cathedral'.

The banker mason put his own personal mark on each stone, as masons have done for centuries, and marked a code number to indicate where the stone was to go in the final design. There was a hole in the top surface of every stone so that a 'lewis' – a lifting device – could be inserted to enable the derrick crane to lift the stone into position. The stones were bedded on to a half-inch layer of mortar and checked with a plumbline by the mason fixer, assisted by his labourer.

Day in, day out, in all weathers, the team of masons was at work on the new site on the Mount, and thousands of templates for stone in the Lady Chapel, Chapter House and chancel were made by Mr. Pittaway. He had moved to Liverpool to find a satisfying career, but he could have had no idea that his expertise was to promote him in 1921 to the key position of Clerk of Works. He was to supervise the building of the great Vestey Tower, and to be awarded the honorary degree of Master of Arts by Liverpool University before his eventual retirement after 46 years.

Masons' marks that have been used in the Cathedral, from a list prepared in 1961.

J. Kitching	A. Stone	E. Calland	T. Rowbottom	J. Rowbottom	P. Whitehead	P. Flynn
R. Hayson	W. Calland	G. Vidler	C. Cowley	B. Millen	N. Hales	J. Kelly
K. Sekora	J. Scott	D. Holland	P. Dunn	T. Crickson	R. Goodall	B. Whitehead

CHAPTER
- Four -

Lady Chapel

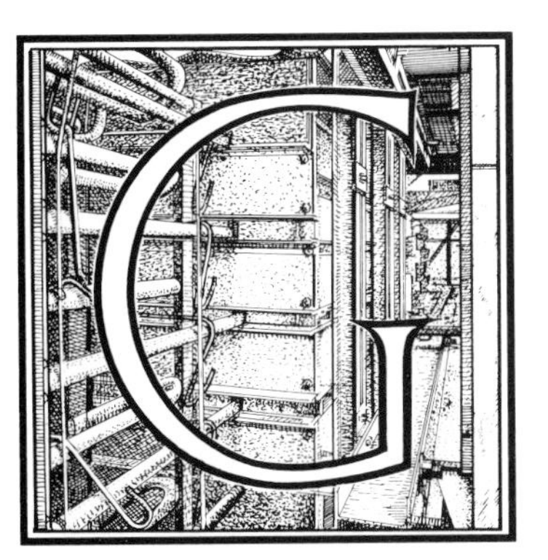

ROUPS of visitors to the site during the first decade of the century must have been bewildered by the range of activities being undertaken over such a vast area: all the foundations had been put in for the whole of the east end of the Cathedral; the walls were rising slowly for the areas we now recognise as Chancel, Chapter House, Ambulatory, Vestries and Undercroft; walls were rising more quickly for the Lady Chapel. A great effort was being made to finish even one small part of the building, so that Cathedral services could begin.

The Lady Chapel under construction in March 1907. Note the form-work still in place in the far archway and one of the large cranes that were to tower over the site for many years to come. It is hard to believe that a building as elegant as the Lady Chapel (see the photograph on page 48) could emerge from such apparant chaos.

There is remarkably little timber to be seen in the completed building; but timber, and the men who worked with timber, were crucial to the progress. Whenever an arch was to be built, the skills of the carpenters were required to prepare the timber form-work upon which the brick and stone of the final arch would be set. The technique employed was to build a heavy wooden framework or 'centre' in the exact shape of the arch. The first stones were placed on top of the timber shape to create the lowest 'ring' or 'order' of the arch, and the stones were separated by wooden wedges the exact width of the joints, which were then mortared and allowed to harden. When the lowest ring was finished, the next was built on top, the weight being taken by the first ring until the next keystone was in position. The top surface of each ring was smooth, so that each layer of arch was entirely separate, allowing for any movement which might be created by minor settlement. Until after the Second World War, as the photographs show, all the scaffolding necessary for the building was timber – in many cases great rough tree trunks like gigantic pit props, lashed together with rope.

In very few places does the solid brickwork of the Cathedral show today, though millions of bricks were employed in its construction. Bricklayers and fixer-masons worked closely together, the bricklayers bonding in their

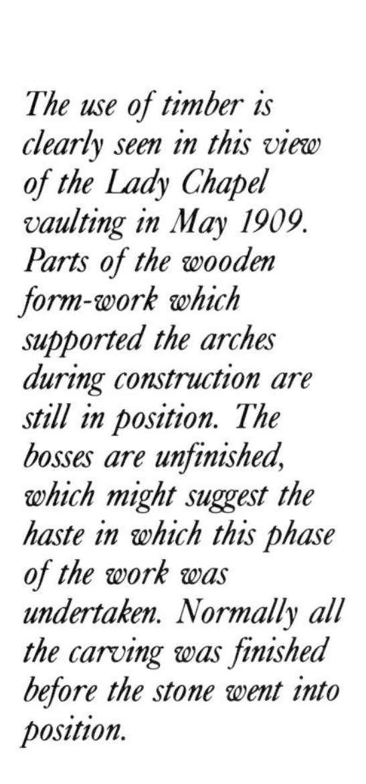
The use of timber is clearly seen in this view of the Lady Chapel vaulting in May 1909. Parts of the wooden form-work which supported the arches during construction are still in position. The bosses are unfinished, which might suggest the haste in which this phase of the work was undertaken. Normally all the carving was finished before the stone went into position.

bricks once the surface blocks were in position.

The builders were hard at work, and so were the architect and the various committees, many decisions of great significance being taken as the building progressed. As late as 1908, the drawings for the exterior elevation of the Chapel were approved only to the heads of the windows; there were still doubts as to the eventual height of the Chancel, and whether or not the vault would be of stone or timber. Plans had to be advanced for all the stained glass windows, and contracts for the Chapel windows were awarded to James Powell and Son of Whitefriars.

Plans for an octagonal Chapter House were approved early in 1909, even though (as was discovered in 1990 during excavations to renew a collapsed drain) concrete foundations for a much larger structure had already been put in. By the spring of 1909 the Lady Chapel walls had reached their full height of 55 feet, Morrisons were at work on the vaulting, and the walls of the choir were up to 40 feet.

In May 1909 the Committee gave Scott so many urgent tasks to carry through that it is surprising that he had any time or imagination left to think about the details for a part of the Cathedral which would not even be started for many years:

> The Architect was *inter alia* instructed to prepare forthwith designs for the choir stalls in both Lady Chapel and Choir, for six electroliers in the

Lady Chapel (at a cost not to exceed £100 each), for gilding and painting the Lady Chapel Reredos and presumably, to ensure that Satan did not find mischief for idle hands, in addition to design the Choir Reredos and redesign the Chapter House. It was perhaps fortunate that Mr. Scott was a young man still in his twenties.

The Lady Chapel in November 1908 is filled with the timber scaffolding supporting the platform (see photograph on page 45), just below the vaulting. The wedges which were used to keep the ropes tightly lashed are clearly evident..

At the June meeting, the Committee decided that the Lady Chapel would be opened at 11 a.m. on St. Peter's Day, June 29th, 1910, by Francis James Chavasse, Bishop of Liverpool, and the Most Reverend Cosmo Lang, Lord Archibishop of York.

There was considerable interest in the service, because no interior photographs of the Chapel interior had been authorised, and many people were very curious to gain a first sight of it. However, congregational numbers were severely limited by the size of the Chapel, and by the large number of visiting clergy. Most of the invited congregation were those who had been generous in their financial contributions to the building fund. 'Official dress' was the order of the day, and all present who were entitled to wear a uniform did so, the Bishops wearing their Convocation robes. The organisers had, reasonably, expected good weather at the end of June, but they were disappointed by heavy grey skies and more or less incessant rain throughout the morning. Fortunately, just before eleven o'clock the rain stopped, and though conditions remained unseasonable, the lengthy procession stayed dry.

The undercroft was crowded with civic and church figures, who processed out through the central door into the courtyard which was flanked by the wet and windblown members of the Third Batallion of the Liverpool Regiment of the Church Lads Brigade, and a detachment of the Incorporated Church Scouts Patrols. Church of England companies of the Boys Brigade were also represented. The procession was headed by the civic regalia, the Lord Mayor, the Town Clerk, members of the Executive Committee, marshals, Cathedral choir, clergy, archdeacons, twenty bishops and their chaplains, the Archbishop of Dublin, various other officials, the Bishop of Liverpool and the Archbishop of York and their attendants. During the singing of the hymn *Blessed City, Heavenly Salem*, this long procession moved out of the courtyard and along St. James's Road towards the Lady Chapel porch – while the two twelve-year-old choirboys who had been ordered to attend the Archbishop and see that his robes were in order, struggled to prevent him from being blown over by the

Looking down on top of the partly completed Lady Chapel vaulting. Because of the complex nature of the shape of the vault, most of the stones were cut close at hand to the places in which they were to be used.

high wind.

The short introduction to the service was held outside in the porch, and little would have been heard by the congregation inside until the Bishop struck the door with his crozier and cried, 'Open ye the gates'. Immediately the doors were opened, he proclaimed: 'Peace be to this House, from God our Heavenly Father. Peace be to this House, from his Son who is our Peace. Peace be to this House, from the Holy Ghost the Comforter'. Then the congregation (who had been listening to improvisations on the organ by Mr. Burstall) stood, and the Bishop and Archbishop were received by members of the Cathedral Executive: Sir William Forwood, Arthur Earle, Sir Robert Hampson, Frederick Radcliffe, Robert Gladstone, and Giles Gilbert Scott.

As the service proceeded, the ceremony focused upon the different parts of the building and the uses to which they would be put: the congregation was reminded of the reading of the Bible, marriage, confirmation, the

Right: *St. Peter's Day, 1910. Bishop Chavasse moves in procession through the courtyard at the east end before the service of consecration. Representatives of the Boy Scouts and the Boys Brigade, the latter with rifles, line the way.*

Left: *The Lady Chapel, Altar and Reredos. The oldest surviving photographs are poor, but this shot from the 1920s shows the original window which was destroyed by bomb blast in the Second World War. The choir stalls in this picture were specially designed and built for the Chapel but were later moved to Childwall Parish Church.*

singing of the choir, and Holy Communion. The Chancellor of the Diocese read the sentence of consecration, and the Bishop signed the Instrument of Consecration, saying, 'By virtue of our sacred office in the Church of God, we do now consecrate and for ever set apart from all profane and common uses this House of God, under the name of The Chapel of the Blessed Virgin Mary, and to the glory of the Ever Blessed Trinity, Father, Son, and Holy Ghost'.

The quiet solemnity of that important step in the history of the Cathedral was followed effectively by the choir, who sang Sterndale Bennett's setting of the words 'God is a Spirit' before the Archbishop of York stood up to preach on the text 'The Lord is in His holy temple: let all the earth keep silence before him'.

Either the Rev. Charles Harris, Cathedral Organisation Secretary, had an extremely retentive memory, or he had access to the text of the sermon, because he was able to report the sermon in some detail. He recalled that the Archbishop first brought greetings from York Minster to her 'youngest daughter', the beginnings of the new Cathedral in Liverpool, then:

> After alluding to the thirteen centuries since York was founded, and tracing the decay of Roman Power and the rise of King Edwin in Northumbria, he asked, Who can join these fleeting generations together? He contrasted the new worlds to which men went who sailed from the river Mersey with the old Roman world, and asked, What can

> bind these wide regions in one? Not blood, not mere land, but two things more powerful still - the faith in which King Edwin was baptised, and the Divine Society which preserved great vivid memories and handed down the same words, the same Scriptures, the same Sacraments of unfailing grace through the presence of Jesus Christ, the same yesterday, today, and for ever. The Church, he continued, is the most permanent element in our civilisation. The ever-changing voices of the world must prove of less abiding influence. After emphasising the need that faith must express itself in service, he made a stirring appeal that the Cathedrals of the future should add new and fuller help to the life of the people, and be not only homes of learning and repose and worship, but inspiring centres of work.

After the sermon, the holy vessels and ornaments were presented to the Bishop, who placed them on the communion table and blessed them, and the service concluded with the singing of the hymn *O God, our help in ages past*.

A few informal memories of the occasion have been left for posterity by a former chorister:

> Writing nearly thirty years after, it is interesting to recall the fact that the writer of these notes - then a chorister of twelve years of age was one of the two very proud small boys who, bearing the train of the then Archbishop of York, were, presumably, the first laymen officially to enter the completed Lady Chapel. Recollection is dim, and its sole stimulant now is an autographed photograph of the Archbishop, Dr. Lang, then a striking personality, with jet-black hair, who afterwards, in the robing room which served as a vestry, promised that services well rendered should be commemorated in this way.

The Bishop knew that many people would be disappointed at not being allotted places at the consecration service, and so he wisely arranged twelve special services over the next fortnight. Eight of the bishops who preached had former connections with Liverpool. Eight thousand people worshipped in the Chapel during that time, and another eight thousand visited during the day. A little over nine years after Bishop Chavasse had spoken at the Town Hall meeting which had formally decided to build a cathedral in Liverpool, he was able to write to his people in the *Diocesan Gazette*:

> The Consecration and the Opening Services of the Cathedral chapel are now matters of past history, and the Diocese has reason to look back upon them with the deepest thankfulness to Almighty God and with the brightest hopes for the future. The details of the Consecration Service had been carefully thought out, and no hitch marred them. The ceremonial was simple, dignified, and most impressive. The stillness of the people, the spirit of reverence, the fulfilment of long cherished hopes, combined to produce a sense of God's Presence, a joy, and an awe which will never be forgotten by many of those present.

The early history of the Lady Chapel, and indeed of the Cathedral as a

The first Cathedral choir to sing in the new Cathedral. F. H. Burstall, Organist and Choirmaster, is seated in the centre of the front row.

whole, was dominated by men; but a group of remarkable ladies was determined that women should also play a significant and, in their eyes, appropriate role in the establishment of a great new cathedral. Miss Rosalie Stolterfoht had it in mind that a group of ladies from the diocese might become responsible for preparing all the fine embroidery and linen which would be needed as part of the worship in a great church. The Cathedral Embroidery Association which came into being to carry through the ideas of the group of ladies had two simple, though important, reasons for coming into being: 'to give the women of the Diocese a definite share in the great undertaking of building the Cathedral, complementary to the men's larger part' and 'to provide the Cathedral with frontals, burses, linen and other embroidery'.

After a number of diplomatic conversations, the Cathedral Executive Committee agreed to the formation of the Embroidery Association, provided that all the design work be undertaken by Mr. Bodley, and all designs submitted to the Bishop, the architect, and the President of the Executive.

The intrepid band of ladies faced considerable scepticism: 'failure was predicted, notably by our friends in the South, who seemed to think that it was almost presumptuous to suppose that skilled workers could be found in the Liverpool Diocese, or that churchmanship and knowledge was sufficient for success'. Mr. Bodley was uncertain as to the abilities of this unknown group, and requested that each worker submit to him an example of her work, which had to pass the highly professional scrutiny of the firm of Watts and Company. They were also advised not to attempt

Three altar frontals made for the High Altar by the Embroidery Association. The top frontal, the red, has heavy gold embroidery on fine rich velvet. The middle one, the white, is the richest of all and is covered in figure-work, much of it in gold. The sight of the Altar at Easter and Christmas is truly glorious. The lowest frontal, the green, has been used more than the other two because it is appropriate throughout the long Trinity period.

figure work. However, when he saw the quality of their work, he immediately changed his mind, and the ambitious character of his designs indicated his confidence in the precision and skills of the Liverpool group. The first design he gave them was in 1905 for a festal frontal for the Lady Chapel, featuring vases of lilies worked in gold on cream damask.

After Bodley's death, the design work was given to Mr. C. G. Hare, his partner, and a most fruitful partnership was established between him and the Liverpool Association. By 1910, a complete set of altar frontals was ready, together with matching veils and burses. Not content with producing fine embroidery, the ladies were determined to provide all the linen and 44 surplices, all to be made to the pattern provided for them by St. Paul's Cathedral, and they also raised all the money necessary to finance the whole venture. The maintenance of the embroidery, linen and ornaments would have to be undertaken with care, and after gaining the permission of the Bishop, a Guild of Service was established to take charge of all the necessary care of the Sanctuary.

Even before the consecration of the Lady Chapel, they were at work on the frontals for the High Altar, fifteen feet in length. The first to be completed was the superb gold festal frontal with its 35 figures and

One of Hare's beautifully executed cartoons for a section of the Lady Chapel frontal.

thousands upon thousands of meticulous stitches of gold thread. The fame of the Liverpool work spread worldwide, and the architect of Montreal Cathedral came to see their work twice. Randall Davidson, Archbishop of Canterbury said, when he saw the Lady Chapel work, 'The half was not told me'. Lord Halifax went down on his knees to examine the details before remarking, 'There is not a bad bit of work in them'. Before the end of the whole enterprise, when Hare saw the way in which his designs had been carried through, he declared, 'It is the best amateur work I have ever seen'.

Even when the Lady Chapel had been formally dedicated, Scott was not free from adverse criticism from such Committee members as Robert Gladstone, who wrote to the Bishop on 7th July 1910 complaining at length about the details and positioning of the Altar and Reredos – these complaints, it seems, being based largely upon his opinion that 'Tryptychs are not in harmony with English churches'. The extent of the pressure upon the architect was recognised by Sir William Forwood, who noted to the Bishop that Scott 'had been bombarded with letters . . . and I have been really sorry for him'.

It is interesting for us now to stand quietly in the Lady Chapel and think of all those men and women whose skills saw the building through to completion. Young Owen Pittaway the stonemason; Mr. Joseph Phillips, sculptor, who undertook much of the fine decorative stone carving; and Radcliffe and Scott, whose friendship and co-operation were preparing for the next massive phase of building. Little did any of them know that the horror of war would split Europe in the following decade.

The Great War and a Chancel

CHAPTER
- Five -

URING the construction of the Lady Chapel, one man seemed to grow steadily in importance. Present, in a rather insignificant position, at the luncheon table in the Town Hall in 1904, was Frederick Moreton Radcliffe; a lawyer who was to become one of the greatest guiding forces in the history of the Cathedral enterprise. He was born in 1861, the eldest son of Sir David Radcliffe, who was Lord Mayor of Liverpool from 1884 to 1886. In 1901 Frederick became one of the two honorary treasurers of the Executive Committee. When in 1903 the Committee had doubts over the appointment of such a young and inexperienced architect, it was he who helped to formulate the compromise which made the appointment acceptable, and who travelled in Spain with the young Scott, seeing some of the great buildings which were to leave lasting marks on the design of the new Cathedral. It may well have been Radcliffe with

Bishop Chavasse at work with his papers. He worked very long hours and was a great letter-writer. Much of his correspondence, in tiny writing, has been preserved and is lodged in the Bodleian Library, Oxford.

whom Scott discussed his very first ideas for a single, massive central tower.

The early plans and drawings of the Cathedral show a building with a single transept over which rose twin towers: the only evidence for these towers observable today are the lower stages of the Eastern Transepts, which are clearly more massive than they need to be. We are told by people who knew him well that he would frequently make quick sketches on any piece of paper which might be to hand; a couple of these sketches have been preserved in the Radcliffe papers in the Liverpool Record Office, and give some clue as to what was starting to happen in Scott's mind.

We know Scott and Radcliffe became life-long friends, and Scott certainly stayed with Radcliffe at Lyme Grove, his house in Prescot. It is easy to imagine enthusiastic conversation between the two, Scott suddenly reaching out to pick up a piece of Radcliffe's notepaper on which to make two quick pencil sketches. One is a very rough sketch of what we now know as the Chancel, the great Central Space and the Eastern and Western Transepts. The other drawing is of the south elevation of the building; a building at this stage without any tower at all. These sketches were dated August 1909, and we know that in the autumn of that year Scott began to mention to the Committee the possibility of fundamental changes. At this time, though, the Committee's attention was firmly focused upon the plans for the service of consecration of the Lady Chapel, and nothing could divert their attention from that event.

The original floor plan of Scott's design had been traditional, in that twin towers rose above the arms of the transept at the junction of chancel and nave. In the new plan, the nave was shortened to balance the chancel, and a great central tower was flanked to east and west by transepts. The tower spanned the full width of the Cathedral, and the central space produced a breathtaking area capable of accommodating thousands of worshippers. Even though the foundations for twin towers had been put in and the piers themselves had begun to rise, the Committee (no doubt with the support of Radcliffe) had sufficient confidence in their young architect to accept his new ideas.

It must have been with some trepidation that he took his fully revised plans to the Committee in October 1910. In his own words, spoken many years later: 'It has always astonished me that the Committee allowed a young man in his twenties completely to alter a design chosen in a competition by two eminent assessors'. The Committee must have had total confidence in him as they accepted his changes, which 'very much commended themselves'. Scott estimated that the revised plan would be cheaper to build at 1/3½d per cubic foot, as against 1/6d.

We know from the records that in 1909 the walls of the Chancel had reached forty feet in height and the piers 29 feet. Excellent progress was being made, and they anticipated that the Chancel would be ready for use

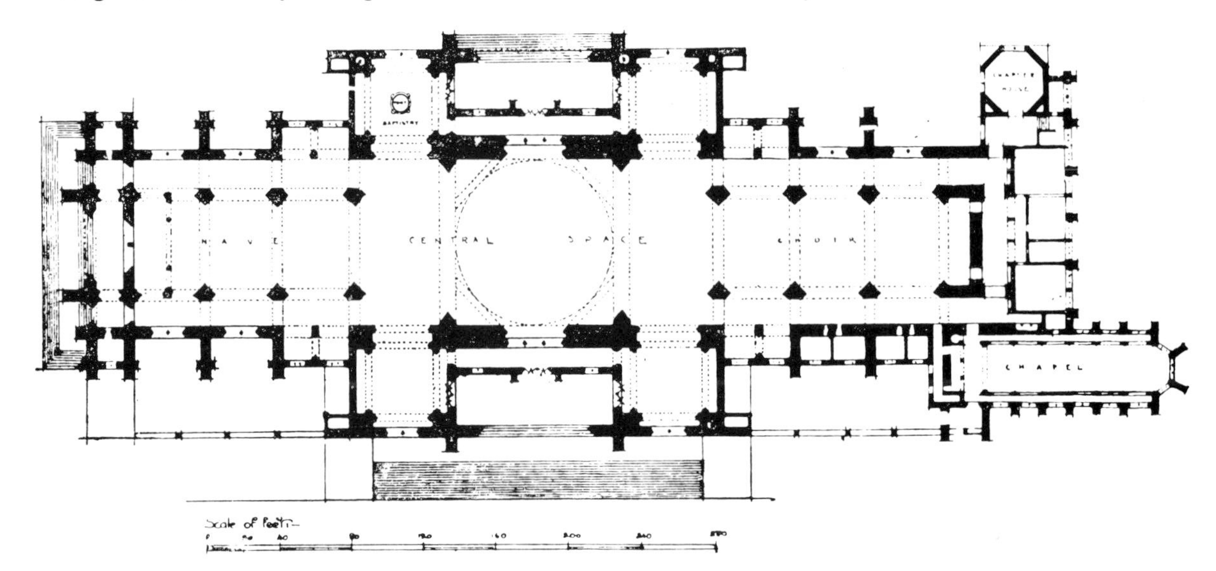

Left: *The 1910 design with a single central tower and a huge central space underneath it.*
Below: *Three photographs taken over a number of years trace the progress of the east end of the Cathedral viewed from the courtyard. This first one was taken around 1908. Work has just begun above ground level.*

by 1917. International politics, however, made this completion date impossible.

Several years earlier, diocesan politics almost caused a major upset in the plans for the Chancel. The actual planning of many of the main features was years ahead of the building process, and the negotiations surrounding one feature provoked the most unfortunate violent hostilities within the diocese. Mr. H. Douglas Horsefall was a member of the original Cathedral Committee. Autocratic in manner, and a very rich man, he was generous in his gifts to the Church – he had been personally responsible for the building of St. Agnes Church in Ullet Road, one of the foremost Anglo-Catholic churches in the diocese. He was a man used to having his own way.

His giving was always specific: 'that money must be used to further the

& SONS
LIVERPOOL

Morrison & Son
Builders
Wavertree

A view across the east end of the Chancel, looking towards the Reredos and window in about 1918. The photograph shows clearly the massive nature of the timbering which was needed in such a vast and lofty building.

interests and extend the teaching of what we may term the Catholic party in the Church of England'. Mr. Horsefall did not make any donation to the general building fund, but was anxious to donate £5,000 for the provision of the reredos. His letter to the Bishop reveals something of his character and mode of operation:

> Had there been no one to consider but myself, I should have liked to have put a great Crucifix with the simple legend *Sic Deus dilexit mundum*. But this I recognised as impossible, and should be content with a pictorial representation of the scene of the Crucifixion and if this is declined, I am quite content to believe that the money which I had destined for the glory of God 'in a holy and beautiful house' is required

Previous pages: *Two photographs of the east end under construction. Only two years separate the two images and the progress both to the Chancel and to the Chapter House is remarkable, particularly since the work was going on in war time.*

One of a series of photographs taken from the Upper Parliament Street end of Hope Street This photograph dates from around the end of the First World War and shows the east end covered in scaffolding, with the octagonal Chapter House in the foreground nearing completion and work just beginning on the Eastern Transept to the right of the photograph. The earlier Lady Chapel stands on the left, dwarfed in size by the emerging main part of the Cathedral.

> by him for another purpose, and that good will come out of what I could not but regard as a serious evil. For it will indeed be a serious matter and have far-reaching effects if such an offering is declined.

The threatening tone of these words is unmistakable.

Sir William Forwood, for one, felt considerable animosity towards both Horsefall and his plans: 'I think he must have known that the Reredos he wished would not be acceptable and the new offer would place us in a difficulty and therefore I cannot feel kindly disposed towards him'.

In a letter to Mr. Bodley who had been approached by Horsefall, Bishop Chavasse described the potential donor as 'a good and devout man', but as Bishop he was clear in his mind that the acceptance of such a gift would be deeply offensive to some members of the Church:

> The Diocese has put a trust in me of which I am unworthy. Men of all schools of thought have subscribed to the Cathedral on the definite understanding that, as Bishop, I should allow nothing to be introduced into the building which can offend reasonable churchmen. If, when they enter the Choir, the prominent object upon which their eyes rest is a large Crucifix, if when they come to Holy Communion the prominent figure before which they kneel is that of our Lord upon the Cross, they will think not unnaturally that they have been betrayed. From the very

Left: *The same, Eastern Transept, seen from inside the building, when it was nearing completion in 1919.*

Below: *Bishop Chavasse had wanted a building to stand out over the city's rooftops and, as this splendid photograph shows, he got just that, with the incomplete Cathedral already dominating the skyline. This view from the Pier Head also shows the old Custom House with its dome and classical columns.*

A beautiful photographic composition by Stewart Bale: the view up Nile Street to the Children's Porch of the Lady Chapel. It is interesting to compare the comparative scales of the houses and the Lady Chapel in this view and then to compare the Lady Chapel with the main Cathedral (see, for example, page 61).

first I have publicly stated that the new Cathedral will not be used as a Propaganda for any one particular set of Church views; and when it was known that a good and devout man like Mr. Douglas Horsefall declined to give any subscription to the fabric of the Cathedral and desired only to present the Reredos, a certain amount of feeling was created in the Diocese and outside it. Mr. Horsefall is a most munificent churchman, but . . . he declines to subscribe to any Diocesan object in order that he may concentrate his generous gifts on promoting in the Diocese what he calls 'the Catholic Revival'.

All the correspondence from the Bishop, Bodley and Forwood indicates their wish for compromise. The Bishop was anxious that, among other elements, the Reredos would feature the risen Christ more strongly than the dead Christ. He felt able to accept a crucified Christ along with other scenes from his earthly ministry, but the letters from Douglas Horsefall indicate that he was not looking for compromise. He was demanding a simple answer - positive or negative - to his offer, and was unwilling to enter into any negotiation. When no simple response was given, he

Preparations inside the Chancel. The pier in the centre divides the Chancel, to the right, from the North-East Transept. The gallery to house the organ console is visible on the north wall of the Chancel. Above, the frames of two of the organ cases are almost complete but they are without the large metal case pipes. *For the organ, see also page 107.*

This famous view of the partially built Cathedral towering over the rooftops must have given Liverpool people some idea of the vast scale of what was still to come. Older Liverpool residents will recognise the famous David Lewis building, long since demolished, in the centre of the picture.

threatened to put the whole matter in the hands of the press: and this he proceeded to do.

The ensuing article in the *Church Times* of the 23rd March 1906, under the heading 'A Generous Offer Refused', becomes an open attack on the Bishop by a highly partisan correspondent:

> Such discourtesy and bungling would appear to be incredible. Unhappily, they are significant of much which has happened recently in the Diocese . . . A prominent member of the Evangelical section said the other week in my hearing, 'Law is not administered in the Liverpool Diocese; it is manufactured'.

The *Church Times* correspondent seemed determined to present the idea that the Church in Liverpool, High and Low, was suffering at the hands of an intolerant autocrat. The writer reveals his scorn not only for the Bishop, but for the Evangelicals:

> The Protestant party which the Bishop emphatically calls 'some of our best churchpeople' are not likely to be appeased by the suggested change from Crucifixion to Ascension. They detest the idea of a Reredos. That they should be considered in this way, puny minority as they are, to the extent of slighting a Churchman who has shown his devotedness repeatedly and munificently is symptomatic of much which has happened recently.

The whole affair reveals something of the bitterness which existed even within the Church of England, to say nothing of the strength of animosity between Roman Catholic and Protestant Churches. Friendly working relations did exist at the top between such men as Canon Major Lester and Monsignor James Nugent, but at the grassroots in general there was little love lost between Catholic and Protestant in Liverpool during the first decades of the century.

As in other dealings in the diocese, the Bishop was able to steer a middle course. The Horsefall Reredos was never carved, but building work on the chancel went ahead.

In 1913, before the outbreak of war, Sir William Forwood retired and Frederick Radcliffe became the chairman of the Cathedral Executive, and also retained his chairmanship of the Stained Glass Committee. Under Radcliffe's astute eyes, decisions were taken over the details of the glass and sculpture which were to influence for ever the final form of the building. Various important features of the Chancel were donated by wealthy individuals: the organ was to be the gift of Mrs. Barrow; the Reredos of Mrs. Mark Wood; the East Window of Mrs. Ismay; the choir stalls of Lord and Lady Waring; the Bishop's Throne of Miss Watt, the last owner of Speke Hall. Tremendous attention was given to every aspect of design and decoration, and the notes of the Stained Glass Committee's meetings often strike a comic note as the members questioned the hair style of a long-dead saint, the size of a camel, or the thickness of a prophet's ankles. Over such matters the Bishop and Mr. Radcliffe seem to have been meticulous.

The onset of war soon led to two shortages: in labour, and in the inflow of new money. The Committee was determined that work should not cease, though they knew that the time was not right for a major fund-raising drive. Initially the monthly expenditure was cut to £2,000 and work continued. Various schemes were considered, but slowly work was moving ahead to complete both the Chancel and the Eastern Transept up to the tower arch.

Economic difficulties were considerable, though they faded into insignificance in comparison with the human problems. The carnage on the fields of France began to affect a high proportion of the Cathedral's workforce. In 1915, Mr. Sutton Timmis lost his only son in battle at the age of nineteen – a son later to be commemorated for all time in one of the great transept windows. 1916 saw the death of Captain David Radcliffe, once again an only son. In the following year, Bishop Chavasse received the news that his son Aidan was missing, and within a month came the news of the death of Noel – the only man in the Great War to be awarded the Victoria Cross and Bar for outstanding bravery.

Inevitably, there was a drastic slowing down in the progress of the building. Economic problems became even more serious, and a large portion of the workforce was in the armed forces; but work never ceased, even though the quarry was temporarily closed and did not become fully operational again until 1920. With monumental courage, determination and faith, the Committee continued with its work, even though by the end of hostilities one third of its members had lost close relatives. Personal grief was not allowed to impede progress, and the various committees met regularly, and painstakingly dealt with the thousands of detailed matters. To make matters worse, by the end of the war, building prices had doubled.

On 14th July 1919, eighteen years after the Bishop had made his great proposal to build a cathedral, the General Committee met in the Town Hall, and he spoke again about the nature of their achievement:

> In an age of materialism, uncertainty and doubt, the great Cathedral rising on St. James's Mount is a witness to the fact that there are still men and women amongst us who have convictions, to whom God and Christ and Eternity are real, and who are animated by a faith which is able alike to sustain a nation in the agony of an appalling war, and could lead its citizens to consecrate part of their wealth to glorify God by the erection of the most noble Houses that they could devise for His worship and honour.

An amusing snapshot of the new and old Bishops. In physique the two men could not have been more unlike, but both men can be seen as having been right for their times: the inspirational qualities of Chavasse were followed by the cool, organisational skills of David.

DR. CHAVASSE WELCOMES DR. DAVID, OCTOBER, 1923

At the 1901 meeting, the Bishop had spoken of a great building which would 'speak for God' in the middle of the city. Miraculously, through the years of war, that was what started to happen. The rising of the immense building above the slate roofs of Liverpool must have been every bit as dramatic as the appearance of the Octagon at Ely, or the spire at Salisbury in the Middle Ages.

We tried to imagine the thoughts and feelings of Francis James Chavasse as he was driven down to the Town Hall in 1901. We must again try to look into his mind as he was driven there, this time in a motor car, on Monday 24th September 1923. It was to be his last formal visit there as Bishop of Liverpool. After careful consideration, thought for his wife's health, and with his typical humility, he resigned the See so that a younger man could preside over the consecration of the great Cathedral he had inspired his diocese to build. On that day, the people of his diocese presented their beloved 'little Bishop' with an illuminated scroll, a silver tea and coffee service, and a cheque for £3,807.

As the Cathedral and the diocese sadly said farewell to the old Bishop, the new man at the Palace was arriving with great enthusiasm, and the eyes of the Church of England looked on with eager anticipation. Albert Augustus David had spent most of his working life in education: assistant master at Rugby, headmaster first of Clifton and then of Rugby. He had turned down a series of bishoprics before eventually accepting Bury St. Edmunds in 1921. He was imaginative, enthusiastic, an innovator and educator strong on organisation and administrative structures, liberal and yet autocratic in his ways. He appointed the Rev. Charles Raven, a future Regius Professor of Divinity at Cambridge, as provisional canon. Not only the Church in England, but the Church worldwide, must have become aware of events in Liverpool, and the imminent consecration of its new Cathedral.

CHAPTER
— *Six* —

Consecration

I wonder whether ever again in the history of Christendom a group of people will accomplish what was accomplished by the Cathedral community as it prepared itself for the day of consecration. Somehow, the new portion of the Cathedral, Chancel and Eastern Transepts were ready in time, the windows installed, the furniture in position. The choir stalls caused some concern, as the original pieces were destroyed by fire, and the whole set had to be re-made. The organ, though not complete, was more than adequate for the size of the completed section of the building.

There were worries about the building itself, but an even greater worry surrounded the form of service. The consecration of a cathedral is a very rare event and, not surprisingly, the *Book of Common Prayer* has not provided a form of service: the last cathedral to be built and consecrated on an entirely new site was Salisbury, in 1225. As Canon Raven wrote later:

> It was evident that to mark such an occasion no repetition of a traditional form would suffice; that it would not be enough to collect together a variety of ancient ceremonies and formulae and to combine them into an Office. What was needed was a service which, while fulfilling all that past experience could suggest, should possess a coherence, a rhythm, an appropriateness of its own for the circumstances of today. Such a service must be the work not of a liturgies expert (if this means a student of past precedents) but of a creative artist who perceived what the ceremony signified, knew how to interpret its significance in apposite technique, and could enable the congregation to experience and share in the dramatic movement of the whole.

Frederick Dwelly, Vicar of Emmanuel Church, Southport, was appointed Ceremoniarius to devise and run the service of consecration in the still far-from-complete Cathedral.

In Giles Gilbert Scott, the Cathedral building had a creator of genius, and, in the Rev. Frederick William Dwelly, a priest with the genius to use the building well. It has been reported that Augustus David, the recently-appointed Bishop, had admitted that he was unsure about creating an order of service worthy of the occasion. F. W. Dwelly was the Vicar of Emmanuel Church, Southport, a man known to both the Bishop and Canon Raven. Dwelly was invited to create the order of service for the consecration, and to take on the role of Ceremoniarius. It must be remembered that Liverpool did not then have a dean and chapter: the overall responsibility for the worship and running of the Cathedral lay temporarily in the hands of the Bishop. Scott created the body of the building: Dwelly brought it to life. For the next thirty years he was the poet and choreographer of worship in Liverpool Cathedral, and his influence is powerful even today.

He was born in Chard in 1881. Having started work in commerce in London, he went late to Cambridge, graduated, and was ordained in 1906. He served his first curacy at St. Mary's Church, Windermere, where he remained for four and a half years. He was extremely popular, and involved himself whole-heartedly in all branches of parish and town life. When he left, among many smaller gifts, he was presented with a grandfather clock, a leather-bound *Encyclopaedia Britannica*, a silver ink stand, an embroidered stool, a diamond and sapphire pendant for his wife, and a cheque for £420. He moved to become the senior assistant clergyman at the parish church of St. Matthew, Cheltenham.

Old newspaper reports show that he was clearly an eloquent and very popular preacher – people did not glance at their watches when he was in the pulpit. He had wide responsibilities in the parish because of the serious ill-health of the Rector, and he carried the parish and its two churches through the interregnum. Two hours before his final service at St. Matthew's, more people than the church could seat were queueing outside in the road. Extra chairs were placed in all available spaces, and he preached that night to a congregation of 2,000 on the text 'Whatsoever things are lovely, whatsoever things are of good report, think on these things'. At the end of the service he went immediately to the parish's other church, so that he could speak to the congregation there.

In 1916 he came to the Liverpool Diocese to become Vicar of Emmanuel Church in Southport. Soon there were reports of very impressive services at the church, and spirited, powerful preaching from the new incumbent. He was clearly a man with special gifts of leadership

The view from the temporary wall to the High Altar. Only the north case departments of the organ (seen here on the left) were completed by the date of the consecration. The steps in the Sanctuary were later modified to raise the height of the Altar so that it could be seen better from a distance.

and the ability to organise people and arrange memorable events. He marshalled all the youth organisations in the town for the Armistice thanksgiving service, and in November 1923 he devised the service for the unveiling of the town's impressive war memorial. Augustus David had been present at that service, and both he and Raven were aware of Dwelly's flair as an imaginative liturgist.

Dwelly could never be thought of as a scholar in the way that his friend Charles Raven could, but he was zealous in all his researching of old consecration practices. More significantly, he could write memorable prose, and his genius translated the results of his scholastic researches into symbolic actions and memorable choreography. Dwelly's gifts needed a cathedral - and the new Cathedral needed Dwelly.

No aspect of the services was to carry the taint of empty theatricality - like the decorative features within the building, the words, gestures and movement were to be meaningful, and the Bishop was anxious to ensure that the people of his diocese took seriously the event which was to take place. All the parochial clergy had details of the service in advance, so that they could spend time with their congregations in helping them to appreciate what was to happen in their new Cathedral on Saturday 19th July 1924 - exactly twenty years after the laying of the foundation stone. As Scott and Radcliffe walked together round the recently-completed works, they must have thought back to that earlier service, open to the sky, with the congregation seated on rough wooden benches.

No great service involving thousands of people is ever a happy accident. The whole had to be planned with military precision and rehearsed so as to minimise the chance of anything going wrong. There are reports of long rehearsals with Dwelly, clad in flannels and cricket shirt, racing round the building organising the arrangements for the main processions. Dwelly has since been described as 'an erratic genius' and 'a liturgical maniac', but he had a keen eye for ceremonial. An incident involving his friend Raven is revealing:

> The story has often been told that when rehearsing for a great occasion Dwelly became aware of the need for colour in a certain blank area in the Cathedral. 'What we need over there,' he exclaimed, 'is a splash of colour. You, Charles, in your chaplain's red cassock are just what we want. Please go and stand over there.' To which Charles's answer is supposed to have been: 'I was not aware, Mr. Dean, that when I was ordained to the sacred ministry it was in order to be a splash of colour in any situation.' But in general Charles accepted and delighted in the splendour of what he felt was a living pageant related to the contemporary world and not an imitation of some ancient glory.

That essentially was the challenge of the consecration service: the splendour of the past linked to a meaningful present. Dwelly was, of course, faced with a basic difficulty in that the previous consecration of a wholly new cathedral had been in pre-Reformation days, with much being made of the sealing of a religious relic within the Altar. Dwelly had to undertake careful adaptation to make the service relevant and acceptable to a Low Church Protestant diocese.

The serious spiritual tone of the whole day was set quietly and prayerfully in a night-long vigil in the Lady Chapel; a Watch of Prayer and Meditation began at 6 p.m. on Friday 18th July, and each of the twelve rural deaneries of the diocese was allotted one hour for the watch. The service was plain and without pageantry, and ended just before the hour with the Gloria and the final blessing. As people filed quietly out into the night sky, a queue of four hundred or so people waited to take their places. The final group emerged into the freshness of a superb summer morning, and almost five thousand people quietly meditated on 'The Cathedral', 'The Bishop and Clergy', 'The Faithful', and 'The City, the Country and the World'.

At the Bishop's wish, there was a celebration of Holy Communion early on Saturday morning in every parish church in the diocese, and a vast number of people made their spiritual preparation for the day. Saturday morning saw the city thronged with people. King George and Queen Mary had spent the night at Knowsley as the guests of Lord Derby, and they attended a ceremony at St. George's Hall before lunching at the Town Hall. All Mr. Dwelly's plans had been precise and thorough, but he must have been slightly concerned that human failings might intervene.

The congregation were all in their seats by 1.50 p.m., in order to be a part of the preliminary ceremonies. At a medieval ceremony, the bishop and all the people would have been outside; but in the twentieth century service, the Bishop in his purple cassock entered almost unnoticed and, accompanied by his Chaplains and the Ceremoniarius, inspected the building to see that all was ready. He said the Lord's Prayer and instructed

Ceremoniarius, Bishop and other diocesan dignatories outside the building.

the congregation in the Transepts to prepare themselves for the ceremony. He then withdrew to robe, leaving the whole of the Chancel empty.

Out of the silence emerged the first chords from the great organ – never before heard in public. Even though the organ was not complete, its effect on the listeners was electrifying, and the expectant congregation saw the first of the many processions begin to enter and take up their places. The assistant clergy, the beneficed clergy, and visiting choir members representing each cathedral in the Northern Province, followed each other in a steady stream.

While this was proceeding, the Bishop, now wearing his scarlet convocation robes, stood outside the central doors and spoke the words of the first prayers. He then knocked on the doors with his crozier, but his knock remained unanswered, and the Bishop and his procession moved off to circle the outside of the building while chanting the litany of the diocese. They paused at a spot along the north wall to mark a small consecration cross, subsequently to be carved into the stone. While this procession was moving slowly on the outside, other processions of dignitaries were making their entrance into the building – deans, bishops, archbishops, metropolitans and lord mayors. Mr. Dwelly's careful timing ensured that all was moving without a hitch, until sudden cheering from the crowd along St. James's Road heralded the unexpected.

Through some unexplained error, the King and Queen had arrived at the Cathedral some fifteen minutes ahead of schedule, and the news was taken to Mr. Dwelly and the Bishop. 'What shall we do?' asked the Bishop.

A poor-quality snapshot taken before the start of the service. It is of interest because it shows the King and Queen, having arrived too early, waiting outside the doors as they watched the arrival of the processions.

The Bishop at the High Altar during the service of consecration. The fine stone-gilt figures of the Reredos, depicting the entirely appropriate scene of the Last Supper, can be seen. To left and right of the Altar are credence tables flanked by stone angels. When the Sanctuary's steps were later raised, these tables became seats and the angels disappeared!

'That is for you to decide, My Lord,' replied Mr. Dwelly; to which the Bishop could only respond, 'Well, go and ask if the King will kindly wait.' This message was conveyed to Lord Derby, who was in attendance upon His Majesty. 'Can the King wait?' The response was explosive. 'Damn it, the King can't wait.' Mr. Dwelly replied in the now-famous words, 'My Lord, this service is not for the King but for Almighty God'. His Majesty must have approved of the sentiments, and agreed to wait and watch the processions. It gave him the opportunity to cross the road and inspect the youth organisations lining the route.

The Queen, meanwhile, was standing outside the door at the top of the great flight of steps, and she became curious as to exactly what was on the other side of this door – a door to be kept closed on the orders of Mr. Dwelly. The Queen became very curious, and when a Queen asks to be permitted to go through a door, it must be hard to refuse her request. The steward inside, seeing the door suddenly pushed open, exclaimed, 'Oh my God, it's the Queen.' But the Queen entered the building unseen, and was able to watch part of the great clergy procession – an interesting activity for a monarch more usually part of a procession than watching one.

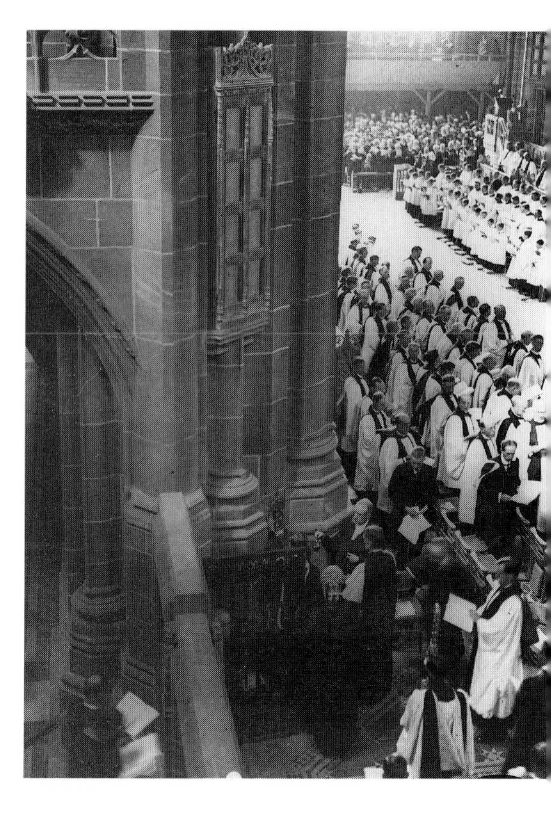

The consecration cross being marked on the pillar. The balcony erected against the temporary wall can be seen on the right. Though built specifically for the consecration, it proved very popular and remained in use for many years. The congregation felt very close to the preacher.

At the appointed time, and not before, their Majesties entered through the main door, a loud voice called 'God save the King', and the congregation rose to sing the national anthem before Sir Frederick Radcliffe and the Earl of Derby led their Majesties to their seats on the south side of the Chancel.

When they were seated, there was a loud knocking as the Bishop struck the west door with his crozier and called, 'Lift up your heads, o ye gates, and be ye lift up ye everlasting doors, and the King of Glory shall come in.' He was answered from inside with the question, 'Who is the King of Glory?', to which he replied, 'The Lord of Hosts, He is the King of Glory.' Sir Frederick Radcliffe formally opened the doors, saying, 'Right Reverend Father in God, we pray you to consecrate this Cathedral Church,' and the Bishop replied, 'I am ready to proceed to the Consecration.' Lord Derby presented him with the Cathedral keys, and the Bishop entered at the head of a great procession.

Almost immediately upon entry, he knelt in prayer while everyone else moved to their appointed positions. As the Bishop continued his prayer, the choir sang Sir Hubert Parry's anthem *I was glad when they said unto me we will go into the House of the Lord*, and the whole building awoke to the music. Only when the final resonating chords had faded into the silence did the Bishop rise and ask the whole congregation to kneel silently in prayer for the new cathedral. Ashes had been scattered on the floor in front of the desk where the Bishop had prayed, and with his crozier he drew alpha and omega, and the cross of St. Andrew. This was an acknowledgement that every human faculty belongs to Christ, and through his action the Bishop claimed for Christ the whole field of learning, of science and of art. Probably the Bishop did not realise that the marks he made that day would be retraced annually by the youngest chorister, on the Sunday closest to the anniversary of the consecration.

Two old friends of the Bishop then walked through the crowded

Chancel carrying the Book of the Gospels and the Book of the Ordinal, which they placed symbolically upon the Altar. Only then did the Bishop move slowly to the east, carrying the keys in his right hand and the crozier in his left. So, as with any man, when we draw near to God we must go alone yet strengthened by the Gospels and the authority of the Church. His walk was in silence, and every eye in the Cathedral was upon his progress. In its simplicity this was one of the most memorable and significant moments in the whole ceremony.

No human error spoiled the significance and solemnity of the movements but, once again, human frailty almost caused disaster. The Bishop's Chaplain was to go ahead with the Archbishop's procession and leave the Bishop to walk entirely alone, but half a dozen choir boys had become detached from their part of the procession, and Mr. Dwelly ordered the Chaplain, 'Take these boys to the Narthex'. Unfortunately, the Chaplain did not know the meaning of the word. He took them quietly to the west entrance - accidentally finding the Narthex. One disaster thwarted, the Chaplain had the embarrassing task of getting himself right up to the other end of the building. 'My legs melting from under me, my knees quaking with fear,' the poor man embarked upon his lonely journey, wondering what its symbolic significance might be.

After members of the Cathedral clergy had led prayers of dedication for various parts of the building, the Bishop led the Solemn Prayer of

Queen Mary signing the Deed of Consecration. King George stands to her left and Bishop David to her right.

Consecration, immediately followed by the rejoicings of the people: 'Alleluia, the Lord is in His Holy Temple, Alleluia! The Lord is here to bless. Alleluia! Amen.'

As organ and congregation combined for the Doxology, the Bishop came down out of the sanctuary and processed to a pillar in the south-west wall of the Chancel where he made a stencil mark of the consecration cross, and almost immediately Mr. R., Cooper, stonemason, began to carve the cross into the stone. The sound of mallet and chisel could be heard at times through the singing of the hymn *Christ is made our sure foundation*.

Next the focus of the service shifted to the Chancel steps where a table had been placed ready for the ceremony of witness. When he had assured himself that all was in order for the ceremony, the Bishop signed the document, followed by the King and Queen, the Archbishops, Lord

An unusual view of the Cathedral from the east end. The King and Queen lead the procession away from the Cathedral on their way to Knowsley.

Derby, Sir William Forwood, Sir Frederick Radcliffe, and the Lord Mayor. As everyone stood, the Bishop, arms outstretched, pronounced:

> By virtue of the sacred office in the Church of God we now declare to be consecrate, and for ever set apart from all profane and common uses, the House of God under the dedication of the Cathedral Church of Christ in Liverpool, in the name of the Father, and of the Son, and of the Holy Spirit. Amen.

During the singing of the hymn *City of God*, the Archbishop of York moved in procession to the site of the pulpit to preach his sermon. He began by reminding his listeners that, above all else, the Cathedral was evidence of the city's Christian faith, unshaken through years of great political, social and spiritual turmoil. The preacher praised the laymen of the diocese for their faith, determination and perseverance:

> In the heart of the people of Liverpool there is an unshaken confidence that whatever the changes and chances of history may be, the spell of Christ's religion will stand firm in the hearts of men . . . [through the presence of the great Cathedral, the people would be refreshed and restored] . . . souls wearied by the toil, bewildered by the sorrows, haunted by the doubts of human life, entering these doors will feel a touch of the rest that remains for the people of God, and in the stillness know that God is with them.

The Archbishop's words were spoken in a cathedral as yet only one third of its finished size, yet his words were prophetic, as day after day the Cathedral speaks its silent message to the steady streams of visitors.

After the taking up of the collection, representatives from all parts of the diocese carried in the ornaments and sacred vessels to the Cathedral clergy, who placed them on the Altar together with documents about the Cathedral and its builders. When the Archbishop had pronounced his blessing, the Bishop and the Cathedral clergy moved out in procession, while the choir sang William Blake's *Jerusalem* to the music of Sir Hubert Parry. After the singing of the hymn *Praise my soul the King of Heaven*, the congregation processed out into the sunshine of a beautiful summer day.

It must have been with a sense of exhilaration and relief that some of the principal characters walked out into the light. Scott, now 43, eager for the next phase of the building, and later that day to be knighted; Forwood, whose early determination to raise money and enthusiasm had been successful; Radcliffe, deeply involved in so many aspects of the whole project. Sadly, the 'Little Bishop' was not present: Chavasse was not sufficiently well to leave Oxford.

The craftsmen builders with their families in the streets outside the Cathedral could say with complete justification, 'We built it'. But as the *Church Times* reporter commented, the consecration day was the brainchild of one diocesan clergyman: 'If any person at all is entitled to take credit for the events of this week in Liverpool Cathedral, that person, above all, is Mr. Dwelly'.

Two sides of a brick wall

CHAPTER
- Seven -

UNTIL Consecration Day and the week of services that followed, there had been one single-minded focus of labour and attention: the finishing and the consecration of the Chancel and the Eastern Transept. The next phase of the Cathedral story has to reflect divided attention between the two sides of the massive temporary brick wall. On the one side, the Cathedral company and its patterns of worship were being established while simultaneously, on the other side, a building programme even more adventurous than the first was under way.

Before the consecration, Sir Frederick Radcliffe issued a challenge to some of the Cathedral clergy: 'The laymen of Liverpool are giving you this great gift: I sometimes ask myself if you will be able to use it'. Many people must have realised that 'success' on the consecrated side of the wall would be a crucial factor in creating the moral and financial support essential for the building of the rest of the Cathedral.

If one man is to be thought of as being at the centre of Cathedral growth between 1923 and 1931, it must be Charles Raven, one of the greatest theological scholars of his day. He was born in 1885, five years after the formation of the Diocese of Liverpool, and had contacts with the region from the early years of his boyhood; his family spent their holidays at Parkgate on the Wirral, where he was able to pursue his passion for observation and natural history. A glittering undergraduate career at Cambridge was crowned by a double first after which, to most people's astonishment, he accepted the post of Assistant Secretary for Secondary Education with Liverpool City Council.

His work and life in lodgings in Canning Street, less than a quarter of a mile from the Cathedral, did not give him great satisfaction; but he was greatly excited and influenced by his contact with a boys' club at The Colosseum in Fleet Street, a little back street parallel with Bold Street. One feature of the club was a Sunday night service held in Picton Hall, with youthful congregations numbering over eight hundred. The influence of the Colosseum experience seems to have been strong. While his mind was set on ordination and a curacy, there came the news that he was being considered for the post of Dean of Emmanuel College, Cambridge; he was elected unanimously.

He had no notion when he left his lonely rooms in Canning Street that in 1923, Augustus David would bring him back to Liverpool as a residentiary canon to be centrally involved in education and work with newly ordained clergy. On Tuesday mornings young curates, fresh from theological college, attended at the Cathedral for what must have been unforgettable sessions with Raven and Dwelly. A young curate from Liverpool Parish Church was one of the few students able to approach Raven in intellectual capability; Michael Ramsey, one day to become Archbishop of Canterbury.

Charles Raven had been appointed Provisional Canon Chancellor only

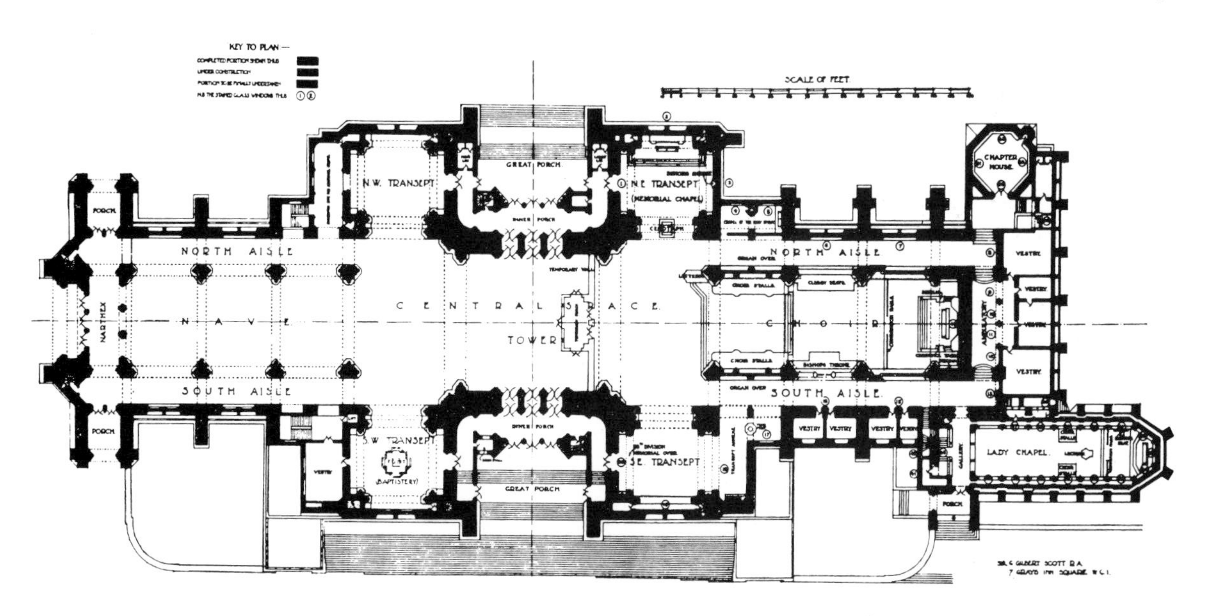

The Cathedral plan in 1927. By this date the Cathedral had taken on more or less its final design, except for the extreme west end (the left of the plan). Transepts to both east and west of the great porches produce the huge Central Space, while the Nave has three bays to match the Chancel. These features produce the symmetry of the modern design. Note that the disabled access has given way to a flight of steps down to St. James's Road.

months before the consecration, and Frederick Dwelly joined him as a canon a year later. These two figures were central to the establishment of the worshipping Cathedral, and we have some insight into their thinking through the pages of a little book written by Raven in 1933, *Liverpool Cathedral – An Impression of its Early Years*. Raven's book, and the preoccupation of bishop and clergy in the early years, rightly focused upon 'the function of a cathedral in relation to the world in the twentieth century'.

Many of the medieval cathedrals had unbroken traditions dating back to their consecration, whilst other more recent cathedrals were established upon existing parish churches with their own styles and traditions. The great city of Liverpool had established a wholly new foundation, which had to face the challenge of the 'creative adventure' of developing:

> a life worthy of the community and of the age that had produced it. The eternal revelation in Christ must be presented in terms that can be

An overview of the site taken from the roof of the North East Transept in June 1926, showing the timbering in position ready for the concreting of the foundations of the Central Space. The area to the right will become the North (Welsford) Porch and the present-day Refectory. The Oratory can be seen in the distance.

> understood by the people of today. Its theology must be a real interpretation of God to minds thinking along lines of modern knowledge: its ceremonial, its music, its services must enable modern folk to experience worship: its organisation must display the aspiration after fellowship and the ability of the Church to rise above legal and mechanical relationships.

The theological basis of any cathedral is going to be as fundamentally important as the rock upon which its physical foundations are laid. Meetings of the diocesan clergy were held in the Cathedral to discuss theology and general matters of religious significance. Much of this was preparation for the Church Congress held in Southport in 1926. A Cathedral School of Divinity was established, and a wide range of courses at different levels was made available. There was no exclusiveness of attitude - labels of churchmanship were avoided, and the life of the Cathedral was for the whole city and diocese:

> The great communal services, medical, educational and artistic, financial, industrial and commercial, were in fact ministries and vocations; and that the first task of the church was to arouse the consciousness of God, to foster worship and the practice of His presence, and to show how this experience could be related to and must transform the whole conduct of our daily life.

It is too easy for religion to become, for many people, divorced from the rest of life, and the Cathedral community was determined to be outgoing and practically involved in all aspects of life. Strong links were established with the arts and sciences, learned professions, industrial and social services, 'illustrating a basic principle of the Cathedral's theology, that all such callings were in fact ministries of the Spirit, and thus creating living links between religion and the other human interests'.

The service of consecration had been so effective and memorable that it was obvious from then on that such a building demanded enormously high standards in the performance of its ceremonial, and the devising of its services: 'every great service must be in the highest sense a work of art'. The Cathedral community knew that they possessed a building likely to rank among the great buildings of the world, and the conduct of the consecration revealed that F. W. Dwelly's liturgical skills were a match for those of the architect. Here was someone who understood how the building could be used, and could inspire and marshal the whole community. The splendour of the great services remains imprinted on the mind, and the words and movements are woven into a unified experience within the glory of the building. As a later bishop was to remark, 'You have to go to Liverpool Cathedral if you want to see how to walk to the glory of God. Every procession is an act of worship'.

The Cathedral did not set out to function as a kind of high-grade parish church, ministering only to its small group of regular worshippers; indeed, part of its work was to attract into worship many people who were not themselves regular members of a parish congregation. The Cathedral services might well be a form of evangelism which could then be more effectively followed up in the greater intimacy and continuity of the parish: 'Hence its services aimed rather at inspiration than at edification, at arousing desire more than satisfying it, at attracting outsiders more than ministering to a regular congregation'.

'The 8.30' became legendary throughout the diocese and among all age groups, and at the centre of the success of this venture were the figures of Raven and Dwelly. A later Cathedral figure, Frederick Dillistone, describes the extraordinary preparations for the weekly preaching:

> Dwelly would lie flat on one of the great oak tables in a darkened vestry before going in to preach. Raven would pace up and down, almost physically sick, rehearsing his words and gestures like an actor. Dwelly captured his audience by sheer informality of approach, talking to them as his friends for whom he really cared, about important matters which they had not perhaps sufficiently taken into account. Raven captured them by his looks, his gestures, his command of his subject, perhaps most of all by his ability to relate to the great themes of the New Testament, to personal needs and duties . . . There seemed to be in Charles a quality of incandescence; his burning spirit set his whole personality alight and this communicated itself in an extraordinary way to his audience. Incandescence, imagination, charisma, electrifying – these were words which have been used by people of widely different backgrounds in an attempt to describe the effect of his preaching. The ultimate secret, as for all forms of genius, remains a mystery.

For almost twenty years to the time of consecration, the work on the site involved building upwards in the form of piers and walls, windows, vaults and roofs, but 1925 saw a change of focus as all the attention moved back down to the ground. For months, the appearance of the site to the general visitor would have been chaotic.

On July 21st 1925, the first anniversary of consecration, the first soil of the new site was formally turned and the next phase of the foundations began, though at the same time most of the working plant had to be relocated. A cottage was demolished; the setting-out shed and office were moved. The old stone saws were completely overhauled and resited, and the crane track was modified. Only when all this had been completed could the new work be seen to be under way, under the careful eye of Owen Pittaway, now Clerk of Works.

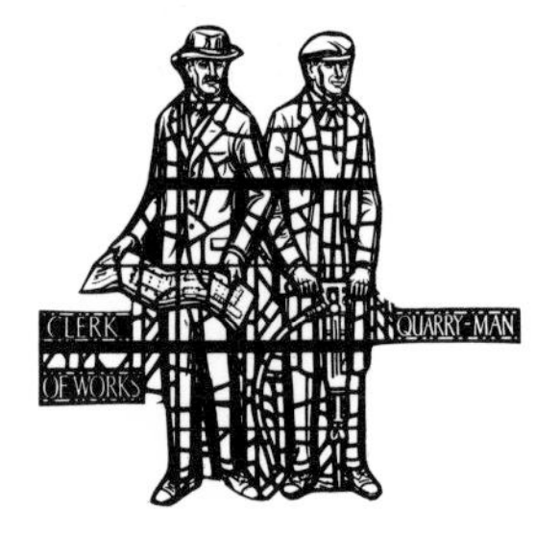

The position of the new foundations was marked out on the ground in wood before the topsoil was removed to lay bare the underlying rock. The immediate surface rock was too soft for load-bearing and had to be excavated. Pick and shovel had been used twenty years before for the Chancel foundations, but now the pneumatic drill speeded and eased the whole operation. The first signs of progress which might have been noticed by the people of Liverpool would have been the steady stream of lorries carrying the spoil from the site to a tip at Broadgreen. By the

View westwards through the new section of the building. Again, the view can be located by the Oratory in the distance; the modern Visitor Centre is on the right. At last the size and splendour of the Central Space could begin to be appreciated. The banker masons seen here were able to work close to the places where finished stones were to be fixed.

autumn of 1925, three hundred tons of spoil were coming out every day – twelve thousand tons in all between August and December. On the river side of the site, good rock was exposed between 17 and 23 feet of the surface, while on the ravine side a maximum depth of fifty feet had to be reached.

Excavations of such magnitude required large quantities of heavy timbering. Fourteen thousand feet of foot-square timbers were set in place by skilled operatives. The work was difficult in that the timbers placed last and deepest in the excavations were those which had to be removed first as soon as the concreting began. The men who carried out this specialised work moved on to other sites, but much of the timbering was used again later, when platforms to support the roof vaulting were being constructed.

By March 1926, concreting was being done at the rate of 150 to 200 tons of concrete a day, and employing 110 men. This section of the foundation work was the most extensive of its kind in the whole history of the

The Gambier Terrace view in the early summer of 1930. Work is well under way on the second set of Transepts. These had to be completed in order to allow the construction of the Tower, which they helped to buttress.

building, because it would eventually support not only the Central Space and Western Transept, but also the massive central tower which Scott planned to build when funding became available.

The most urgent task was to find space for the banker masons whose progress in preparing the stone determined the speed at which building could proceed. To make much-needed space, the old timber refectory was dismantled, and another one constructed in the courtyard at the east end. It was not a beautiful building, but one necessary for the life of the Cathedral.

One group of people watched the new work on the site with special enthusiasm and interest: the 'Cathedral Builders'. The Builders were an increasingly large group of people who wished to be associated with, and to support, the enterprise, but who were not able to make large financial donations. Instead, each gave what he or she could afford through a team of voluntary collectors. An annual Builders' service became an important feature of the organisation, and at the end of these well-attended gatherings, the Builders were conducted out on to the building site to see the progress of the work. One of the most significant features of this movement was the publication of the *Cathedral Builders Quarterly Bulletin*, a little journal which has done much to preserve the building's story for posterity. The very first Cathedral Builder was Master Simon Cotton, a boy whose parents Vere and Elfreda were to become the scribes of the Cathedral's history as they edited the *Bulletin* from 1925 through to the one hundredth edition in 1977.

By June 1931 the rapid progress on the building was clearly visible on the skyline, and preparations were under way for the construction of the massive western tower arch. Great balks of timber were being delivered to the site to form the platform on which the arch was to be built. The uprights were of Oregon pine, a foot square and up to 86 feet in length. Nearly half a mile of timber was erected, which would have to support three hundred tons of masonry during the construction of the arch.

On 29th June 1931 the Dean and Chapter of Liverpool Cathedral were incorporated by Order of Council - making history again, because such an event had not taken place since the Reformation. Before incorporation, the Bishop had been in charge of Cathedral affairs, but from now on the Dean and Chapter took full responsibility for their great building and their great worshipping community. The Deanery is in the patronage of the Crown and His Majesty appointed Frederick William Dwelly first

The foundation of the Dean and Chapter in October 1931. This is one of the few Cathedral photographs to show Canon Raven, here shown in the centre of the Chancel steps.

Dean of Liverpool.

The culminating service for the foundation of Dean and Chapter was celebrated at 11 a.m. on Sunday 4th October 1931. Even the slightly carping correspondent of the *Church Times* had to admire the ordering of the service:

> Though the ornateness of the Liverpool Ceremonial made some of us thankful that in our ordinary churches we have the simple Western rite, yet I am glad to admit that every detail of the elaborate service was carried out with perfection. There was a total absence of fussiness. Every official knew his part, merged himself into it, and did it without self consciousness. The result was a miracle of naturalness; there was nothing of that 'play acting' feeling so often manifest in Anglican ritualism.

Timber platforms way above ground became centres of the building process. This view of the start of the North-West Transept vault was taken early in 1931. The first stones of the arch are already in position on the timber formwork.

Right: *The massive timbers on which the western tower arch is to be constructed dwarfs the figure of Owen Pittaway, Clerk of Works, in the spring of 1932.*

Below: *And, from the outside, a dramatic view of the same tower arch viewed from the west. Without the Nave this end view of the central section of the Cathedral gives a good indication of the impressive width of the building. Note the clutter of buildings at the base of the building, and the gravestones from the old cemetery.*

By the summer of 1932 the brick and stone of the new arch are going into position. Still the traditional scaffolding techniques are being used, with timber wedges to help ensure the tension of the ropes.

The canons had formally been installed on the Wednesday, and they met in the Chapter House where the service commenced as the Chapter Clerk read the greeting from the Archbishop of York. The choir led the Cathedral procession into the Chancel as they sang *I was glad when they said unto me we will go into the house of the Lord.* A very junior member of the choir on that day was one R. Woan, later to become Choir Master.

The sky was overcast for most of the service, but at a high point in the ceremonial, as Dean Dwelly knelt before the Bishop in the centre of the chancel, the sun broke through the clouds. The East Window is acknowledged by most people as being too dark unless the mid-day sun is

The same arch viewed from the side shows a bricklayer at work on the ring of bricks soon to be overlayed with stone. Successive layers of building material were not bonded together, so that any minor movement or settling could be accommodated without damaging the arch.

behind it, but for a few minutes the near-lifesize figures blazed in rich colour, surrounded by great shafts of gold light shining through the plainer glass.

An interesting feature of the service was the installation of a College of Counsel; a group of laymen from the diocese and beyond whose wisdom and expertise could give valuable service to the new chapter. Sir Frederick Radcliffe was one member, as were John Masefield the Poet Laureate, and the composer Martin Shaw. Dean Dwelly had the knack of attracting to the service of the Cathedral a range of talented people whose artistry was to enrich the worship in many ways. In the field of music Martin Shaw, Vaughan Williams and Gustav Holst contributed their talents in the early years. The invitation and Order of Service book for the occasion were designed by Edward Carter Preston, whose elegant, powerful sculpture was to enhance so many parts of the building.

After a lunch at the Adelphi Hotel, John Masefield addressed the company, speaking on what a cathedral was and should be:

> To most of us a Cathedral is a big and beautiful building, made from four to seven centuries ago by men of extraordinary genius, as an offering to God, and as a house for the throne from which the Bishop might watch them draw near. Usually such a building is kept in good repair, it is often thronged with sightseers, who sometimes in the course of a year contribute large sums towards its upkeep. Sometimes the sightseer is slightly inconvenienced by the presence of a few old infirm men and women, gathered in a corner to listen while a man in vestments gabbles something, but the inconvenience comes seldom and is always slight. The sightseer is usually more pestered by guides, who will tell him that such an arch is late thirteenth century and the other window is early fourteenth, and expect money payment for the information. Looking into his guide book, he will read that Ruskin thought that such a tracery was the last quite pure tracery to be traced by an upright heart, and that somebody else thought that the profound knowledge evident in every line of the Bishop's Tomb marks the culminating point of the Cinquecento.
>
> Coming away from such a place, the sightseer sometimes reflects that the place is dead and had better be buried.
>
> As it happens, I have only once, and then only for two weeks, lived sufficiently near to any Cathedral to have felt its influence in my life. Cities today have become too big for the citizens to have a civic sense; a city dweller may well be five miles from his Cathedral: so it has happened to myself. Often a city dweller cannot see his Cathedral without making a special journey. This brings me to my first point of

what a Cathedral should be.

It should be, first of all, a place plainly to be seen by the citizens, and by those in the district. The Parthenon at Athens is the most perfectly placed of all great temples. The sites of many castles would be perfect for Cathedrals. Amiens is well placed, so is Durham; so are York, Gloucester, Salisbury and St. Paul's Cathedral. So is this great Cathedral of Liverpool. A Liverpool Cathedral should be readily seen from many points of the city, and, above all, by the life of the city, the river, with its ships and docks. All Cathedrals should be specially conspicuous by tower or spire, and these again should be made more conspicuous by some great figure of white or gold, the guardian of the city; and some further glory of windvanes telling the windshifts, and great bells telling the hours and their quarters, and ringing for the city's joys; in this city for the ship launched or the ship come home. And in this city I would have the tower such that mariners, who are the life of the city, could adjust their compasses by it, and see the storm signals and the time signals upon it, so that it should be their tower pre-eminently.

Then Cathedrals have been made great in the past because their citizens have believed in them, and have given greatly of their best to make them glorious. In their great times they have provided for all great artists the opportunity to indulge the imagination to the full. They have used the best skill of their time. The skill in a nation does not vary greatly from century to century, but in some centuries it is encouraged, and greatly used, in others it is neglected, in others it is depressed and abused. Cathedrals in the past have taken the very best skill of their time and encouraged it to the full. Their builders, sculptors and painters, their metal workers, paviors, glaziers and carpenters have been of their best. All the skilled ones of the time have had the joy of contributing; and the rich ones have had the joy of helping. Poets, perhaps have been looked at somewhat askance by Cathedrals in the past (I do not here blame the Cathedrals wholly), and the results of the coolness may be seen in the hymnals. Still, some of the noblest Cathedrals' decorations known to me are illustrations of Dante; and there was a time when at York and at Coventry, if not elsewhere, poets gave of their best to link the life of the city with the city's holiest place.

Certainly a Cathedral, besides being visible at a distance, should be splendid within, with the best that all artists and citizens can offer. This splendour should touch and mark all her parts and precincts, and not only her building, but the many institutions attached to her, for teaching, healing and relieving. She should be the place to which all the generalities of her citizens, as well as those of the artists of the time, should turn and flow.

Then since the main purpose of a Cathedral is worship, and the Dedication of a Cathedral is to some special attribute of what is ever to be worshipped. That Dedication should have its Feast of a solemnity great and touching, in some way that many might share and all feel. Here the arts are needed, for by the arts men are linked, as by the intellect men are kept asunder.

> How the touching of all souls may be wrought, is for inspiration to show, but no Cathedral can be serving Life that does not draw Life into it, all the Life of its community. Sports, contests, exhibitions, draw whole communities; they always did and always will; contest and spectacle cannot fail. Yet they have always yielded their place as chief attraction to the sincerity of men in earnest.
>
> This Cathedral of Liverpool, the greatest of modern Cathedrals, is a Church of the Resurrection. It comes into the life of our time, in a decade when all the ways of life known to us from childhood have to be remade, when the nation has to be recreated, with what difficulty we do not yet know, but no doubt with much. This Cathedral, therefore, should be the symbol of that Resurrection: and at the same time its standard. What has been muffled and in shrouds and buried down deep after being broken by the soldiers, should emerge here and be triumphant. Then indeed it would be a Cathedral that Is and Is as it should be.

'The greatest of modern Cathedrals' Liverpool certainly was, and with men of the stature of Raven as part of the chapter the quality of its thought and worship could be a match to the building. Raven did not look into a medieval past, but into an exciting future: 'Religion is not static, but dynamic and adventurous, not as a system of duties, but as a way of living'. His vision of the cathedral and its functions was wide:

> It is in a unique sense the spiritual home of the people of Liverpool, and should serve particularly to express their corporate devotion to God and their fellowship with one another.
>
> The Cathedral should be above all sectional and divisive influences and

Sir Giles Scott and Owen Pittaway at one of their many planning meetings.

> able to unite us all in whatever makes for true service to God and man . . . It should be a centre for unity, where all men can sink their divisions in the sole adoration of Him in whom there is neither Jew nor Greek.

The people of Liverpool and the wider church may well have been able to accept the notion of Jew or Greek, but shortly after Raven went back to Cambridge as Regius Professor of Theology, parts of the Church of England found themselves unable to accept a Unitarian.

Unitarianism has always been strong in Liverpool, and such families as Rathbone, Holt and Melly had for years been at the centre of social work amongst the poor. Dean Dwelly invited two eminent Unitarians, L. P. Jacks and Lawrence Redfern, to preach at non-liturgical services in the Cathedral and thereby ignited a fury in parts of the Church of England. The sequence of events in the famous case are not relevant in this context, but parts of the outcome were unfortunate for the Cathedral and the diocese. Although the Bishop publicly supported the Dean, the affair opened up a serious rift between them. For eight years prior to the foundation of Dean and Chapter, David had correctly assumed the position of Dean, and after 1931 he had difficulty in resigning himself to the change. Even in the carefully measured words of Dr. Dillistone, Raven's biographer, we read, 'To put it bluntly the Bishop found it difficult to keep his hands off the Cathedral'.

A spectacular view over the smoky rooftops to the city was opened up when all the timber had been removed from the tower archway in the winter of 1932.

CHAPTER
- *Eight* -

'Specially conspicuous'

THE Cathedral story has been unfolded through the words and eyes of eminent men – Bishop, architect, Dean, Chancellor – but the next phase is best seen through the eyes of a lad of sixteen. John Rowbottom came from a family of stonemasons. His father had worked on the Lady Chapel but, like so many of the earlier Cathedral workforce, he did not return from France, leaving a widow with the difficult task of bringing up a growing family in hard times. When John left school there was no work to be found, but as a war widow Mrs

Rowbottom managed to persuade Colonel Alan Tod, Chairman of the Executive Committee, to give the lad a start to follow in his father's footsteps on the Cathedral site.

One morning in 1932, young Rowbottom arrived on the site not knowing what to expect. Today, as an old man sitting happily in his armchair, his eyes twinkle and his round face creases into a smile as he admits that on that first morning he was scared out of his wits because he seemed to be surrounded by the biggest, ugliest men he had ever seen. Right from the start he was put to work with an experienced banker mason, to begin to learn his trade in the sheds where the straightforward ashlar blocks were being prepared. He had to stand still and watch, ready with a small brush to keep the stone and the banker clear of fragments. He had a mallet and chisel in his hands from the first day, but he soon discovered that any misdemeanour or poor work was greeted with a swift clout from the master mason. He was also kept busy as 'can lad'. In those

Part of the veritable army of banker masons required to keep up with the building progress in the 1930s. They had little protection in bad weather. This is exactly the scene that would have greeted young apprentices like John Rowbottom on their first day at work on the site.

A dramatic view of the under-tower space in the summer of 1931. The Chancel roof can be seen in the background. Piles of bricks and stone wait for expert hands to raise them to their final positions. Note the brickwork in the top right of this photograph – alternate courses jut outwards to provide a key for affixing the blocks of facing stone.

days, each workman had his own metal tea can with a wire handle, and a lid which doubled as a cup. The 'can lad' poured on the boiling water, and delivered the cans round to the men all over the site, receiving two or three pence a week for his labours. To speed up the efficiency of his delivery service, he had a long piece of wood with nails hammered into it, so that he could deliver eight cans at a time. Some of his customers were over 150 feet in the air, up ladders and along wooden scaffolding planks lashed in place with lengths of rope – planks that sometimes slipped a foot or so if the rope had dried and the wedges loosened. At dinner time he was sent off to a shop at the bottom of Knight Street, to buy 36 steak and kidney pies at a penny a time.

Apart from a period away from the site on military service, John 'Dick' Rowbottom was to work on the site for the rest of his working life, and to become one of the key fixer masons during the building of the Nave. As a lad he lived through the most complicated phase in the whole building history, and watched the steady growth of a massive and superb tower, 331 feet high, which would house the highest and heaviest peal of bells anywhere in the world.

In his speech after the service to mark the foundation of the Dean and Chapter, John Masefield declared that all cathedrals should be 'specially conspicuous by tower or spire'. Hearing this pronouncement, both the Executive Committee and the architect must have had mixed feelings: the one because there was not enough money to build even an inconspicuous tower, and the other because he had still not finalised his design. He knew that the tower was his greatest architectural challenge to date, and that any misjudgement would mar the building for all time.

There had been excellent progress during 1931. The old and new sections were almost joined, despite the cramped conditions in which bricklayers and masons had to work. The Western Transept arches and the heads of the windows were completed. Over the whole of the new section was a sturdy timber platform from which the work on the vaulting could proceed. The final work of the year had been the construction of the timber centering for the Transept vaults. Banker masons had been steadily at work, and the site showed evidence that stone was all ready for the vaulting and for the massive western arch.

By the end of 1932, the casual visitor walking past the site would probably have been unaware of the rapid progress. The Rankin Porch arch had been completed; a superb rounded arch joining East and West Transepts. The great west tower arch was now visible to people walking along Rodney Street, though they could not see the complex work as the Transept vaultings were completed. In 1933 followed the construction of the vaulting of the western crossing – the area between the arms of the Transept – 4,200 square feet in all. As work proceeded aloft, work began below with the excavation of the robing rooms below the Transepts, now known as the Western Rooms.

It was not until 14th March 1934 that the Executive Committee was able to announce to the public that a benefactor had been found for the Tower. Lord Vestey and his brother, Sir Edmund Vestey, had donated £226,450 for the building of a tower in memory of their parents. The entire cost of the completed Tower eventually rose to over £300,000, all of the extra money being given by the Vestey family.

Before building commenced on the Tower itself, Vere Cotton thought it useful to lay before the readers of the *Quarterly Bulletin* some staggering statistics. Work had been in progress on the new central section of the Cathedral for ten years, during which time immense quantities of building

The timber work being prepared for the construction of the complex under-tower vaulting, one of the most spectacular areas of vaulting in the whole building. See also the photograph of the completed vaulting seen from inside the Cathedral on page 162.

By the summer of 1934 the stump of the Tower was visible. This photograph, taken from the roof of Lewis's building looks along Renshaw Street to St Luke's Church, later to be devastated by an incendiary bomb.

materials were handled. As the basic raw material, two million cubic feet of rock had to be quarried at Woolton; 4,700 lorry loads of stone, weighing 26,000 tons, had been delivered to the site and set as finished stone 310,000 cubic feet in volume and 21,000 tons in weight. As well as all this mass of stone 4,750,000 bricks had been set in walls and piers. Placed end-to-end, these bricks would have stretched 675 miles – from Liverpool to Berlin – and piled flat on top of each other, would have made a column forty times the height of Everest.

Cotton was also preparing his readers for what was to come, by making comparison between the newly-opened Queensway Tunnel under the river between Liverpool and Birkenhead, and the yet-to-be-built Vestey Tower. The new tower would accommodate four tunnels the size of the Queensway, as well as a fifth, eighteen feet in diameter.

A fine tower is one of the greatest challenges to be faced by any building enterprise, and demands three distinct fields of expertise: those of the architect, the structural engineer, and the mason and builder. Scott spoke and wrote extensively on the challenge of the Tower, which occupied his attention from 1910. The final design to be adopted was the sixth fully worked out plan. The tower is the most prominent feature of a building, visible from many angles and often over considerable distances. The finished piece must satisfy the eye from all points of the compass, and from near and far – correct proportion is crucial.

As well as calling for great aesthetic expertise from the architect, tower design also requires great engineering skill on the part of the structural engineer, and in our adulation of the architect we too frequently ignore the engineer's mathematical and design skills which ensure that the building is structurally sound. Mr. Burnard Geen, the structural engineer for the Tower, had a dual set of problems. The Tower itself was immense: square at the base, octagonal on the top, and containing a great weight of stone, brick and concrete. The second complication was to be the great ring of bells. Mr. Thomas Bartlet had left £5,000 in his will for the provision of a peal, and the Vestey family were adding to this the funding for a great Bourdon bell. The combined dead weight of the fourteen bells would amount to over thirty tons, and the forces generated by the bells being pealed caused even greater problems. How do you prevent the highest and heaviest peal of bells in the world from plummeting straight down into the Crypt?

The stonemasons, banker and fixer mason alike, faced further immense difficulties because the whole tower tapered – as Scott explained to a local newspaper:

> The tower with its battered verticals – the whole thing tapers – is very elaborate, and the tapering of that elaborate masonry is a remarkable technical feat. It would be much easier if it were all vertical, but when it tapers, as everything is wider at the bottom than at the top, it is difficult. There are octagonal turrets on the four corners of the tower and these taper in themselves and they are very elaborate at the top. These turrets

Various stages of progress in the design of the Tower. The final design can be seen above.

give the skyline or silhouette of the tower and are tapered 1 in 80.

Not only the outline shapes of Tower and turret tapered, of course, but every stone within their structure. Owen Pittaway the Clerk of Works, Jack Kewley the Setter Out, Bill Meredith the Foreman, and everyone right down to young John Rowbottom, were going to have to produce their finest work.

Building work in 1934 and 1935 might have been described as 'the seen and the unseen'. The under-tower vault was for ever to be a visual marvel, but the concrete girdle at the base of the Tower was later encased in brick and stone, and the great steel cradle supporting the bell structure remains hidden from all but the bell ringers.

Mr. Burnard Green's solution to the weight of the bells was to design a massive girdle of reinforced concrete running round the walls at the base of the tower proper. This feature was to prevent any vertical cracking in the tower, which might have been caused had the walls tended to splay outwards under the weight. The concrete band was to be 6 feet 1½ inches high and six feet wide, all reinforced with 1½-inch steel bars. The whole girdle was divided into 44 sections, and the concrete for each section poured separately, and the finished structure contained 32 tons of steel bars and six hundred tons of concrete - all this over 170 feet in the air. While work on the concrete girdle was in progress, all stone fixing on the vault had to cease because the big crane was taken up with the hoisting of the concrete.

Once the girdle was in place, work commenced on constructing four, 21-inch-deep steel girders 74 feet 6 inches in length spanning the diagonals of the Tower. These massive girders were fixed at one end only, being on roller bearings at the other end. Eventually a whole cradle of girders rose to support the mass of the bells and their fixings and tranfer the weight outwards and downwards into the walls of the Tower. To finish the job and prevent corrosion, two coke-fired boilers such as those used in road mending were installed on the Tower so that all the steel could be sprayed with hot bitumen.

So the Cathedral skyline changed yet again, as, for a short time, the stump of the Tower was crowned with a nest of steel girders. From below it might have looked flimsy, like something made out of Meccano, but close to it was seen to be immense and capable of supporting the highest and heaviest peal of bells anywhere in the world.

This shot in 1935 shows the scale of the bell frame through the comparison with the men at work on it. Sitting stop a huge concrete girdle, this structure, devised by the engineer, Burnard Geen, was essential both for housing the bells and to ensure the Tower's stability.

A general view from the cemetery. The cage lifts can be seen on the side of the Tower, as well as the top girders of the bell frame.

CHAPTER
— *Nine* —

Fixtures and fittings

ISITORS to the completed Cathedral with the energy and determination to climb 288 stone steps to the floor of the ringing chamber will see an ornate metal casket in a ledge above the door. This is the somewhat unusual resting place for the ashes of Thomas Bartlett, the man who in 1912 gave a sum of money to provide a great peal of bells.

The focus of the Cathedral story has been on the site at St. James's Mount, but the stories of the great fixtures and fittings begin many miles away in studio and workshop. Bells, organ, stone statues and massive stained glass windows all had their origins somewhere else. The bells for Britain's newest cathedral were cast by the world's oldest bell foundry. The Whitechapel Bell Foundry can trace a continuous line of bell production for over five and a half centuries: Robert Chamberlain was casting bells in Aldgate in London in 1420. The firm itself, now known as Mears and Stainbank, was established by the master founder Robert Mot in 1570, during the reign of Queen Elizabeth I, and the foundry's insignia of Mot's initials and three bells is still in use.

The techniques of the bell maker have altered very little over the years.

The process begins with the making of a mould in two sections, the core and the cope. The core forms the inside shape of the bell, and is made from curved bricks with a coating of loam; the cope forms the outer shape of the bell, and has a coating of loam inside an iron moulding case. The loam surfaces are carefully shaped with moulding boards called strickles. When the shaping is completed, the letters forming the name or inscription are pressed in reverse into the loam. The moulds are then oven-dried and finally coated with graphite to give a very smooth surface. This done, the core and the cope are clamped together, and the molten metal (an alloy of copper and tin heated together in a furnace) is poured into the mould.

In December 1938, Sir Giles Scott and several interested people from the Cathedral arrived at Whitechapel to be present for the casting of the great tenor bell, four tons in weight and 6 feet 4 inches in diameter. The actual casting took only 9 minutes and 45 seconds, but the bell had to be left to cool very slowly for a week before it could be removed from its mould and the finishing process started.

The tenor bell on the tuning machine in the Whitechapel Bell Foundry.

The casting process has remained the same for centuries, but the subsequent tuning procedures are modern and sophisticated. The Whitechapel Foundry pioneered the process whereby a rotary machine is used to shave off metal from the inside of the bell until the precise note is achieved. The harmonics of bells are complicated. The dominant note is called the strike note, but four other notes are tuned as well: the 'hum note', an octave below; the 'nominal', an octave above; and a minor third and a fifth above the strike note.

Every bell is a unique instrument, and by tradition has a name and an inscription. The Executive Committee obviously enjoyed themselves when devising these for the new ring, and they honoured the memory of Thomas Bartlett, the donor, in an interesting fashion. The initial letters of the psalm texts on each bell spell out his name – they had to cheat ever so slightly by putting two texts on the final bell. Each one was formally named by significant members of the Cathedral community, and we can imagine the ingenuity and scholarship of Sir Frederick Radcliffe at work on the dedications. Sir Giles Scott designed new lettering for the inscriptions, and this style is now used on all the bells coming out of the foundry.

The ingenuity and wisdom of Mr. Hughes of Mears and Stainbank were employed in the design of the bell frame within which the great peal was to be hung. They decided against a metal structure because of the

Twelve of the bells photographed together after their delivery to the Cathedral in 1940. The headstocks have not yet been bolted into position.

problems of corrosion and the regular painting which would be necessary. Sufficiently large quantities of massive, well-seasoned timber were unavailable, and so the firm made history once again by designing a framework of reinforced concrete. The size of the bells and the vast size of the tower might have caused some problems, but the space gave the opportunity for a new and ideal layout for the ring. They designed a radial frame in which each bell swings to the centre of the tower. The headstocks of the bells were re-designed, and the result achieved for Liverpool is now standard on all the Whitechapel bells.

Each bell moves on bearings and is fitted on to a large timber wheel to which the rope is attached. Before a peal commences, the bell is pulled gradually until it 'sets' upright at a point of balance. The bell is prevented from swinging right over by a weighty wooden stay attached to the headstock. At each pull the bell turns a full circle, first in one direction and then in the other. The clapper strikes the side of the bell just before it reaches the vertical position.

Liverpool people who travelled by tram along Great George Street were familiar with the organ works of Henry Willis and Son. Willis was, and still is, one of the great names in the world of organ building; the name was especially well-known in Liverpool because Henry Willis had been responsible for building the superb instrument in St. George's Hall. Henry

Willis I, usually referred to as Father Willis, produced one of the greatest concert hall organs in the world while still a comparatively young man; his grandson, Henry Willis III, was entrusted with the building of the organ for the Lady Chapel.

The story of the main organ began in 1905 when the Cathedral site was little more than a series of foundations at the east end. Mr. W. J. Ridley, a Liverpool banker and organ enthusiast, revelled in the music produced by the instrument in St. George's Hall, and was anxious that the new Cathedral should be provided with the finest possible instrument. He had an enthusiasm for organ building – and he also had a very wealthy aunt who was the widow of Mr. James Barrow. He persuaded his aunt to endow a large sum (later considerably increased) for the building and maintenance of one of the biggest organs ever to be built.

The St. George's Hall organ was the work of a young man, and the new Cathedral project was entrusted to Henry Willis III, then only in his mid-thirties. A small Organ Committee was established including Willis, Ridley, Scott and Burstall. The name Willis had for years been associated with some of the great old cathedrals: to provide an instrument for an important existing building was challenging; to design an organ for a new building, as yet little more than a vast building site, was a major undertaking. An organ builder would normally test the acoustics of a church before he began his planning, but Willis had nothing more helpful than the architect's drawings – and his own genius. Even when the instrument was installed, he knew that he would have to wait many years before he could test out his greatest work in the completed building.

A single section of one of the largest of the case pipes, seen here in the workshop of the manufacturer. These big pipes, whose size can be gauged by comparison with the tools and equipment around it, were welded together down on the floor of the Cathedral itself.

One of the most important decisions was in the hands of the architect who, with advice, had to decide where to position the instrument – an instrument so large as to be visually one of the most significant features in the building. After toying with the idea of placing the organ on a choir screen, it was decided to position it in cases high up on either side of the Chancel, taking up a complete bay on both north and south sides and projecting slightly into the Choir. The console was to be on a gallery on the north side, right above the voices of the Cantoris side of the choristers. Eventually the organ cases themselves were to be seen as superb examples of craftsmanship, employing elaborately carved oak and high-quality plain metal for the pipes.

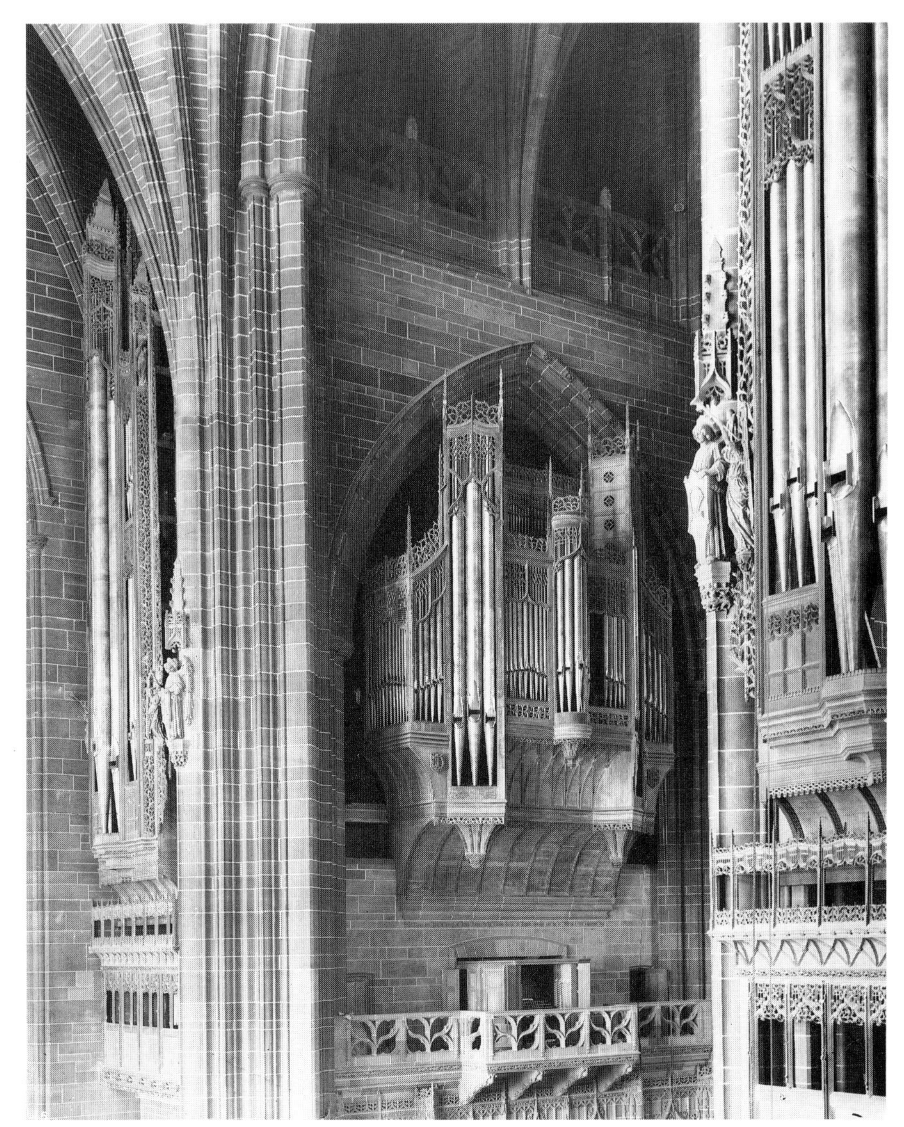

The view across to the organ console, situated on the north wall of the first bay of the Chancel. In all there are four ranks of pipes – two facing each other across the Chancel, and two (seen here on extreme left and right) facing into the Central Space. Wind from the blowing chamber situated in the Crypt is fed to the pipes through trunking within the piers of the arch to the left of the console.

When Scott decided to alter the design of the mouldings on the piers half way up, he introduced the stone figures seen here to try to mask the change. Unfortunately, the adjacent organ cases also carry (wooden) figures and these just happened to be at the same height, producing a somewhat incongruous effect.

Both Ridley and Burstall died long before the organ was completed, but in 1917 Henry Goss Custard was appointed Cathedral Organist, and was actively engaged with Willis on the final design for the instrument.

Of all the 'fixtures and fittings' of any great church, the organ is the most complex both in terms of the range of materials used in the building, and the range of skills employed in its design. The blowing chamber resembled the engine room of a small ship. It was built in the Crypt on the south side, to house three motors and rotary blowers with a capacity of 48 horsepower. The wind is fed through to the various departments by means of great lengths of ducting under the floor and in the piers, right up to reservoirs convenient to the sound boards.

The size alone of some of the great pedal pipes is staggering. Willis insisted that the timber for the 32-foot double open wood should be in one piece and without blemish. The planks are three inches thick, and the lowest 'C' pipe measures 3 feet 2 inches by 2 feet 9 inches and weighs 1 ton 2 cwts. Tons of the highest grades of 'spotted metal' (a mixture of lead with a high percentage of tin) were employed, and every single pipe from less than one inch to 32 feet had to be individually hand-crafted. The pipe maker begins with sheets of metal which have to be cut, precision planed, rolled and shaped, welded, voiced and tuned. The sheer range of pipes had never been attempted in one instrument, and the pneumatic action needed to make over nine thousand pipes speak, was complex indeed. The wood of the swell boxes in which some of the departments are housed is four inches thick, and one pedal swell box measures 13 feet by 13 feet 1 inch by 28 feet.

Many stories, true or apocryphal, have come to surround this great instrument. One re-told by R. Meyrick-Roberts in *The Organ at Liverpool Cathedral* (1926) is probably true:

> Close to the Willis factory is a school; and the noise created by the voicing of the heavy pressure reed stops so distracted the attention of the young scholars that the master sent over a polite note to the organ-building firm suggesting (it is believed) that the noise might be discontinued during school hours. Mr. Willis expressed his regret at his inability to do anything in the matter, as the work had to go on; and gently intimated that he feared there was worse to come, having in mind

Not part of the engine room an ocean-going liner – just part of the organ blowing chamber!

October, 1926, the blessing of the newly completed organ by Bishop David. Every year the event is celebrated at the Anniversary Recital played by the Cathedral Organist.

the tuba magna, which had not yet been voiced. Worse did come – and worse than our famous builder had bargained for. In his own words: 'To deal with the high pressure, the mechanism of the action is partially balanced; but once a temporary wind-trunk conveying the wind to balance the action blew out, with the result that every one of the sixty-one notes ciphered. The noise was positively appalling, as can well be imagined.' The school has since been replaced by a huge block of flats.

To gaze at the console, as many Liverpool people did when it was displayed in a shop window before its installation, might have prompted sceptics to ask whether such a vast instrument was necessary or playable. Goss Custard was able to answer the sceptics by saying, 'If necessity had been the only consideration, most of the great artistic achievements of the world would never have been accomplished'. And the mechanics of the mighty instrument responded with sensitivity to all the demands of the organist:

> The electric controls to the shutters of all the swell boxes are perfect; in fact, so sensitive are they that they respond instantly to the slightest pressure of the foot, and every shading of tone, from a slow crescendo or decrescendo to a sudden sforzando of great intensity, is obtainable without exertion.

Early on the morning of Saturday 18th October 1926, over four hundred people assembled on the platform at Euston to board an excursion train to Liverpool. They were all organ enthusiasts heading for the dedication and opening recital of the great Willis masterpiece in Liverpool Cathedral.

At the consecration service in 1924, only choir, swell and part of the pedal were completed, so the excitement amongst the organ enthusiasts was high in 1926. The splendours of the completed organ were matched by those of the dedication service itself. Before the processions moved into the Cathedral, some words of Milton were sung, which became the keynote of the service:

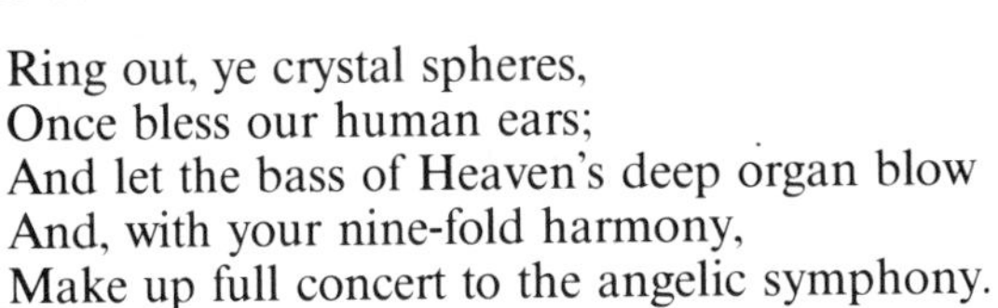

> Ring out, ye crystal spheres,
> Once bless our human ears;
> And let the bass of Heaven's deep organ blow
> And, with your nine-fold harmony,
> Make up full concert to the angelic symphony.

Bishop David addressed the congregation after a spell of 'absolute silence'. After the singing of Versicles and Responses, the congregation took their seats to hear the organist playing Bach's *Fugue in E Flat Major.* Meyrick-Roberts was present at the service, and later reported:

> It was now that the organ was heard for the first time, the organist giving a dignified rendering of the great master's music, building up the tonal qualities of his instrument to a superb fortissimo. This was followed by the choir singing *Praise of all created things* (Gustav Holst) – a highly effective work, and well sung. The organist now made more music, playing in brilliant manner Basil Harwood's *Paean.* In this work many tonal combinations were displayed; contrasts of one department with another; and a gradual working up of tone towards the exciting finale, until the cathedral was ringing with joyful sound; when, suddenly, the ear was arrested by a new tone. The mighty tuba magna, with its colossal and glorious voice, was heard for the first time.
>
> Three prayers followed; then (the congregation standing) the Bishop left his throne and, with pastoral staff in hand, stood beneath the lofty chancel and between the north and south organ cases. Facing the high

altar, with uplifted hand, he made the Dedication, saying:

'In the joy of our Lord Christ we dedicate this organ for the worship of His Holy Church unto God Immortal, in Whom all harmonies are one, Who made us so that in music we can hear His voice, to Whom be praise and glory in the Eternal Spirit here and in the world to come.'

Between 1958 and 1960, the organ underwent a complete re-build at the hands of Henry Willis IV. The old pneumatic action was replaced by electric and some tonal alterations were made, and the old unenclosed choir section was discarded and a new positif section substituted. In its re-built state the organ had 9,704 pipes in six sections: pedal, choir, great, swell, bombarde, and solo. The organist sitting in front of his pedal board and five manuals has at his disposal one of the most fully developed, rich organs in the world, and the whole is essentially the conception of Henry Willis III. Other large and famous organs have been modified and added to during their lives - but Willis got his plans right from the very beginning.

During that re-build, a young man made his first inspection visit. David Wells, who cares for the organ to this day, takes up his own story:

It was in April 1959 that I first encountered the Grand Organ of Liverpool Cathedral. I was a boy of 15; Mr. Willis Jr. (as he was then) took me on that short trip up the hill from his works to L.C.O. [Liverpool Cathedral Organ]. To him this was another of his inspection visits of the restoration work in progress at that time, but to me it was a whole new world. Since that day I have retraced my steps many times whilst tuning and caring for this very special instrument.

Eventually, David Wells was to establish his own organ building firm, and to be the custodian of one of the greatest organs in the world.

Most visitors would assume that the parts for the organ were made elsewhere and later assembled on site, but there is also an assumption that the large number of carved stone figures were created from start to finish *in situ*. The strength of many of those carved figures lies in the feeling which they convey, that they have been conceived and created in the positions in which they stand: many of them appear almost structural, and the word 'decoration' would not come to mind. It will be a surprise to some that these figures were originally modelled in clay in the sculptor's studio. The overall design for the Reredos behind the high altar was by Scott, influenced, we have been given to understand, by features he had seen in Spain, especially the gateway to the College of San Gregorio at Valladolid. The figures in the Reredos are the work of Walter Gilbert, who was mainly responsible for the design, and Louis Weingartner, responsible for the modelling. The final figures were carved in Wooler sandstone, lighter in shade than Woolton, by Arthur Turner.

A visitor to the Cathedral during the 1980s who was fortunate enough to be taken to the less accessible parts of the building, would have been very surprised - almost shocked - to find a quantity of large plaster figures

The plaster working model for a small section of the Reredos – the work of Weingarter and Gilbert. The final piece in stone is so high that it is not easy to appreciate the excellence of the work.

stacked roughly, many upside-down, in a remote turret room. The discerning viewer would have recognised these shapes as being identical to the figures in the two porches and in the Central Space; these figures were all the work of Edward Carter Preston.

He was born in Walton, Liverpool, in 1885 and studied for a time at the 'Art Sheds', part of the University School of Architecture and Applied Arts. Life classes had been taken by Augustus John, and modelling classes by C. J. Allen, though Gerard Chowne remained the greatest influence on Preston's artistic development. He was well established in a variety of artistic work before he had any part to play in the building of Liverpool Cathedral, though it is interesting to remember that the inscription on the foundation stone laid in 1904 was carved by his brother-in-law, Herbert Tyson Smith.

Carter Preston had become known for fine lettering, but it was as a watercolour painter and medallist that he had begun to make his name. The first evidence of his contact with the Cathedral is in a letter from Bishop Augustus David to Radcliffe in January 1931:

> You will have heard of Carter Preston, the sculptor here. Scott was much impressed by a piece of his work which Dwelly showed him, and has given Carter Preston a commission for Stations of the Cross in a church

Right: *The Lady Chapel, the first part of the Cathedral to be completed. The influence of G. F. Bodley can be seen in the more ornate decoration of this part of the Cathedral. After Bodley's death Scott was sole architect for the rest of the project.*

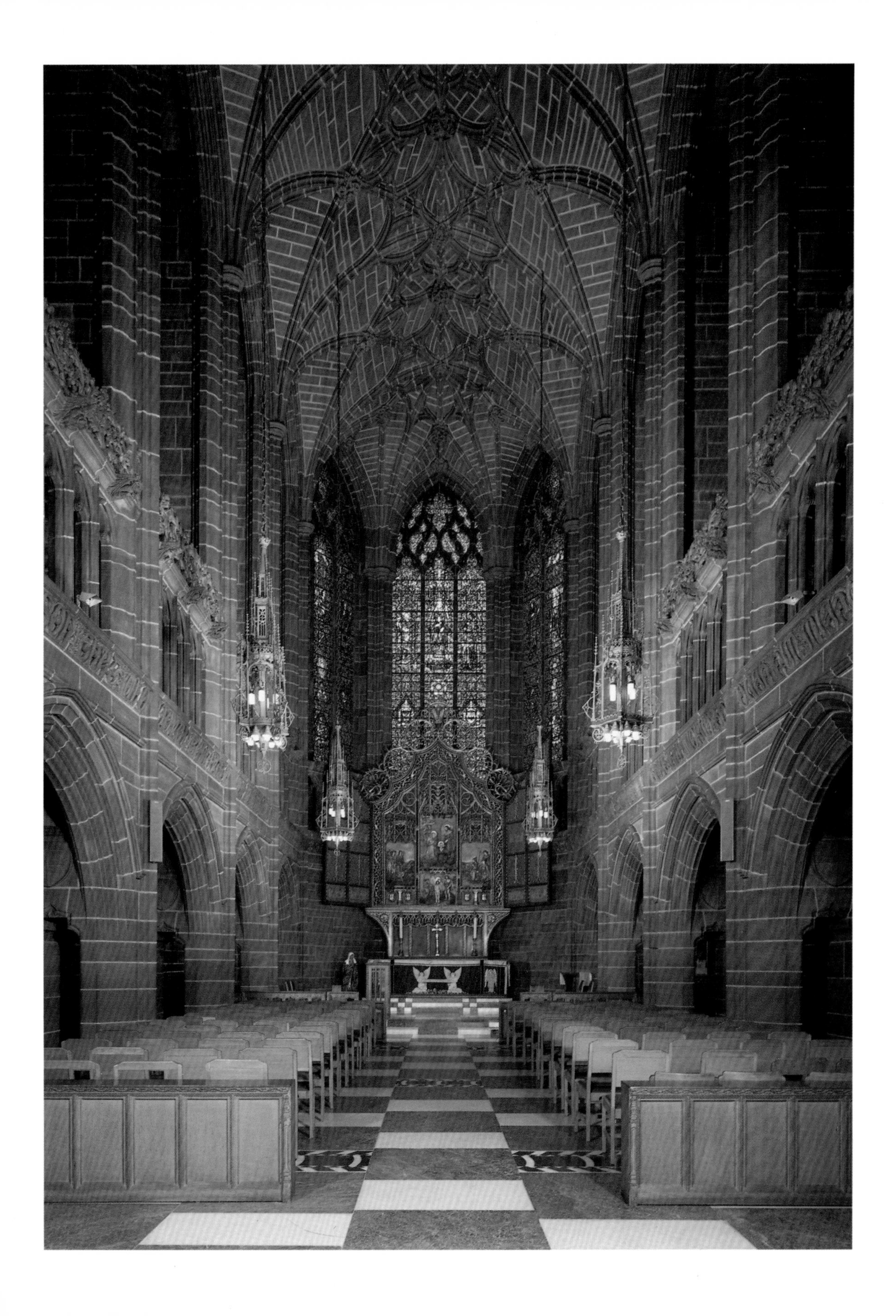

Left: *The interior of the octagonal Chapter House, erected by the Freemasons of West Lancashire.*

Detail of the richly decorated Festal Frontal.

Detail of the Red Frontal.

Below: *Another finely embroidered section of the Festal Frontal.*

Left: *Detail of the superbly worked Lady Chapel Reredos.*

Below: *Detail of a figure from the depiction of the Last Supper on the High Altar Reredos.*

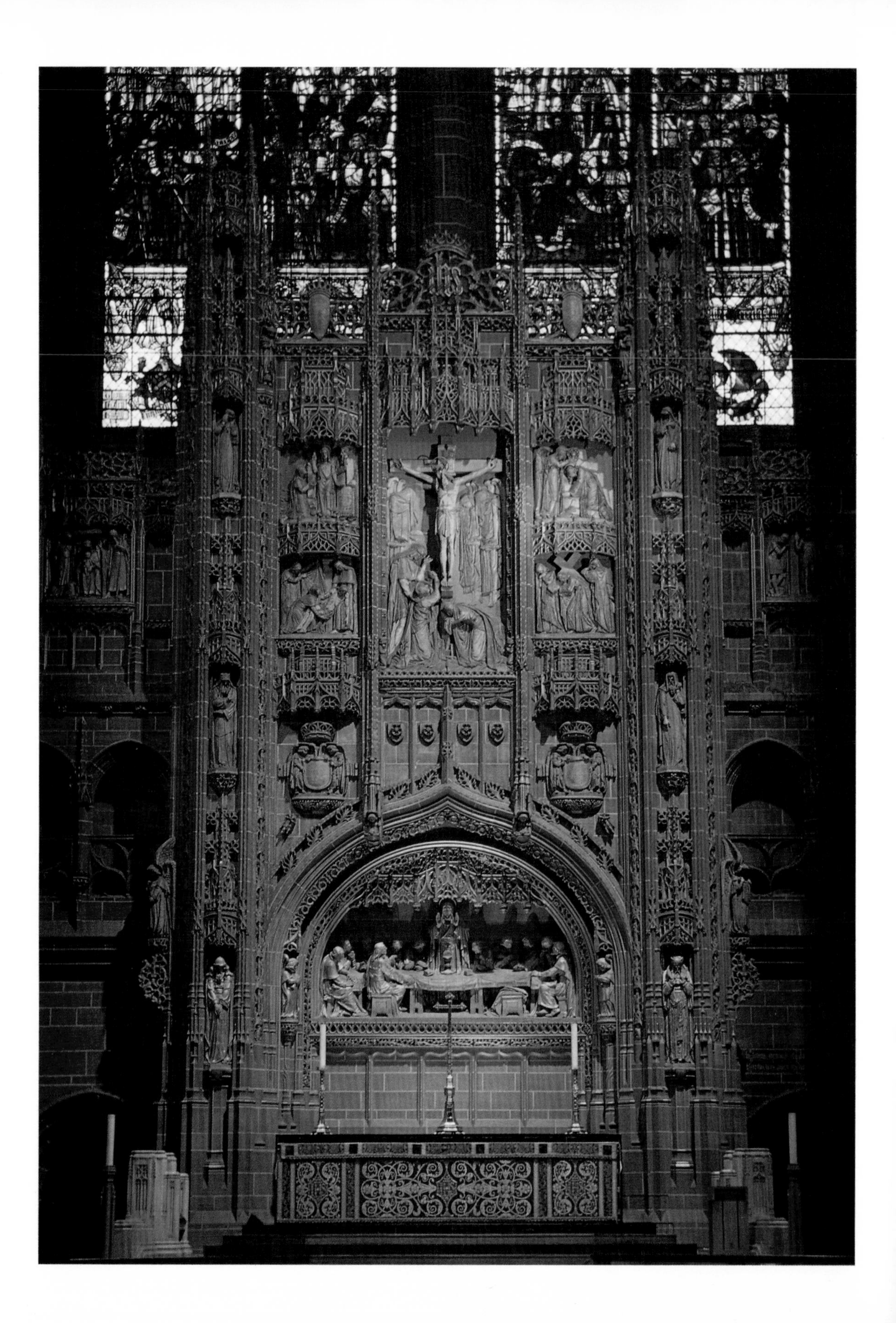

A Liver Bird on one of the choir stalls.

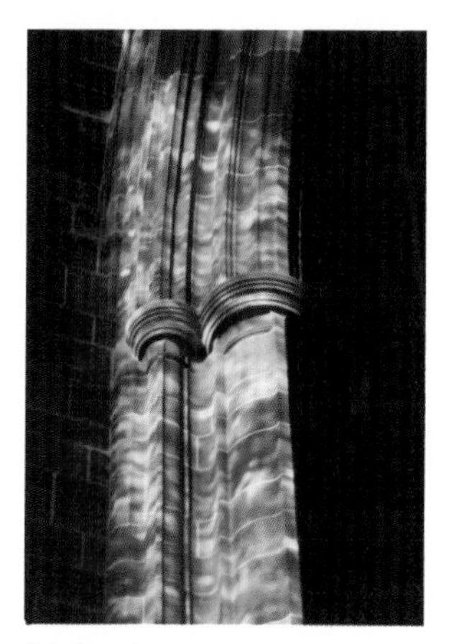

Light plays on stone to produce dramatic effects.

Modern stained glass.

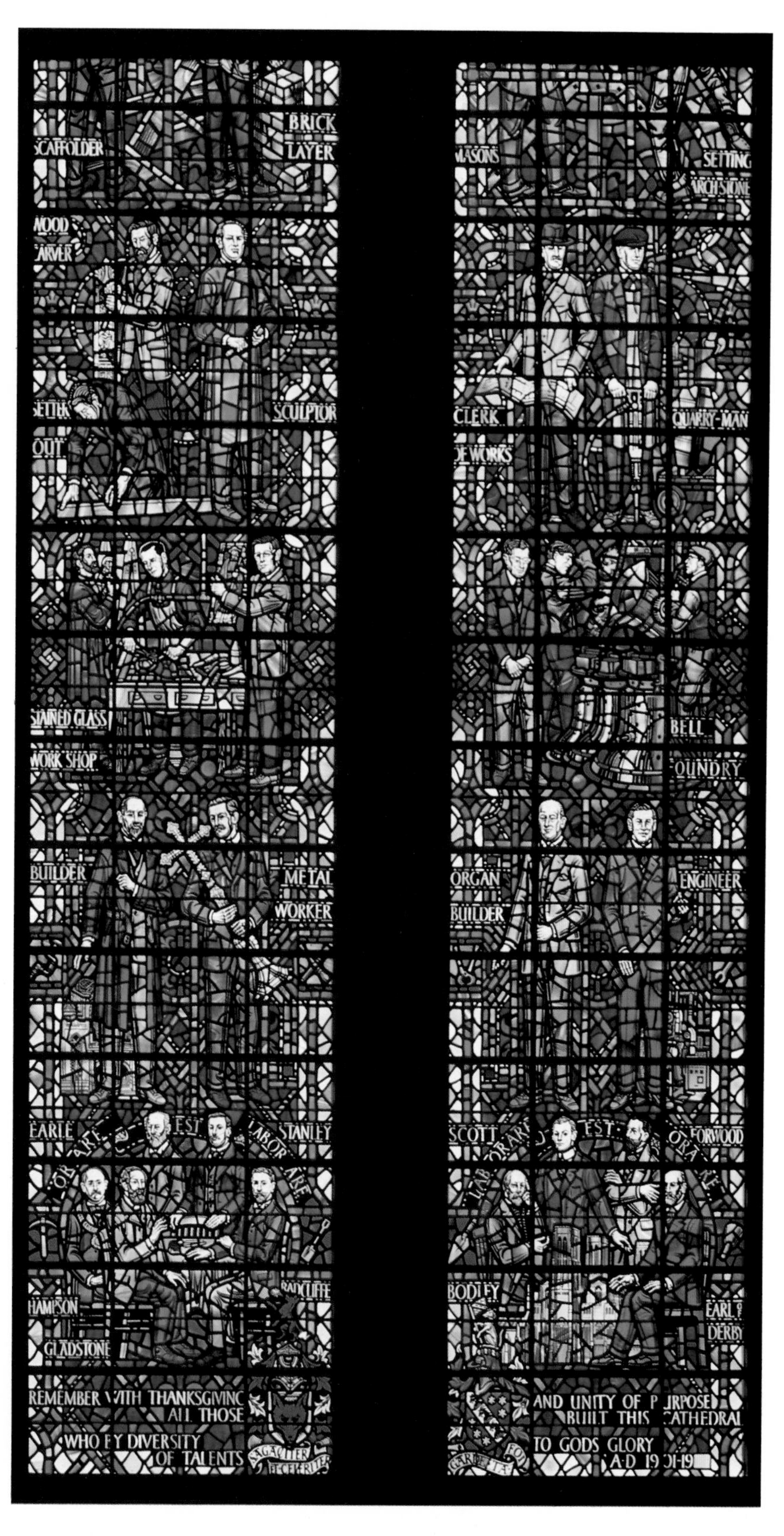

Left: *Surely one of the most dramatic views of the inside of the Cathedral is from the Corona Gallery, looking down upon the Central Space and Chancel.*

Right: *Scott's masterpiece by night.*

Below: *And, from the old cemetery, by day.*

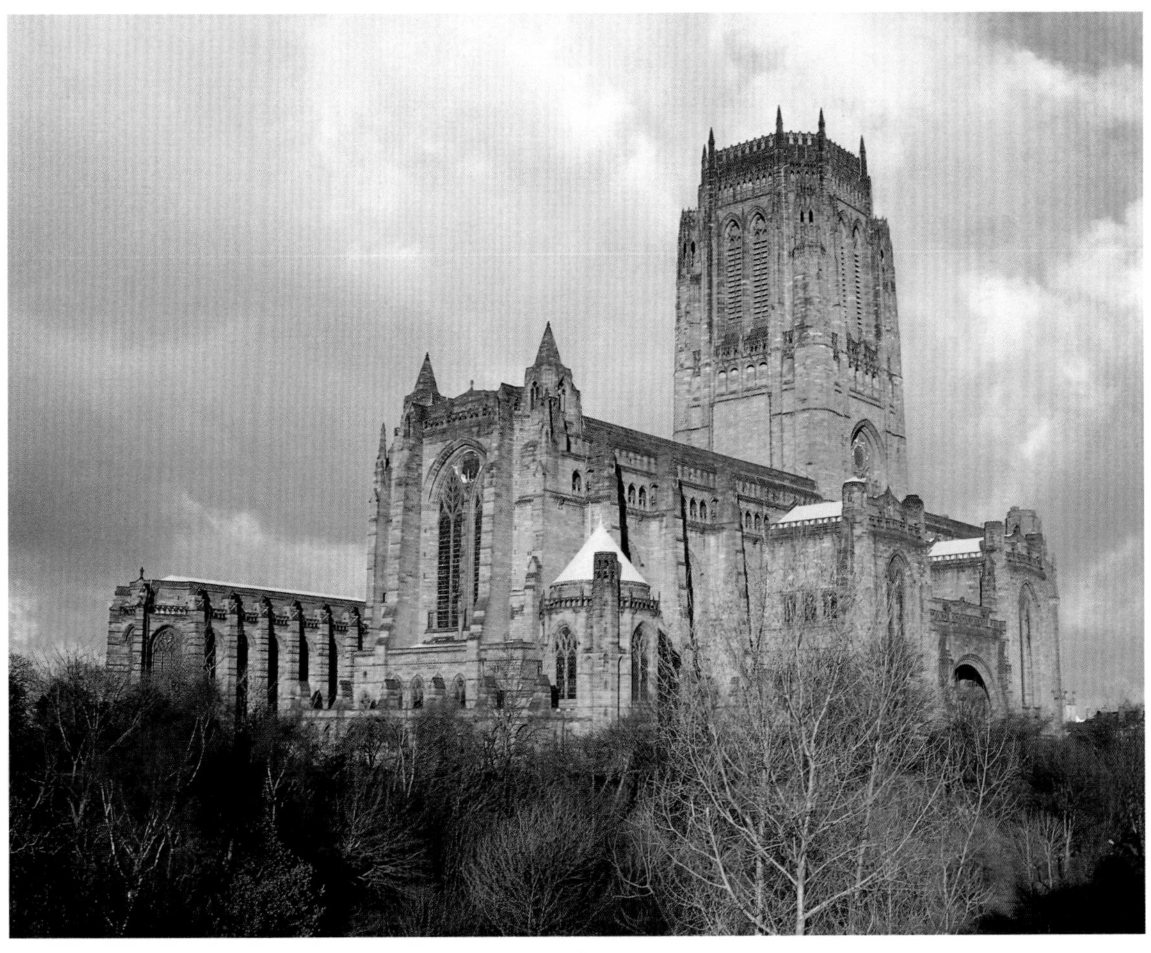

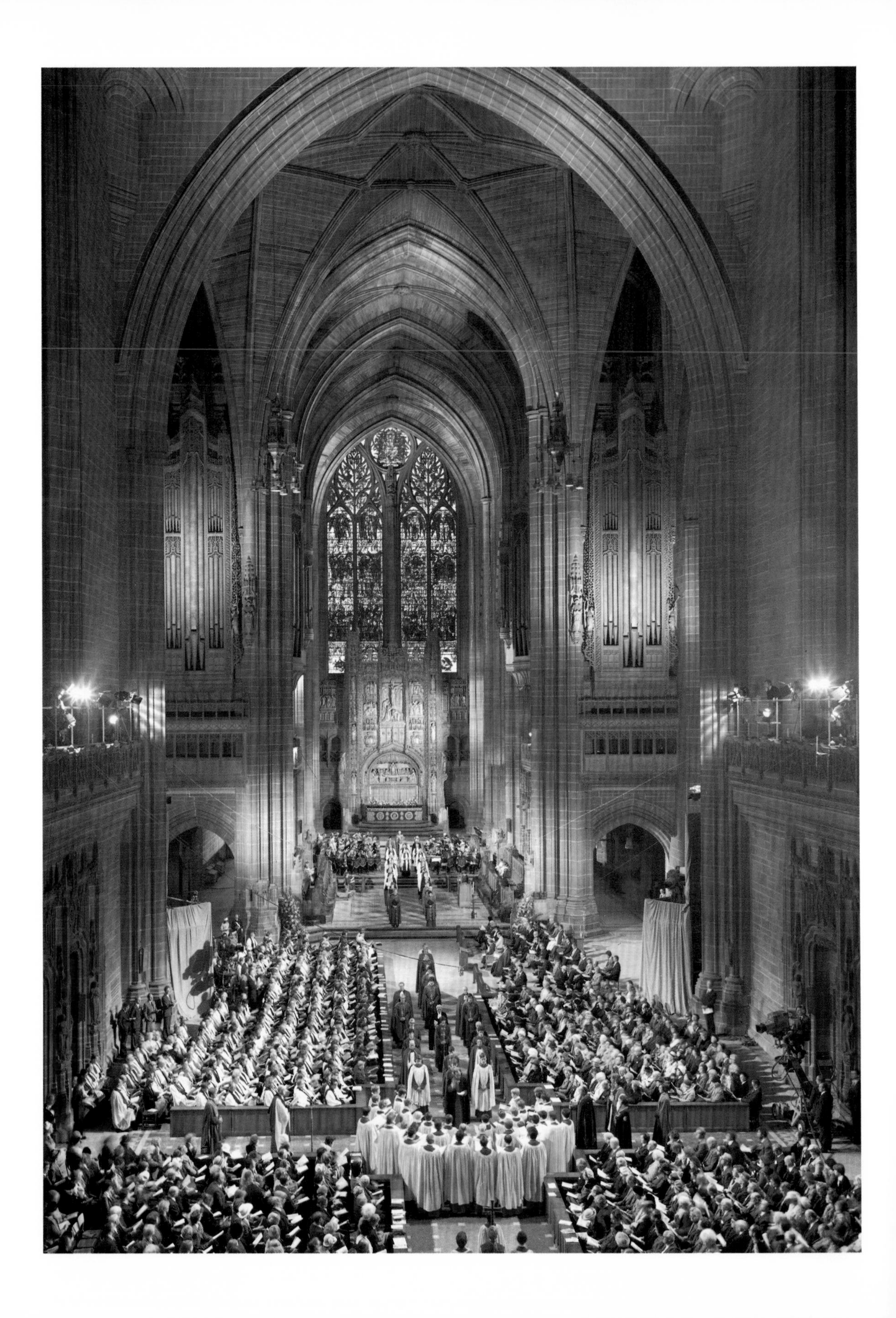

Edward Carter Preston with a plaster working model of one of the figures to be carved on the Rankin Porch. Carter Preston was also an accomplished artist, as seen from his line drawings which are used to illustrate the first page of each chapter of this book.

> he is building somewhere. I rather hope you will get designs for your four figures. Carter Preston who is the finest kind of agnostic wandered into the Cathedral on Christmas Day and said to Dwelly afterwards, 'You came very near to the ineffable'. He is a kind of prophet like Blake and lives very high.

His first Cathedral commission was for the Bishop Ryle Memorial, and his period as 'Sculptor to the Cathedral' extended from 1931 to 1955. These years mark an extremely interesting period of co-operation between Scott, Radcliffe and Carter Preston. As Carter Preston wrote, 'Radcliffe acted between myself and the Committee in matters of symbolism, Sir Giles acted in a similar capacity in the matters relating to the fitness of the designs to his architecture. It turned out to be a very efficient method of getting things done and also saved me a good deal of worry.'

With such an extensive commission in front of him, Carter Preston moved into 88 Bedford Street South, within half a mile of the Cathedral, and converted the coach house into a studio. There he worked in clay, first producing miniature figures known as maquettes. Once the Committee was satisfied with the maquettes, the complicated process began which culminated in the carving of the final figures in Woolton stone. First, full-size figures were made in clay. Carter Preston would have executed much of the finer detail in hands and faces, though he would have been assisted by technicians in some of the plainer parts of the work. When the artist was quite satisfied with a whole figure, a technician skilfully created a plaster mould around the clay. A plaster model, the exact replica of the original clay, was later cast in the mould, and it was this working model which was given to a stone carver to copy exactly.

The windows of Liverpool Cathedral are probably the most prominent visual features in the whole building. The great west window is so powerful that many visitors are almost mesmerised by it, do not look where they are going, and fall down the steps into the Nave. Sir Frederick Radcliffe's words may sound rather rhetorical in these prosaic days, but he does suggest the great power which is exerted by a good window:

> A rapture of colour will carry a youth, if only for a moment, into a realm of wonder, when the familiar pleasant skies and trees and the outside world would only create a longing for release. Since painting has disappeared from the walls of our churches, either by the ravages of time

Left: *Complete at last – the Queen joins a packed congregation for a service in 1978 to mark the finishing of the work of construction.*

Carl Edwards, centre, in his studio. A completed section of the Parsons Window is displayed at the back. Edwards holds the design for a window in his hands and examines the full-size cartoon.

The leads around some pieces of glass are being fixed and soldered in the foreground. A kiln for firing pieces of glass can be seen at the back.

> or the malice of men, little in the fabric remains for teaching or magnificence except the splendour of glass.

Good windows are very powerful, but as James Hogan (one of the most influential stained glass artists to work on the Cathedral) wrote over fifty years ago:

> In my long connection with the Art of stained Glass it still surprises me to find how few there are who have any knowledge of the subject, or who have taken the trouble to find out anything about it . . . The fact is that stained glass has no relation whatsoever to picture painting. It is an art of its own, dealing with the transmission of light through coloured material, whilst painting is the application of a coloured pigment on a flat surface upon which light is reflected.

The stained glass artist is somewhat akin to the organ builder in that he has to possess wide-ranging artistry and craftsmanship, and considerable aesthetic, technical and scientific skills. Like the organ builder, he also has to design his creations long before the building that will receive them is complete.

Sir Frederick Radcliffe was the Chairman of the Stained Glass Committee for many years, and through his writings we have an insight into the long process which brought a window into being:

> Under the guideline of Sir Giles Scott, while full scope is allowed to the individual talents of the artist in glass, the spirit of the whole design dictates the designs of every window. According to our practice from the beginning, the architect first confers with the committee as to the main lines on which the design of the windows should be based and the extent to which it is to be of clear glass or coloured. When he has settled this, the committee selects subjects capable of being depicted within the limits assigned. The stained glass artist is then instructed to prepare a design which, after careful consideration by both architect and committee, is put in hand. The glass thus observes its limits as a necessary part of the total effect aimed at, while contributing its particular glory to the beauty of the whole.

The minute books give evidence as to the diligence of the Stained Glass Committee, though we may find the subject of their deliberations faintly comic. Radcliffe had an eye for the smallest detail, and

> those who knew him well will appreciate the horror with which he discovered that the sketches for the Ambulatory windows submitted in June depicted St. Columba with a Roman not a Celtic tonsure. Equally characteristic was his insistence that efforts must be made to discover if St. Patrick, St. Andrew, St. David and St. Columba did or did not have beards.

At another meeting concern was expressed over several matters: a shadow from the right hand of the centre figure looks like a pistol . . . St. Peter's head is too far separated from his body . . . St. John the Baptist's hair should be less and his left shoulder reconsidered . . . St. John the Baptist's head was too small; was he carrying a large locust, or a baptismal shell? Radcliffe was not trying to be awkward; he simply recognised the great significance of the windows:

> When the service is over and the organ has ended, and the pulpit is silent, the building and its windows will still continue the work of teaching and inspiration.

Eventually, the artist was able to produce a very detailed watercolour sketch of the window, from which he and his craftsmen could move on to the second stage. The whole window had to be drawn out on paper full-size, showing the size and shape of every single small piece of glass. This very large drawing is called the cartoon, and has to be used for the cutting of all the separate pieces of glass. The making of the glass itself is a very skilled and complex process, whereby different oxides are used to produce the range of colours demanded by the artist. The glass itself is not a mass-produced factory product; it has to be blown by a skilled craftsman. Much of the later glass at Liverpool was blown into a metal mould in the shape of a box, the resultant product being known as slab glass. When examined closely, the variations in colour, thickness and texture are considerable, and all add to the final brilliance of the good window. The glass is cut to size to fit the cartoon shapes, and then the thousands of pieces are joined together by means of metal strips into manageable panels, which are eventually wired on to the strong metal fixing bars.

A revolution in stained glass making came about during the history of Liverpool Cathedral, and today the visitor can see that most of the original windows are very dark, particularly on a grey day. From the late 1930s, James Hogan was the chief designer with the firm of James Powell, Whitefriars Studios. His work moved away from techniques which made use of painting on to the glass in an attempt to produce a sense of shade or depth, and returned to the ideals of the medieval artists who – apart from facial features and other details – simply made use of pure colour. When Hogan's huge under-tower windows were seen by visitors for the first time, they must have been staggeringly powerful in their pure, jewel-like use of colour. Hogan's chief assistant was a man called Carl Edwards whose further developments of Hogan's methods were later to produce the varied, glowing windows which are such a striking feature of the Nave.

CHAPTER
— *Ten* —

'Keep going . . .'

PETER sat as he did every evening, by the kitchen fire listening to the radio: Children's Hour and the 6 o'clock News. 'What do they talk about on the news when there isn't a war?' For a generation of Liverpool children, the conditions of the Second World War were normality: the skyline a forest of grotesque barrage balloons, sandbags, searchlights, blackout precautions, air-raid shelters, gas masks, anti-aircraft guns and devastating bomb damage. But for the people who were building the Cathedral, 1936, '37 and '38 were optimistic years of progress, and confidence that June 1940 would see a service of splendour

R. JONES & SON (HAULAGE) LTD

By 1938 good progress had been made on the Tower. The decay of many of the houses on the slope below the Cathedral is evident even before the wartime bombing.

Excavations to provide rooms and storage areas at the west end. Much of the stonework is unfinished and the carving is protected by timber. The brick temporary wall can be seen on the right.

and pageantry as the Central Space was opened up for worship. That great service was not to be.

While the Rankin Porch was taking shape and the Vestey Tower month-by-month becoming a more dominating landmark, other more formidable changes could be observed on the continent of Europe. German troops occupied the Rhineland in 1936; by the end of 1937 Hitler was re-arming Germany, and Austria was over-run in 1938. The Cathedral Builders had to press on with enthusiasm and determination; they had lived through one war at great cost; they could not slow down now.

It was in optimistic mood that Vere Cotton listed the work to be completed before the new section was ready for use. James Hogan's giant under-tower windows were almost finished, though much else remained, including the completion of the Welsford and Rankin Porches; the erection of the Radcliffe Library; the fabrication of the doors, the font and all the light fittings; as well as further excavations for underground rooms and heating ducts. It was a long list of works, but with 220 men on the site, the projected dates were not unreasonable.

By the end of 1937 a start had been made on the removal of the massive balks of timber which still obscured any view of the exciting new space, and slowly the vast beauty of the new area began to show itself. As the readers of the *Quarterly Journal* were informed, at 183 feet tall, Nelson's Column would very nearly have fitted under the Tower vault.

No sooner had the scaffolding come down than excavations began to remove three thousand tons of soil and rock in preparation for a further room and storage space below the floor level of the building. Extensive excavation was required for the central-heating ducts. It had been decided to heat the Central Space by the method employed two thousand years earlier by the Romans: hot air would be drawn by fan along the ducts, so making the entire floor a low-temperature radiator. Later experience was to show that though the Romans may have found the hypocaust effective, the Liverpool system did not manage to make the congregations comfortable in the winter. By the end of 1938 the contract for the marble floor had been placed, the design of the font agreed, and the Tower walls were 267 feet above floor level. It was hoped that the final pinnacle would be in position by 1941.

Fixer masons at work on the Tower. This photograph gives no sense of the height at which they are working.

At 7 a.m. on Sunday 3rd September 1939, a mother and her twelve-year-old son set out to walk from their home in Everton to the Collegiate School in Shaw Street. This was a journey the boy made every day, but this day was different. He carried a small haversack on his back with a complete change of clothing; round his neck was a brown cardboard box, and tied to his lapel was a luggage label with the name 'Finnegan' inscribed on it in bold capital letters. At the school the two parted, and young Robin joined his fellow pupils in a long crocodile that wound its way down to Lime Street Station. He had no idea as to his destination. His mother, convinced she would never see her son alive again, walked all the way back to Everton by way of the back entries and alley-ways, her face streaming with tears. The evacuation of children from the cities had begun.

The congregation arriving for the morning service in the Cathedral realised the effect of evacuation upon them, when they read the little note at the head of their service sheets:

> Because of the evacuation of the Children of the Choir the daily services

Bricklayers and masons at work over 200 feet in the air. They are working on one of the corners of the Tower, above the level of the vaulting. In the centre can be seen one of the octagonal turrets that were built at each corner to change the shape of the Tower from square at the bottom to octagonal at the top. These can be seen clearly in the photograph on page 176.

> in the Cathedral will be non-choral. The Congregation is asked to sing with full heart and voice all the music of the Sunday services.

The psalm for the day could not have been more appropriate: 'Lord, how are they increased that trouble me: many are they that rise up against me. Many one there be that say of my soul: There is no help for him in his God.' Maybe the Bishop in his sermon reflected upon these words, and upon the final verses of the same psalm: 'Lord, lift thou up the light of thy countenance upon us. I will lay me down in peace, and take my rest: for it is thou, Lord, that makest me dwell in safety.' Before the end of the day, radio sets all over the country broadcast the voice of Prime Minister Neville Chamberlain, as he informed the British people that their country was at war with Germany.

Vere Cotton's words on the first page of *Quarterly Bulletin* No. 57 have an almost Churchillian ring to them, and their tone clearly expresses the feelings of the group of Liverpool people determined to carry on building their Cathedral:

> For the second time during the building of the Cathedral England finds itself engaged in a struggle of such magnitude as to demand the concentration of all its resources of man power and material if victory is to be achieved.
>
> In what must still be known as the Great War, though work on the

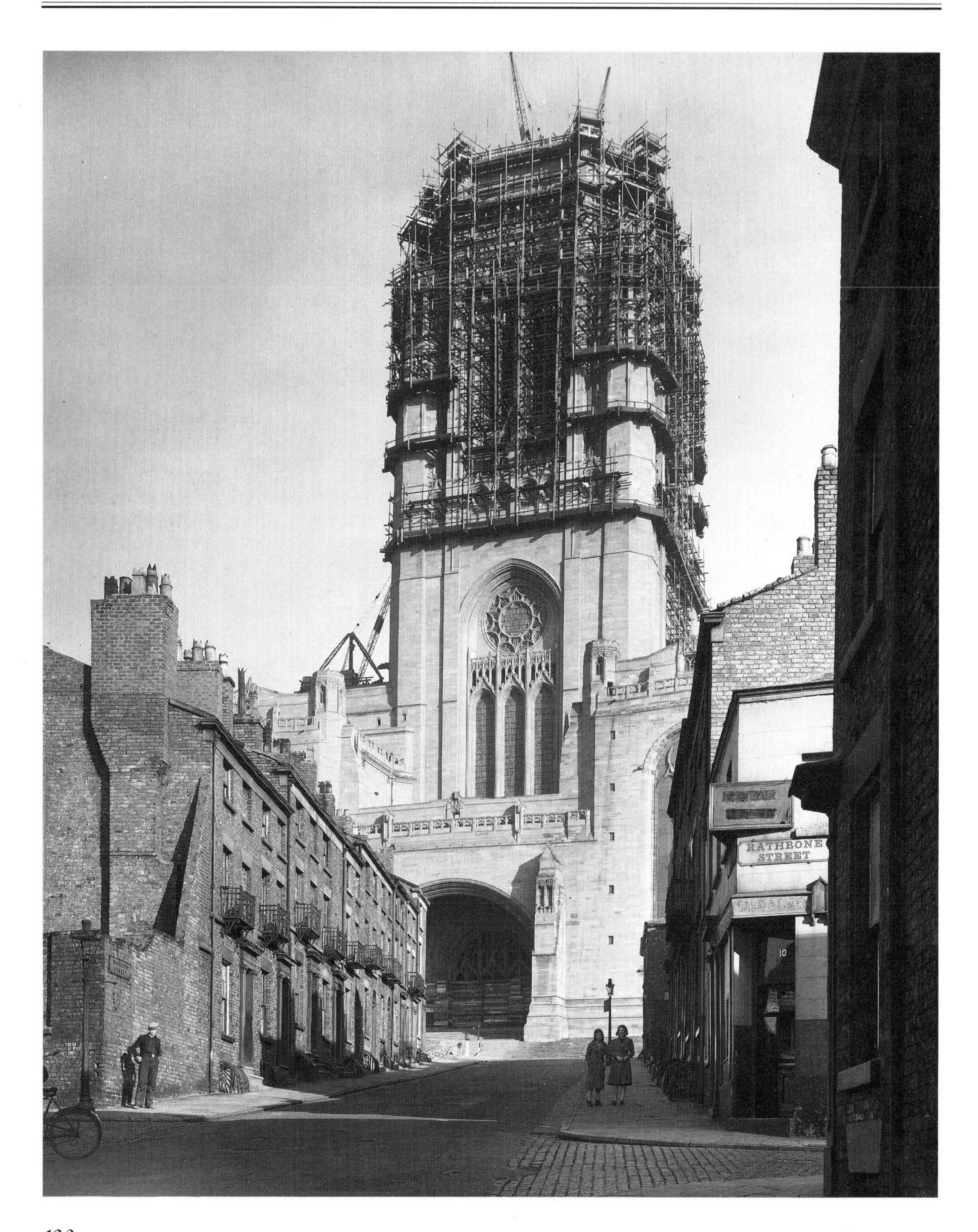
RATHBONE
STREET
10

> Cathedral gradually slowed down as more and more men left to join the Colours it never stopped completely, and while it is impossible to forecast the course of the present struggle, it is reasonable to foresee a similar slowing down of activity on the New Section as men and materials become scarcer. Already nineteen men have joined the forces, a number of others have been diverted temporarily to A.R.P. work, and Government control of cement is severely restricting the supply urgently needed for concreting.
>
> The policy of the Committee can be stated quite shortly – it is to go steadily ahead as far as human and material resources permit, but of course no attempt will be made to claim that work on the Cathedral is in any sense a reserved occupation and any hope of completing the work by next summer must in the changed circumstances be finally abandoned. In any case a great inaugural service, or rather series of services, such as had been planned would be unthinkable in war time and whatever progress is achieved with the actual building must be postponed until peace is once more restored to a troubled world.
>
> The heavier the toll that war takes of the treasures of the past the greater the need that this generation should call new beauty into being to redress the loss and while the Committee cannot with propriety during the war issue any general appeal for funds, they hope that now, as was the case 25 years ago, they may continue to receive memorial gifts and a steady flow of donations and bequests. As regards the Bulletin, as long as publication is practicable and the editor in the intervals of military service can do his part, it is hoped to continue issuing it, not only because the Committee are more than ever anxious to maintain interest in this great task, but because it is felt that many readers whose thoughts are inevitably concentrated on the war, will turn with refreshment to a publication which tells the story of a building which expresses (as does no other modern building in this country) man's unquenchable faith in the supremacy of spiritual values in a world assailed by materialism and brute force.

However confident the words, those at the heart of the Cathedral enterprise knew that it was going to be a daunting task to go on stone-by-stone building the rest of one of the finest towers in the world by day, when the city was going to be under attack from enemy bombers by night.

It was because of the fears of bomb attack that so many children were evacuated to less strategically important parts of the country. Apart from the words 'North Wales', young Robin Finnegan had no idea where he and his Collegiate colleagues were being taken. They arrived at an unknown station at about two o'clock and marched off to a reception centre to be provided with sandwiches and cups of tea. At some time during the long process he discovered that he was in Bangor – all road signs and station names had been removed in case the Germans landed – and at four o'clock he and his friend were loaded into a car to be driven to the home of the family upon whom they had been billeted. He asked the driver of the car if there was any news: 'Nothing since war was declared at

The mighty Tower now begins to dwarf the houses on Washington Street.

eleven o'clock.' Both boys sat silent, convinced that they would never again see the families they had left behind.

As fate would have it, the bombing of Merseyside did not commence until after most children had returned to Liverpool in the following year. Meanwhile, the weather rather than Hitler's blitz hampered the building programme. The winter of 1940 was the most severe on record. Ice flows were sighted in the Mersey, and the intense cold of early January was followed by severe blizzards over several days. Work was brought almost to a standstill until March.

The Port of Liverpool, with its line of docks from Dingle to Seaforth, was of enormous strategic and economic importance during the war. Inevitably, Liverpool was going to be the target of enemy action, and Scott's great architectural masterpiece stood out like a beacon on the Mount. Immediately, the copper roofing of the building, with its bright green patina, was painted a non-reflective black. Sandbags protected the Rankin Porch with its Carter Preston statues, but full protection for a building of that size was unthinkable. Cathedrals such as Canterbury and York had their irreplaceable medieval glass removed and put into safe storage, but Liverpool had to take the brave decision to leave its windows in place. The task of boarding up and replacing with plain glass would have been immense and costly. All the work was modern: if the worst happened and windows were damaged, many of the original cartoons and some of the designers themselves were still available. Modern windows could be replaced.

In comparison with most ancient cathedrals, Liverpool was not in great danger from fire because there was so little structural timber: only the Lady Chapel and vestries had timber roofs. However, fire-watching precautions were essential, and there was also the need to provide safe shelter for some of the people living near to the Cathedral. The two rooms under construction below ground at the west end could clearly accommodate several hundred people.

For sixteen years the Dean had watched the steady growth of his great church, and he was not going to desert his charge in time of war. Part of the Cathedral community became a resident community, and the Dean established his bedroom very close to a danger spot in a little room up near the roof of the Lady Chapel – in the room later to house the Cathedral archive. To the amusement of the choirboys, a bed and a wardrobe appeared in the song room, and Hugh Reid, a Rodney Street specialist and friend of the Dean, took up residence. Miss Christine Wagstaffe, Cathedral Secretary, was tucked away near the old Sacristy, and Mr. Edgar Robinson, the Choir Master, established himself in one of the Undercroft Vestries. A number of the staff of Morrisons the builders took on fire-watching duties, and at the height of the aggressions Owen Pittaway and his family camped out in what is now the works department.

Work was severely curtailed through a diminishing workforce, restrictions on the use of cement, and the government licensing of all building projects. Building was slow, but it was continuous. The average age of the masons left on the site was 59; they were experienced craftsmen, and by the early autumn of 1940 the Tower was 299 feet above floor level. Daily, men risked their lives up on the scaffolding, fixing stone; and nightly, many of those same men risked their lives as fire watchmen. On four successive nights high explosive bombs exploded very close to the building, one on Founder's Plot which blasted in the doors of the Children's Porch and did some damage to the stonework. The effects of the blast on the south-facing windows was devastating. A direct hit on a house on the opposite side of the road caused the instant deaths of Mr. George Siddall, the engineer to the Dean and Chapter, his wife and child and one of the Dean's dogs.

The following day young Mervyn Roberts, one of the choirboys, arrived at the Cathedral for the scheduled practice. The scene was unforgettable. Twelve windows had been damaged beyond repair, and the richly-coloured glass littered the floors of the building. The south choir aisle was ankle deep in the debris which had once been the two Chancel windows. The shafts of clear cold light flooding in through the tangled lead of the windows poured down on to the coffins of the Siddall family, placed side-by-side in the Chancel. At the invitation of their Dean, the choirboys filled their pockets with the broken fragments from the windows – the windows

Clearing the site after the destruction of Mr Siddall's house.

could be replaced; the Siddall family could not. The simple wording on the service sheet printed for their funeral revealed the caring heart of the Cathedral for all of its people:

Wednesday, 11th September 1940

We bless thy Holy Name
for
GEORGE AND MILLIE
AND CHRISTINE
found under the wreckage
of the enemy bombs

Until the shattered windows could be boarded up using the timbers from the old refectory, services had to be transferred through the temporary wall into the unfinished Central Space. Regular members experienced some of the splendour of this great space before the break-through to the Chancel was made. A temporary altar was set up against the timbering of the screen, and the worship of God by the people of the Cathedral community was never interrupted.

From 6th October 1940 for many weeks, the Sunday service sheet carried a simple instruction to all the members of the congregation:

> If an Air Raid warning sounds during a Choir Service the act of worship will be immediately transferred to the Crypt; members of the Congregation will please follow the gentlemen of the Choir westwards into the Crypt. If the signal sounds during a celebration of Holy Communion worshippers will please follow the Celebrant who will move eastwards to a Crypt Altar, where the service will be continued.

There have been many splendid royal visits to the Cathedral, but one of the most important visits of all was without pomp or ceremonial. King George VI and Queen Elizabeth visited the city in November 1940 so that they could personally identify themselves with the people of the city during the dangerous days of war. The damaged areas around the Cathedral were on their itinerary but, as George V and Mary before them, they saw more than had been planned: their Majesties asked to see the new section of the building. Dean Dwelly, in ecclesiastical frock coat, was unabashed, and led their Majesties by way of the King's Porch and the new Carter Preston statues, through into the Central Space where they were able to wander quietly round, both interested in the depiction of the consecration in James Hendrie's Transept window.

Clearly the King and Queen enjoyed their visit, and were full of encouragement for the Cathedral company during its time of trial. The King's words to the Dean, later quoted in the *Quarterly Bulletin*, must have been an encouragement and a challenge: 'Keep going whatever you do, even if you can only go on in a small way'.

Despite the problems and deprivations of war-time, life 'in residence' continued at the Cathedral, and afforded the architect unique experiences within his growing but vulnerable building. Scott and Dwelly had by that time become devoted friends, and when he visited Liverpool, Scott frequently stayed overnight in the Cathedral, wandering around at will early in the morning and late in the evening. In February 1941, Scott wrote to thank Dwelly for his hospitality:

> . . . how I enjoyed it all. I bet Wren did not have such fun when he was building St. Pauls any way I am quite sure he never wandered through his Cathedral in a dressing gown on the way to his bath!

With the Chancel temporarily unusable because of the shattered windows, services had to be held unexpectedly in the Central Space. An altar was set up against the temporary wall at the west end. Thus the congregation found itself between the brick 'temporary wall' to the east and this wooden wall to the west. When the construction of the Nave eventually got under way in the 1950s this wooden wall was moved westwards as each new bay was brought into use.

A direct hit onto the roof of the Derby Transept in the May Blitz of 1941. Luckily, this bomb was deflected by a brick wall and burst out through the wall before exploding.

For security reasons during the height of the war, little specific information was given on news bulletins, and Scott - back in London - must have been anguished to hear of the bombing of 'a north-western port'.

Thursday 1st May 1941 marked the beginning of the worst week in the whole life of the city - it was the start of the devastating May blitz when Liverpool was singled out to bear the brunt of Hitler's bombs. Night after night the terrifying wailing of the air-raid sirens sent families hurrying to the public brick and concrete shelters in the streets, into metal Anderson or Morrison shelters at home, or simply huddling in darkness and dread under the stairs. In the May blitz alone, 1,453 people were killed in Liverpool.

Under the bright moonlight of 2nd May, St. Michael's Church in Pitt Street, close to the Cathedral, was destroyed; as was Church House with all the Cathedral and Church records it contained. The following night was even worse: between 10.30 p.m. and 5 a.m., approximately five hundred bombers flew over Liverpool. As an historian was to record later:

> At one stage in the night so many fires were blazing that it really seemed as if the whole city was alight and the tower of the Cathedral was floodlit by the red glow. People up on the Fylde Coast, over thirty miles away, nightly watched the glow in the sky which marked the destruction of Liverpool. The tally of famous buildings damaged and destroyed reads like a guide to Liverpool.

The seven storeys of Lewis's department store were almost completely gutted, and along with the other children of Liverpool who grieved over the animals and birds which had been in the top-floor menagerie, I hoped that 'my' special monkey had died without suffering. Blacklers' store was gutted; the Central Lending Library and the Picton Reference Library lost their books to the flames, and most of the museum building was destroyed; the Central Telephone Exchange was demolished, and the General Post Office was struck for the second time. The *SS Malakand*, carrying one thousand tons of high explosives, was hit by incendiaries, causing Liverpool's greatest explosion of the war, in which the whole dock was

The visit of King George VI and Queen Elizabeth to view the damage and offer sympathy and encouragement to the Cathedral company.

destroyed while the vessel took 74 hours to blow and burn itself to bits. But the Cathedral Church of Christ in Liverpool, high up on the Mount, survived.

How the members of the congregation journeyed to the Cathedral on that Sunday morning cannot be imagined: tramlines were distorted and ripped up, power lines were down, hundreds of buildings were still burning, streets were blocked and clogged with brick rubble and broken glass, charred paper blew in the wind. The air stank, and everywhere there were the poignant signs of human loss – the shattered furniture, the broken toy, the kitchen sliced in two, the stray cat. But services were held in the Cathedral, and the Provost of Bradford managed to make the journey to preach at Evensong. Though someone managed to find the time to enter his name in the registers, no-one noted down the text of his sermon that day. All we know is that the hymn just before the sermon began with the words, 'Westward, look, the land is bright'.

Almost exactly fifty years later, a researcher sifting through some papers in the Cathedral archive room discovered a pile of type-written quarto pages giving, almost in diary form, an account of many Cathedral events of 1940 and 1941. All the separate entries were signed only with the initials 'W. J.' and though there was no indication of his name, the detail in some of the accounts indicates that 'W. J.' was a participant in the events that he was describing for posterity.

The Monday night was never forgotten by the community on watch at the Cathedral. The area between the Cathedral and Bold Street was the focus of attack, and the noise of bombs and anti-aircraft guns was shattering. The story is best told in the words of the enigmatic 'W. J.':

> A system of firewatching at nights has been in operation here for many months, regular night patrols being maintained throughout to ensure that any fires due to incendiary bombs are tackled without delay. Imagine, then, the feelings of those inside the Cathedral - including the Dean and Mr. Pittaway - when, on Sunday night and again last night and the early hours of today, hostile planes singled out the building for attack - circling high above in the moonlight as anti-aircraft guns fired away in an effort to drive them off. On Sunday night large numbers of incendiaries fell, ringing the Cathedral, happily without doing any harm.
>
> Then came this morning's attack. Once more incendiaries were dropped near the east end. It is fortunate that the wooden refectory which did duty at this end for many months was no longer there. It had, in fact, been removed precisely on account of this new danger of fire from the air. Incendiaries were also dropped on the north side and here again the value of foresight and precaution in this matter was demonstrated. To guard against the possibility of an incendiary entering the great organ, a wire casement had been placed against the north aisle window at the back of the organ. A fire bomb did actually hit this casement last night but, being unable to penetrate, did no harm. The organ was saved.
>
> An oil bomb capable of setting fire to the largest of buildings dropped at the west end of the Cathedral and a fire raged among the contractor's offices, the setting-out shed and the machinery for sawing up the massive pieces of sandstone which go into the fabric of the Cathedral. Much spare timber also went up in flames. The wind at this time was due east and carried the flames away from the Cathedral; otherwise the temporary wall would undoubtedly have suffered. Tongues of flame reached across St. James's Road. High-explosive bombs followed the incendiaries. One fell into a basement of a house opposite the contractor's yard. A delayed action bomb fell at the foot of the steps to the King's Porch and was removed today by a bomb disposal squad. Two small high-explosives fell just outside the Lady Chapel and while not removing a single stone of the fabric, chipped the steps in numerous places and caused hundreds, even thousands, of incisions in the walls.
>
> The remarkable escape, however, was from perhaps the largest bomb of all. This fell on the roof of the south east transept. It broke through the roof and entered the space between roof and ceiling of the transept. By a happy chance, the bomb struck the top of the inner brick wall supporting the central beam of the transept and, being deflected outwards, burst through the outer wall and exploded in the air high above street level. There the chief damage was to the tall windows of the transept. The havoc that would have been occasioned had the bomb been deflected inwards so that it penetrated the ceiling to explode inside the transept is best left to the imagination.
>
> It may be placed on record that the Dean, subsequently continuing his tour of the Cathedral and finding that the tower had survived and was undamaged, tried to sing the *Te Deum*. In his own words - 'It simply

Sir Giles Scott's plans for the west end of the building were completed and sent to the Dean during the darkest days of the war.

would not come'. Just then a blackbird somewhere in the trees outside burst into song. That was the *Te Deum*. The bird's liquid notes heralded the dawn. The raid having ended, the watchers at the Cathedral were able to look over the city to watch the light rising in the east. The fires left by the raiders were still blazing against the duck-egg blue of the western sky.

It would have needed more than one of Hitler's bombs to destroy so strong a building, but we can imagine the relief in the Dean's heart as he finally managed to send a telegram to Scott, letting him know that, so far at least, the damage was minimal.

In London, Scott was worrying over the dangers being faced by the Cathedral ('my great big child'), and arranging for the measures essential to protect its fabric, while air raids over the south meant that he had his own immediate difficulties to face as well:

> We have been having a chaotic time at the office all the drawings and furniture had to be bundled out on to the pavement when we thought the building was going and they all got into a terrible muddle as all drawings are numbered, its a job to get them back into their correct places, and put in the strong room. I hope we shall not get a direct hit before we get finished!
>
> Poor old Gray's Inn has almost all gone. The Old Hall, Chapel, Library and most of the offices except mine! As all the buildings that butt up against us are now burnt out only a direct hit can do us serious structural harm!

Solemn Entrance

CHAPTER
- *Eleven* -

HEROICALLY, all the Scott letters to the Dean during the desperate summer of 1941 reveal an irrepressible humour and optimism all the more remarkable when one remembers that he was now 62 years old and had been living with his plans and partly built Cathedral for a forty-year period which had witnessed two terrible wars and a great depression which had sapped the economic strength of the city. One letter of July 15th is especially full of excitement and anticipation:

> Many thanks for your cheering telegram, what fun you must be having. The Chancel arch and flanking organ cases will soon be seen for the first

time in their true proportion, and peeps like the one you mention from Derby tomb will provide many thrills to those who have eyes to see! . . . We are greatly looking forward to our Liverpool visit. I shall find it one of the most thrilling of all my visits.

The next visit to Liverpool was to take part in the services to mark the 'Solemn Entrance in Time of War': the plywood wall was coming down and the vast new section would formally be brought into use. Before the war, Dwelly must have had visions of a service to rival the Consecration in

This view from the High Altar shows the demolition of the temporary wall. Before the brick structure was pulled down, another, wooden wall was erected on the Chancel side of it to prevent dust and grit flying everywhere and getting into the organ.

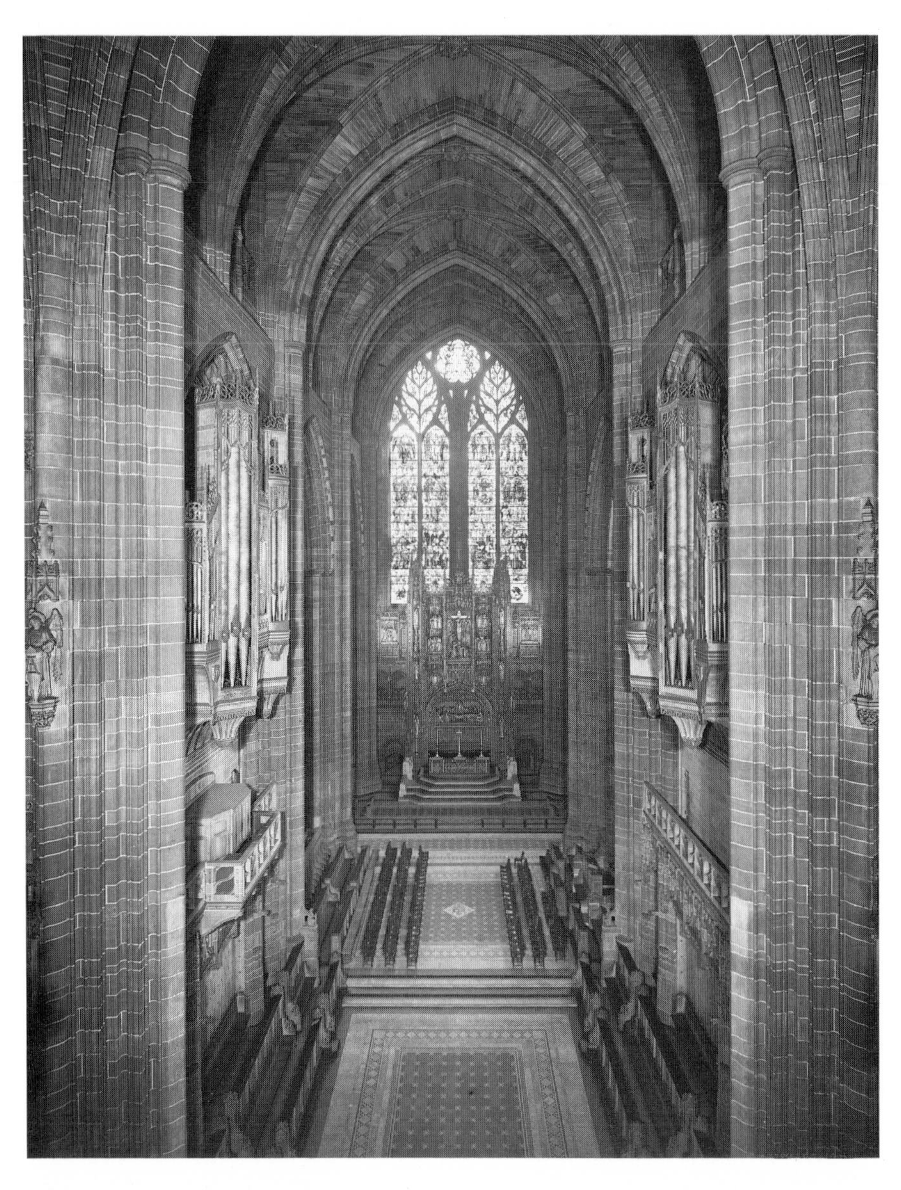

Looking back the other way, this is an interesting view of the Chancel taken from a point on the temporary wall.

terms of splendour. No such service was possible at the height of the blitz, but the service which was held remained indelibly in the minds of all who were present.

Solemn Entrance in Time of War was planned for Sunday 27th July 1941 and the great event was preceeded by important ceremonies on the two previous days. On the Friday the architect formally received into the new portion the Canons Residentiary, the Archdeacons and the General Chapter.

And after the reading of Evening Prayer they recited together this

> declaration, the same as was made by the Bishop on the day of Consecration when he laid his hands upon the pillar of witness: THIS DWELLING IS GOD'S HABITATION, IT IS A POSSESSION ABOVE ALL PRICE WHICH MAY NOT BE SPOKEN AGAINST.
>
> Immediately following, all the Canons assembled in General Chapter to honour the architect, it being the first occasion under the new statutes of nineteen hundred and forty-one.

The most memorable view in the whole Cathedral even to this day is that from the Corona Gallery, that gallery high up and just below the under-tower vault. One can imagine the excitement when the next day Mr. Robinson and the choir boys climbed the spiral stairs in their choir robes and took up their positions on the Gallery. They had been used to looking up to see Mr. Goss Custard on the organ console but on that day they looked down on him over a hundred feet below them. A new sound was heard in the Cathedral that day when they began to sing the hymn *O for a faith that will not shrink, though press'd by many a foe*, followed by *Come down O Love Divine*. After the singing of an anthem by Wesley all joined in the words: 'May the power and presence of God be with you in all you do for Him in this His glorious habitation'.

On the Sunday morning, following Morning Prayer and Holy Communion, 'and the middle wall of partition having been broken down', the service began. Mr. Dwelly's choreography in the old part of his Cathedral had been memorable, but now he had the whole of the Central Space in which to show his genius, and the stark simplicity of one of the first actions became one of the great moments in the history of the Cathedral. The Chairman of the Building Committee led the Dean and Chapter from the old into the new, 'passing over that place in the Crypt where during an enemy air raid a celebration of Holy Communion was begun in the older part of the building and completed at a carpenter's bench in the new; consummating the consecration in the Choir at the first Eucharist in the Nave'. As they moved through the new spaces the choir sang:

> Lord, thy glory fills the heaven,
> Earth is with its fullness stored;
> Unto thee be glory given,
> Holy, Holy, Holy Lord.

The words of the order of service reveal the rich significance of all that was happening:

> The Dean shall say: And first let us rejoice in his assurance, knowing that his promise never fails, Wheresoever two or three are gathered together in his name, there he is in the midst.
>
> A space of Silence shall be kept. Then the Dean shall continue:
>
> It is written, Then came Jesus and stood in the midst, and said, peace be unto you. And they worshipped him.
>
> A space of silence shall be kept.

> Children shall enter into the procession. When the leading boy has crossed the threshold, the reading shall continue:
>
> Jesus called unto him a little child, and set him in the midst and said, Verily I say unto you, Except ye become as little children, ye shall in no wise enter into the kingdom of heaven.

After the Lord's Prayer and the hymn *O worship the King*,

> The Dean standing over that place in the Crypt where a carpenter's bench became the table of the Lord, shall make silent remembrance of that night, when many families and homes were broken and great numbers killed by the malice of the enemy, and after a space of silence he shall say Blessed are the dead which die in the Lord.

The words for an anthem had been written by Sir Frederick Radcliffe, the father figure of the whole Cathedral venture, whose memories went right back to the Town Hall meeting of 1901:

Hail, sovereign Lord, whose all-sustaining power
Transcends the scope of feeble human praise,
Outpour on us the Spirit's glorious dower
Who, unto thee, an earthly temple raise –
Build we, and laud thy Christ in all our ways.

Come thou, dear Lord, true splendour of our race,
Thy presence add to those who worship here,
While in thy name, we seek the Father's face,
And taste the joy of love that casts out fear –
Build we, and sing: 'Our Lord is ever near.'

Eternal Spirit, who dost find a home
In hearts and minds made ready by thy grace,
Renew thy sevenfold gifts in all who come
To seek from strife and stress a breathing space –
Build thou, and make in each thy dwelling place.

Other services followed during the week. The final one was for the masons and all who had worked with their skills on the building. At the end of the service the Dean led Sir Giles Scott to the lectern where he was able to praise:

> The men that bear the burdens, and them that hew the stone, the men that bind the stone to the foundation, and the steel to the concrete; the men that make bricks, and those that pile them high and firm in pillars and walls; the men that have skill to cut timber, and them that are cunning to work in gold, in silver, and in all metals; in ivory, in glass, in lead, and in iron; the sculptors, and the makers of instruments of music, the draughtsmen and the engineers, the men that have skill to grave any manner of graving, and to find out every device which shall be put to them for pillar, and arch, and vault.

The high words and ceremonies over, everyone was back to arduous work: the Tower still had no roof, the final pinnacles had not been set, the

Joseph Phillips, sculptor, at work on the final details of one of the huge bosses in 1934. The quality of workmanship, here as elsewhere, is extremely high and richly deserved the Dean's praise.

drawings for the Nave were not completed. But the architect's delight in the Solemn Entrance simply spurred him on, as is clear from his letter to the Dean in August, 1941:

> Phew! what a wonderful weekend, but especially I wish to thank you for what you did for us, in the midst of all your arranging and organising you still gave the impression that we were the only people you were attending to! Well it was one of the milestones in my life, and a weekend that I shall always remember.

> . . . Now we have the scaffolding off the tower to look forward to and when that is over let us think of the first bay of the Nave with its bridge, drawings of this are making steady progress, and let's hope we shall be able to undertake it as a thank offering for Victory.

The new section of the building was now open and the Cathedral Church of Christ could be seen by all both inside and out as a really great building – not just in Liverpool but in the world. All the more harrowing, then, were the nightly worries over the bombs. In the face of the venom of Hitler's night raids, the precautions the Cathedral company could take seemed very small. Sir Giles ensured that there were plenty of white-painted buckets of sand at crucial spots, and he had agreed that the damping chamber in the Tower could be used as quarters for the fire-watchers.

The Tower, though almost complete, did not have a roof; it was encircled with timber scaffolding which made the whole building vulnerable to incendiary devices. Each night the fire-watchers in their tin hats tried to keep warm and tried to keep awake at their stations. When an attack was on, ears were alert to anything which might come crashing or drifting down from the night skies. Low down in the Tower one night, Jack Kewley, the setter-out, thought his time had come, as he heard something tumbling down from the blackness. But he lived to tell the tale; it was one of the Cathedral pigeons that had fallen victim to a fragment of shrapnel.

Scott had experience of being in his building during a raid; full of concern for it but, typically, more concerned for the well-being of people from the nearby streets who had come in to seek shelter. At the height of hostilities, this did not come just now and again; raids were so frequent that people simply moved in each night, not knowing whether they would find their houses standing when they ventured back in the morning. In October 1941, Scott wrote to the Dean:

> I had occasion recently to visit the public air Raid Shelters under the Cathedral. I went on two consecutive evenings, during one of which an 'alert' was on. I must confess I was shocked to find the conditions under which these poor people spend the night. They were lying about, covered with old dirty bedding, on rough boards supported by a few bricks. Old men and women, children of all ages – a pathetic picture, that made me feel I wanted to cry. Surely something better than this can be done?
>
> Why not lime-wash the upper part of the walls and the ceilings, and colour-wash a warm-coloured, 6 ft. high dado to the walls, and put up proper wood or steel bunks, painted the same colour as the dado.
>
> Put the lights onto local switches; at present all lights have to be on, or all off, which is very trying for those sleeping or those who wish to read. A few pilot lights, and the remainder locally controlled, would be better.
>
> At present, I cannot help feeling that the shelters are a disgrace to the Cathedral, and it is all the more important because I found these shelters were the only ones in the neighbourhood being used; the public street shelters I found to be empty, and some were even padlocked during an

'alert' – but this did not seem to matter much because no one appeared to wish to go into them!

Amazingly, even at the height of the war, with his office bombed and his Cathedral overlooking bomb sites and gutted buildings, Scott was able to plan for the future. He was concerned not just for the Cathedral but for all the land in front of it running down to Great George Street. He did not want a Cathedral stuck up on a hill and cut off from the daily lives of ordinary people. This man who could design the largest cathedral in Britain with the biggest Gothic arches in the world could get the scale right when it came to houses for ordinary people to live in. His note to the Dean contained a beautiful little coloured sketch and plan for one of his early ideas. It did not lie with Dean Dwelly to see any of these plans through to building but the ideas lay dormant for his successors.

Posterity owes a debt of gratitude to the enigmatic W. J. for what might well be the only existing account of the fixing of the top stone on the north-east pinnacle of the Tower, the first to be completed:

> The Dean took the little service, appropriately using the benedictions of the topmost stone of the temple. There were present, in addition to Sir Giles and Dr. Dwelly, Mr. Pittaway, clerk of works, Harry Oxton and Hughie Williams, the masons engaged on the work, together with Mr. 'Joe' Marsh, photographer, who had been specially invited to take a picture of the proceedings. Mr. Marsh's antics will long be a source of amusement although they were not at all amusing at the time. He seems to have had no fear and never even to think of it, and this was the cause of some concern among the others in the party.
>
> The scaffolding erected around the pinnacle was sufficient to serve the purposes of the masons, but it was not intended to serve as a platform for a ceremony. However, all crowded on to it. Up here the fear of heights assails most people and, to make matters worse a gale was blowing. The wind was stronger than it has been for some time and the scaffolding seemed to sway like a ship in a swell. Sir Giles began to feel as if he would be seasick and took hold of the pinnacle for support.
>
> Mr. Marsh needed more room to take his picture and the rest of the party quaked with apprehension as they saw him unconcernedly clamber astride a horizontal scaffold pole overlooking the cemetery and 'snapped' the scene. A false move and he would have fallen some 360 to 370 feet to his death. There was fortunately no such mishap and Mr. Marsh was blissfully unaware that he had done anything particularly daring.

A brief note from Scott to the Dean dated March 6th 1942 comments upon the fixing of the final stone of the final pinnacle: 'The finial photos [are] excellent, better than I expected, we were so cold and they made me take my hat off. I felt blue but it does not seem to show.' Throughout the winter whenever the weather had permitted, the fixer masons had been working over 300 feet up in the air on the eight finials which crown the Tower. For an account of the remarkable events of Friday 20th February

1942 we have once again to be grateful to W. J.:

> Today the thermometer registered five degrees below zero on the ground shortly before Sir Giles Scott and a party ascended to the top of the Vestey Tower. The occasion was the fixing of the last stone on the last of the eight pinnacles, the one standing north- west by compass. When frost is in the air it is inadvisable to continue work in cement or mortar, but the act on which Sir Giles had set his heart had been postponed once already and there was no turning back this time.
>
> The Dean saw Sir Giles prepare to enter the lift that would take him up the tower, but declined the invitation to join him in the stone-laying ceremony. In the party going up were Mr. Dudley Morrison, the contractor, Mr. Pittaway, clerk of works, and Mr. Meredith, general foreman. The lift was not working well. It stopped in mid-air so many times that we thought we should never reach the top. Some of us, indeed, had visions of being marooned half way up the tower for hours. Eventually, amid some good-humoured banter in which Sir Giles joined, we reached the top of the lift shaft on the level of the belfry floor on the cemetery side of the tower. Sir Giles, well wrapped up to keep out the cold, then stepped nimbly up the relay of ladders leading to the broad scaffolding walk which rings the tower along the line of the battlements.
>
> About a score of men were waiting there. The all-important pinnacle was surrounded by a stout scaffolding and platform, and here gathered Sir Giles and his party, together with Harry Oxton, the mason, Hughie Williams, the fixer, and their labourer, Jack Hughes.
>
> While Oxton and Williams prepared the flat surface of the pinnacle on which the finial was to rest, it was interesting to gaze into the space inside the ring of battlements. It looks like a huge crater extending downwards perhaps fifty or sixty feet to the belfry floor. It is partly filled by a large crane so set up on a mass of woodwork that it appears to be on stilts. A little hut on top of this woodwork acts as the brain of the mechanism. Here works the crane driver, James Dixon. It was he who, at a signal, swung the final piece of stonework over to a point above the pinnacle. A serrated copper dowel was seen to be protruding from the underside of the finial where, of course, it was embedded in cement. Now the Snowcrete, a pure white cement fluid, which had been prepared with water heated on the spot in a bucket brazier, was poured into the hole in the pinnacle into which the dowel was to fit. This fluid acted as grouting. Sir Giles gave the word and the finial came down slowly. The architect, trowel in hand, watched this piece of carved stone, weighing, one imagines, at least one hundredweight, drop quietly and exactly into it last resting place.
>
> When the banker mark of the mason who carved this particular stone was observed on the finial's underside, Sir Giles was moved to suggest that that day's date should be carved on the outside of the stone. Mr. Pittaway capped the suggestion by saying that it ought also to have Sir Giles's initials on it.
>
> Instructions were given for the topmost portion of the pinnacle to be

The final pinnacle of the Tower is completed on 20 February 1942.

covered with sacking immediately in order to protect the mortar and cement from the frost.

The important feature of this pinnacle is that it reaches 330 feet 1 inch above the level of the Cathedral floor. This is one inch higher than the other seven. It was achieved by the simple expedient of extending the tip of the pinnacle, the last of the eight crowning the tower, by exactly one inch. It becomes, therefore, probably the highest point in Liverpool.

Photographs of the scene were taken from the scaffolding surrounding the neighbouring pinnacle. This was undoubtedly the sheltered side of the Cathedral; otherwise no one would have cared to stand still for the photographer. The barrage balloons, silver against a clear blue sky, looked down on us and to express approval of what was going on at the top of the tower, broke through to bathe the Cathedral in a warm, friendly light. At this moment it was probably warmer by a degree or two than it was on the ground.

One had an opportunity of studying Sir Giles has he talked to the company present. A tall, well-built man of regular features and healthy complexion, he gives a certain impression of boyishness in spite of his white hair and sixty years. There is nothing of the ascetic in his appearance. He is a genius who doesn't pose as one; he doesn't permit himself any of the eccentricities popularly associated with genius. Always ready to laugh at a quip or joke, Sir Giles is obviously much at home with the men who work on the Cathedral. Today there was clearly no atmosphere of a great man deigning to speak to lesser mortals. He and the workmen appear to regard the work as a comradely adventure undertaken together. He is, in short, not their taskmaster but a friend and fellow-worker. As witness of this, one may call his own words used today:

'Mr. Morrison, Mr. Pittaway, Mr. Meredith, and all of you. We have got to a point which I have been looking forward to for many many years – the highest stone on the tower. At one time I never thought Hitler would let us reach it. But we have got there. In peace-time we would have celebrated with plenty of drinks and smokes, but now we cannot have anything like that. We have to wait until after the war, when you and I are going to have a 'beano'.

'I want to say Thank-you for all you have done and for the grand work you have done in getting this building up. I hope we have a building to be proud of. I think we have. I always say we have the finest masons in the world in Liverpool. We have a really good bit of masonry which I hope will last for centuries. I only hope old Hitler will not blow that last stone off. I cannot adequately express my feelings to you for your help and co-operation'.

Sir Giles Scott and Sir Frederick Radcliffe, friends for so many years, enjoy the open space in the centre of the Cathedral.

As architect and Dean wandered around the Cathedral, relishing the discoveries of early-morning and late-evening light, seeing the Tower on occasions through the mist of the early morning with the sun behind sending great shafts upwards, they might well have remem-bered the words of Bishop Chavasse: 'some-thing to speak for God in this great city'. From the Wirral peninsula, from the flat lands northwards to Southport, from the foothills of the Pennines there was Liverpool Cathedral. As workers crossed the river daily on the ferry boats, up above the dereliction of mangled buildings, through the awful gaps of what had once been great civic buildings, the Cathedral stood – a symbol for the world to see that Liverpool would never be broken.

Thousands of troops from all parts of the world passed through the port during those war years, and many of them found their way up to St. James's Mount to marvel. One visitor was very special. The architect's mother was a very old lady: because of the illness and then death of her husband, she had had the responsibility of the up-bringing of her children. She had wandered round Sussex churches with Giles and Adrien when they were boys, and she had heard so much about the great Cathedral in Liverpool, which she feared she might never be able to see. However, on Monday 13th July 1942 she was escorted round the building by her son and her friend Mr. Dwelly. Her little letter of thanks to the Dean after the visit is full of human warmth, joy, and justifiable pride, and that letter will remain for all time in the war-time archives of the Cathedral that defied all the force of German bombing, and still stands to the glory of God and the indomitable human spirit:

> I was so overpowered and dazed on Monday that I feel I must try to thank you for all your kindness and thought for my comfort. If I had been the Queen you could not have been more careful of me.
>
> I never shall forget my visit, which I had been looking forward to for years, but of late I had given up hope as I was not feeling well enough to undertake it. I was not a bit overtired – it was marvellous. It was a feeling of pride and astonishment to me to think my own son could produce such a glorious building and I am a proud mother of him personally and of his work. (He is rather nice isn't he?)
>
> Forgive the ramblings of an old woman and one who is grateful for living long enough to see the results – Now I feel when my time comes that I have seen the completion of all my hopes.
>
> One really wants to soak in it, 6 hours was not nearly long enough to take it all in, but now in looking at the photos I can wander round at my leisure and thoroughly enjoy myself.

Before the war was over, Augustus David retired as Bishop, and feelings within the Cathedral must have been very mixed. David did find it difficult to accept that after 1931 he no longer held the position of Dean. It must have been very difficult to find full co-operation between Bishop and the autocratic Dean Dwelly. Despite the problems, David was a formative influence upon both Cathedral and diocese, but as one of the clergy commented at the time of his retirement: 'I remember A. D. D. with more respect than affection; and I think he would prefer it so'.

Though there may have been a coldness between Bishop and people during his episcopate, the same was not so of his successor. On 6th September 1944, Clifford Arthur Martin was enthroned in the Cathedral at one of Dean Dwelly's finest services. Hardly anyone in the diocese knew anything about Clifford Martin before his arrival, and in background and character he was totally different from David. He was born in 1895 and lived in North London. Family finances denied him immediate access to higher education, and he enlisted during the opening weeks of the First World War, at the age of nineteen, rising through the ranks to be commissioned. An accident left him blind in the left eye, and so he applied to be an officer-instructor of a cadet battalion. After the war he was able to read for an ex-serviceman's pass degree in theology at Cambridge. As curate, and later as parish priest, his extraordinary pastoral skills were revealed. Just before the Second World War, he was appointed to a parish in Plymouth, a town chosen, like Liverpool, to be the frequent focus for German bombing. His church was gutted by fire and his vicarage badly damaged, but his care for his people never faltered.

The new Bishop, the Right Reverend Clifford Martin.

Martin's arrival in his Cathedral was marked by one of the finest of Dean Dwelly's services and by a great improvement in the relationship between Cathedral and diocese. The service made full use of the fact that the Cathedral was in time of war and incomplete:

> the Bishop, remaining for a space in the carpenter's workshop, shall give himself to thanksgiving and prayer . . . the Bishop will approach the Cathedral Church over the ground on which the Western portion of the Nave of the Cathedral is yet to be built.

His passage into and through his new Cathedral reminded him at every stage of his duties and of the sacraments and services of the Church. With the drama and suspense typical of Dwelly, the service began with the Bishop outside on his building site:

> At five-thirty in the afternoon the Bishop shall knock three times at the door which opens from the carpenter's workshop into the Cathedral church. He shall knock with the same ivory mallet that was used by the late King Edward VII when he laid the first foundation stone of the Cathedral. The Dean shall order the door to be thrown open.
>
> As the door is opened the Keeper of the door shall say in a quiet voice the words: Do justly. Love mercy. Walk humbly with God.
>
> At the Font, before he approaches the Nave of the Cathedral, the Bishop will call to mind the love of Jesus, how he took little children in his arms and blessed them, how of them he said - of such is the kingdom of heaven; then he will call to mind the command of Jesus to the Apostles to go into all the world and make disciples, baptising them, a boy singing:
>
> 'Alone, yet not alone, my God, I journey on my way; what need I fear when Thou art near, O King of night and day.'
>
> Alone, and unattended, the Bishop shall walk through the Nave, through the Choir, through the Sanctuary, to the Holy Table . . .
>
> In the Sanctuary the Dean and Chapter of the Cathedral and the Archdeacons with the Incumbents of the Diocese shall receive the

> Bishop saying: O come, let us worship and kneel before the Lord our Maker. All kneeling shall make an act of worship together. Familiar words from the order of administration of Holy Communion shall be used:
>
> 'Have mercy upon us, most merciful Father. Here we offer and present unto thee ourselves, our souls, and bodies. Grant that we may do all such good works as thou hast prepared for us to walk in. Grant that we may serve and please thee in newness of life. Grant that we may evermore dwell in Christ and he in us.'

Even a fragment of the service reveals Dwelly's mastery of symbol and movement, and his creative use of existing liturgical material. The imagination and vibrancy of Cathedral services were not restricted to a small, closed Cathedral community: throughout the war the Cathedral was host to dozens of organisations whose members took strength and courage from attendance at 'their' special services.

All Clear

CHAPTER
- Twelve -

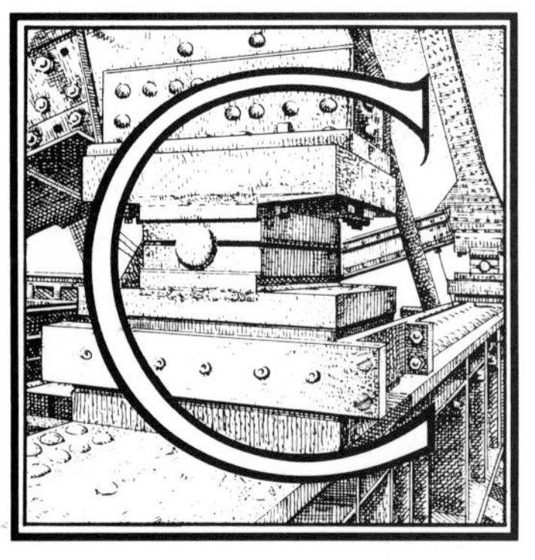

C LOCKS never run backwards. There are times when humankind would like to be able to 'put the clock back', but such nostalgia cannot lead to progress. Of course, the ending of the war was a time of jubilation as well as relief and sorrow; but Europe, Great Britain, and the city of Liverpool would carry for ever the marks of war, and after the immediate euphoria of peace there was the grey exhaustion of the post-war years. Ration books, clothing coupons, coal shortages, utility furniture; no magic potion could turn the world into a brighter, richer, safer place. For a generation of war-time children, a banana was nothing more tangible than an old and faded picture on the wall of the greengrocer's shop. It was over forty years since the prosperous, confident, empire-building attitudes of 1904 had laid the foundation stone of the largest Anglican church in the world. Miraculously, that building had escaped serious war damage, but shortage of materials, money and manpower must have cast an impenetrable gloom over the whole Cathedral world.

One year after the cessation of World War I, Alan Tod had been appointed to the Executive Committee, and throughout the war he had been chairman. All his experience within the commercial world was needed to steer the Cathedral enterprise through war and post-war difficulties. That post-war decade does not make the most exciting episode in the Cathedral story; it is essentially a story of frustration and delay, yet once again it highlights the sheer determination of the Cathedral community who, in a different world, had embarked upon their enterprise and now refused to let down the faith of their forbears.

In 1945, Dr. Cyril Garbett, Archbishop of York, reminded the Cathedral company of the magnitude of their achievement. Such a sermon must take its place alongside Chavasse's words in the Town Hall in 1901, and Lang's at the consecration in 1924:

> Your Cathedral will witness to faith, fellowship and worship. It witnesses to our faith in the reality of the Unseen and of the Living and Eternal God, in an age when He is often forgotten or denied. Usually the parish church was to be found in the very centre of the medieval city, the focus of its life and devotion; but in the modern city search has often to be made for it, for it is overshadowed by vast offices or tenements, or submerged amidst a mass of houses. But here in Liverpool you have set your Cathedral on a site which overlooks the city, and the first glimpse the visitor from across the Atlantic will catch of England will be of a church tower soaring towards the sky. In a city which already has many great buildings the Cathedral will be the noblest. It will speak to all of faith in God . . . If the Christian faith were either dead or dying it would be sheer waste to build this church. It would be an empty cenotaph, the memorial of a faith which had passed from the earth. But it is a living and growing building, filled with the spirit of life, for it is the home of the ever-present Christ. And men and women give the best of their thought, their skill, their labour, and their wealth towards its completion, for they are convinced that He in whose Name and to whose glory it is built is the Eternal and Unchanging God.
>
> The Cathedral witnesses also to work in fellowship. Our ancient Cathedrals are the result of the work of many minds and hands united in a common purpose. Architects, sculptors, masons and builders all had their share in them. Many of them only very gradually reached their present form, for successive generations had to finish a task too great for any one, each making its special contribution to the enlargement, adornment and completion of a building they looked on as the heritage and responsibility of all. It is remarkable how strong is the sense of unity in Cathedrals and churches built in various styles in different centuries. Your Cathedral, please God, will be finished in a much shorter space of

time than most of those which have been built in the past, but it also will be the result of the work of many . . . No great human work can ever be accomplished without the co-operation of many. Your Cathedral should be a symbol of the unity which should pervade all classes and nations in building up the temple of freedom and justice. Without co-operation in a common purpose, we shall lose the fruits of the victory which we have gained at such a heavy cost.

The common purpose which has united all who have given and worked for this Cathedral has been the worship and glory of God. Their purpose has not been to erect an architectural monument, nor a super concert hall, nor a luxury auditorium for ecclesiastical and ethical lectures. Their purpose has been to raise a house in which the worship of God may be conducted with devotion, reverence and dignity. When a visitor enters the Cathedral for the first time, he is at once impressed by a sense of vastness and spaciousness; the grandeur and the majesty of the building fill him with awe, and impel him to adore in worship. But he also is soon impressed by the care taken over every detail. He sees nothing which is cheap and shoddy, but everything is of the best, for all within this building is an offering to God, and is intended to help in His worship. In this you give a valuable example . . Our Cathedrals cannot set too high a standard for the art which should be used as a handmaid to worship.

And the same principle applies to corporate worship as well as to the actual building and its adornment. There was a time when there was fear of using music, colour, and beauty in the worship of the church. It was thought that they might detract the worshipper from the solemnity of the act in which he was engaged. The result was that art became increasingly secular when it found the doors of the church closed to it. But we are learning again that all art should be consecrated to God, and that it should be used as an offering to Him. Here directed by the skill of your Dean, your public worship has been made beautiful with music and symbolism. In the richness of their colour and pageantry, as well as in variety and originality, your services hold a place of their own in the Anglican Communion. The prayers and praises used are both old and new; the worship of the historic liturgies is combined with prayers for modern needs in present-day prose. And the appeal is made to the eye as well as to the ear, and to the imagination as well as to the intellect.

Your services have become popular in the best sense of the word. By this I mean that they have significance not merely to a small group of the faithful who have been brought up to appreciate the ordinary worship of the church, but to the people of a great city. Men of different professions and interests find in the special services of the Cathedral worship which is relevant to their daily work and problems. Our worship should not be separated by a gulf from the ordinary life of ordinary men and women. No Cathedral should stand apart from the life of those who live around it. It is nothing less than a disaster when Christian worship is treated as remote and cut off from the concerns and needs of the average man. Through worship the secular should receive consecration . . .

For we must never forget that worship becomes selfish and self-centred if it begins and ends with the building in which it is held. If here on special

> occasions the offering of work is made to God, it is made so that day by day it may be done for his glory. Worship within the house of God should flow over into daily life. Your Cathedral with all its majesty and beauty would stand as a rebuke unless its influence spreads far and wide. Its splendour and dignity should stir the citizens to emulate it in their public architecture. The wide spaces within it for prayer and contemplation should make them eager to provide without, spaces of peace and quiet for tired men and women and for the play of little children. The colour and glory within it should encourage attempts to bring more colour, variety and interest into the lives which are spent in drab and dreary streets. Its splendour as God's temple should be an incentive to provide houses for those who are meant to be human temples of God, but who herded into slums rarely attain to the greatness of their calling.
>
> As year by year you proceed with the completion of your great task, see that the life of the city grows too in harmony with the Cathedral which will be its crowning glory; so that men may say of the city as well as of the Cathedral that those who are responsible for them are seeking to express in their architecture, their order, their life and their worship something of the loveliness, the fellowship and the joy which are found only in perfection in the invisible City of God.

Over the years, one can almost hear the 'Amen' from the Cathedral company.

In the post-war years, with the centre of the city so scarred by bombing, the Cathedral made an even greater visual impact than it had done hitherto, especially when in 1947 the last of the scaffolding came off the Tower and people were able to see the strength and intricacy of the design for the first time.

The early months of 1947 brought exceptionally severe weather. Sefton Park Lake was frozen for weeks, and children tobogganned down the snow-covered banks and right out across the lake – to the far side, if your sledge was any good. What was fun for the children was a severe hold-up for the building, and work was suspended completely for several weeks.

Despite the blitz and the chaos in Liverpool and London, Scott made good progress with his plans for the Nave, and in the autumn of 1948 a licence was received which permitted a start to be made on the first bay. The cranes were brought down from the top of the Tower so that the steel girders of the roof could be fixed. Most of the people of Liverpool could see very little of all this progress, but the new work was psychologically very important for the Cathedral community. Even by the end of 1949, there were only 37 men engaged on the site, plus eleven masons and a single apprentice.

War had denied the Cathedral and its imaginative Dean the splendour and pageantry of a great service to mark the completion of the Central Space, but the spring of 1949 gave good reason for another royal visit to the Cathedral. On Sunday 27th March, Bishop David was back to preach in the Cathedral, and had some pertinent things to say about cathedrals in the modern world. Not for him the nostalgic vision of the cathedral world of the nineteenth century:

> Most of the Cathedrals seemed to be living for themselves alone, and for the select few who attended their services. They had made hardly any impact upon the life of a city or a diocese, and in themselves they were little more than haunts of ancient peace.

The old Bishop had confidence that Liverpool was creating a cathedral, great and outgoing, for the present and for the future:

> This Cathedral is a standing proof that we of this generation do not lack the power to achieve greatness. Within these walls we may take fresh courage as we face colossal tasks of other kinds crowding in on us now – tasks of rebuilding the national life of our country and the broken life of the world.

Tuesday 29th March was a day which will never be forgotten by the boys and gentlemen of the choir and the Cross Guild: as the beautiful black, red and silver order of service book shows, their attendance throughout all parts of the ceremony was important. It was almost as if their Dean realised that the present generation of the choir needed a special occasion which would always stay in their minds. The occasion was to be the opening of the new doors in the Rankin Porch by Her Royal Highness Princess Elizabeth and the Duke of Edinburgh. Dean Dwelly always rehearsed the ceremonial of the Cathedral with military precision,

Princess Elizabeth, with the Duke of Edinburgh at the right of the photograph, formally opens the Rankin Porch. Sir Alan Tod can be seen behind one of the choristers.

and that day the boys were drilled to polished perfection.

The royal visitors arrived in cloudless spring sunshine and were greeted by the Bishop, who introduced Colonel Tod and Sir Giles Scott, and conducted the party up to the doors. There, a chorister knelt with the key to the door on a cushion, and the doors themselves were manned by other choristers wearing cassocks and ruffs. When the Princess had turned the key, the boys drew upon the doors and the procession moved into the inner porch, passing 25 of the younger boys – one for each year since the consecration of the Chancel.

The visitors were led through into the building site, where they were able to meet some of the craftsmen and watch them at work, before moving back to the completed section of the building, where

> Their Royal Highnesses occupied the Royal chairs, the same as were used by George V and Queen Mary at the Consecration in 1924. Then in the west end of the Western Approaches crossing, the great central space emptied of all furniture, the Royal Guests waited awhile listening to music by Le Fleming, Holst and Bach. They made their mark on the pillar which is the last of the present portion and the first of the new portion of the great Nave of the Cathedral. Then the Princess and the Duke having signed the Cathedral Records moved to the War Memorial

The arrival of Great George, the Bourdon Bell, on St. James's Road.

The Bourdon Bell sits on the floor as the Tenor is hoisted up to the belfry.

Transept and then on to the Choir where the singers left their stalls and surrounded the Royal Guests to sing The Welcome.

There was a brief tour of the building, during which Goss Custard invited the Princess to play the organ, before the visitors left the Cathedral as they had entered. By this time, the steps of the porch were jammed with children from St. James's School, many of them waving union jacks, and the walkway down to the car was flanked by choristers in green, mustard and rust-coloured cassocks, bright in the spring sunshine.

Great progress took place in 1950, when the final work was completed on the roof so that the construction of the bell implacements could proceed. Activity hundreds of feet in the air was matched by labour below ground level, as 1,500 cubic yards of soil and rock were moved in preparation for the foundations of the first bay of the Nave. As the building moved further west, essential re-organisation was completed on the site, and new concrete banker sheds were built near the old mortuary chapel.

Pickfords, the removal firm, have transported many interesting cargoes in their day, but the low-loader lorry which moved rather slowly up to Liverpool from the John Taylor Bell Foundry in Loughborough must have drawn the attention of many people. The lorry was carrying Great George, the 16 ton 10 cwt Bourdon Bell, second only in size to Great Paul at St. Paul's Cathedral. The arrival of the wagon on St. James's Road caused great excitement, and the precious cargo was welcomed by an enthusiastic Dean and some slightly apprehensive workmen, who realised the difficulties there would be in hoisting the new bell some two hundred feet up into the belfry.

Part of the temporary wall had to be taken down and wooden track laid over the marble of the floor. The bell was to be raised by manual winch, and the first attempt failed. Once off the floor, the bell had started to rotate, twisting the cables of the winch around each other and making movement impossible. The whole of the cable was released, laid out on the floor so that the tangles could be eliminated, and guy ropes prepared to prevent rotation at the second attempt.

At 9 a.m. on 7th May 1951, a team of twelve men assembled on the floor of the bell chamber around the two-handled winch. The gang was divided into three teams of four and, with two men to each handle, the hoist began. Though their enthusiasm may have been unlimited, their muscle power

The men who turned the handles to raise the bells up to the belfry.

The arrival of Princess Elizabeth and the Duke of Edinburgh for the dedication of the peal in 1951. A temporary viewing platform had been built on Hope Street.

was not, and the teams were changed every ten minutes. At four inches per minute, the movement was almost imperceptible, and the tension amongst the watchers, at a safe distance on the floor, must have been almost as great as the tension in the cables. Once the hoist was under way there could be no stopping, as momentum had to be maintained.

The cables of the winch disappeared up through the bell trap 175 feet in the air, and as the bell rose, so the smallness of the circular trap impressed itself on the eyes of the watchers. At 7 p.m., after ten hours of non-stop labour, the bell was fixed on to its mounting, to the intense relief of the lifting teams as they crowded around covered in dust, with sore hands and tired biceps. History does not record the name of the man who could not resist taking up a hammer and striking the great bell – just to test that it worked properly.

On Sunday 17th June 1951, the jubilee of the Town Hall meeting at which the momentous decision was made to build the Cathedral, Great George was blessed by the Bishop, and the people of Liverpool heard its cavernous voice for the first time. Below in the Cathedral, the choir sang Beethoven's *Hallelujah*.

The bell inches its way up towards the trap. The bell measured 9 feet, 6 inches, the trap just six inches more. This photograph also provides an excellent view of the spectacular under-tower vaulting, the formwork for which is shown in an earlier photograph on page 99.

The dedication of the Bartlett peal followed on Saturday 17th November. A platform and pavilion had been prepared on Hope Street, overlooking the cemetery, and the weather was perfect with clear skies and full sun as Princess Elizabeth and the Duke of Edinburgh docked in Liverpool after their tour of Canada to be greeted by thousands of Liverpudlians lining the streets from the Town Hall. The Lord Mayor and Lady Mayoress in 1951 were Colonel and Mrs. Vere Cotton, whose long and painstaking devotion to the building and its history rendered them the most fitting of people to welcome the future Queen.

The royal party arrived at the dais at 10.45 a.m., to be presented to Cathedral and civic dignitaries. Six choristers were present in cassocks and ruffs, Geoffrey Bethell presented a bouquet of red roses, and the Dean sought her Royal Highness's permission for the ringing of the bells. Interesting sounds had been floating down from the belfry on several afternoons that week as the team practised – much to the diversion of the one thousand pupils at the Liverpool Institute below. Now the trumpeters of the Central Band of the Royal Air Force signalled to the ringing team waiting in the tower, and the bells were heard in full voice for the first time.

CHAPTER
- *Thirteen* -

'But the continuing'

MANY chapters in the history of the Cathedral are full of excitement and achievement: foundation stone, consecration, Solemn Entrance, the placing of the highest pinnacle. Other chapters seem to be the subject of gloom rather than of sunlight. The Cathedral had survived the war, made good the damage, and pealed its bells, but the pace of new building was painfully slow, mainly through financial restriction; and some of the most significant names in the Cathedral enterprise were now old men. As in all such enterprises, new characters appear, and future progress is assured. The 1952 edition of the *Bulletin*

contained one short paragraph amongst its general notes:

> Canon S. J. Bezzant, who for 20 years occupied with great distinction the office of Chancellor of the Cathedral, has been appointed Dean of St. John's College, Cambridge. He has been succeeded as Canon Chancellor by the Reverend F. W. Dillistone.

Dr. Dillistone – or Dilly, as he was always affectionately known by the Cathedral company – was already a man of considerable stature as a scholar and teacher. He had been educated at Brighton College and Brasenose College, Oxford before holding important teaching posts in England, Canada and America. His early years at Liverpool must have called upon all his natural reserves of faith, serenity and determination.

The first of the Cathedral's great losses came in September 1953 with the death, at the age of 92, of Sir Frederick Radcliffe, who had been centrally involved in the growth of the Cathedral for longer than anyone else. He was present at the Town Hall meeting in 1901, and had served with the utmost distinction for 52 years. Radcliffe had lived just long enough to sign the beautifully-designed scroll presented to Owen Pittaway when he retired after 46 years of service:

> As Mason from 1907 to 1908, setter-out from 1908 to 1920 and assistant Clerk of Works from 1920 to 1921 he acquired an unrivalled practical knowledge of masonry construction which was to prove of the utmost value to the Architect and the Committee throughout the years 1921 to 1953 during which he held the important office of Clerk of Works. In this period the Choir and Eastern Transept were completed, the Under-Tower, Western Transept, Rankin and Welsford Porches and the Vestey Tower were built and the Nave begun.

At the time of the Jubilee Service in 1954, Bishop Martin, though acutely aware of the difficulties faced by the current generation of Cathedral builders, did not draw back from the challenge presented by the good men of the past:

> We to whom the great task has now been committed must be thankful to those who laid such good foundations and pray that we may be worthy of the trust committed to us. So the Cathedral speaks today of the interdependence of one generation upon another. We do not start with a clean slate. We inherit the situation in which we live from those who have gone before us. In our turn we are now making the situation into which our successors must come and in which they must build if the work commenced is to be completed.

For many of the company, the ties with the past seemed to be snapped in 1955 with the retirements of both Henry Goss Custard, the organist, and Dean Frederick William Dwelly. Not only had Goss played at all the great services since 1924, he had also taken a crucial role in the planning of the organ and for thirty years much of the musical success of the Cathedral had been of his making. And the thought of the Cathedral without Dwelly was for many people a contradiction: he had created the patterns and styles of worship which were recognised throughout the world as belonging to Liverpool Cathedral. He was an old, tired man whose faculties were fading, and within two years he was dead.

His body lay in its oak coffin on a high catafalque in the Presbytery, in front of the High Altar, but his living presence could be felt in the whole ordering of the simple funeral service, with its mood of solemn triumph. The choir sang J. S. Bach's setting of the words 'God liveth still', choir and congregation sang the hymns *Who would true valour see* and *The strife is o'er, the battle done*:

> The full Cathedral Choir led a procession of clergy and Cathedral and Diocesan officials into the chancel. The great procession, moving slowly in a measured majesty created by Dean Dwelly himself, took five minutes to pass.
>
> After the last hymn there was a moment of silence. Then, as all the congregation stood, the organ led the choir into Le Fleming's *Nunc Dimittis*, a work commissioned in 1952 as a mark of affection for Dr. Dwelly by the Cathedral Choristers' Guild. Two choristers removed the red and gold Cathedral pall from the coffin. As the coffin bearers took it off the catafalque, a chorister snuffed the four candles standing at the corners. A path was cleared through the wreaths massed round the Presbytery. The *Nunc Dimittis* faded to a silence as the coffin passed

The fineral of Dean Dwelly. Bishop Martin can be seen in the Bishop's Throne on the right.

> between the choir stalls. Then, as the procession reformed and the coffin was borne slowly down the Nave, the Cathedral organ burst into Chopin's *Funeral March*.
>
> Out through the main entrance and down the steps, with the great bell of the Vestey Tower tolling over it, the body of Dean Dwelly went from the Cathedral for the last time.

There was no sermon at the funeral itself, but in December 1960, at the service to unveil the memorial to the first Dean, his old friend Charles Raven delivered the address. One of the great theological figures of the twentieth century, Raven understood his friend, and the contribution he had made to the life of Liverpool Cathedral and the whole Anglican communion:

> He was a man uniquely fitted to his time: a man dedicated to God in Christ and to his own ministry in the Church of England; a man exquisitely sensitive to all the appeals of art, music, poetry, literature, drama, liturgy; exquisitely aware of the intuitive capacities which he possessed and singularly gifted in his approach to people of all sorts, able to get along side of them and interpret almost without spoken word their needs and express his readiness to help. But in addition he had singular gifts of administration, gifts of ingenuity in devising means for recording and storing and making available all the experience that he gathered, whether from his reading or his conversation, from his scholarship or from his contacts with men and things. But above all, he possessed a genius for friendship, the capacity really to care and passionately to help the folk who came to him and with whom he was brought into contact. He was for us a steward of the good gifts of God in this place and we owe him the building up of the community of this Cathedral which has stood the test of economic depression, of world war and of radical changes in its personnel and resources . . .
>
> He had the most extraordinary artistic gift of sensitiveness and intuition. You can see it in his discovery and encouragement of musicians like Goss Custard, or if I dare say so Benjamin Britten: of artists like the sculptor of this Cathedral, Mr. Carter Preston who is responsible for the memorial that we are soon to dedicate: of poets – he brought John Masefield here: of statesmen – some of you will remember Field Marshal Smuts speaking from this pulpit: of doctors and scientists and thinkers, and men of letters: of industrialists and politicians: of soldiers, sailors and airmen – the great Admiral of the Battle of the Western Approaches Max Horton not least – indeed all sorts and conditions of men, craftsmen, and singers, visitors, tourists, all and sundry. To all of them he had an instinctive approach and I think that all of them, as of us, knew that we were joyful in his presence and that we went away from it better men and better women. He gave life and life abundant. And if he had singular difficulty in explaining the reasons for his intuitive judgements, he was always conscious of the need to consult others and by the end of his life when he gave his pastoral theology lectures in Cambridge, he startled me by the brilliance with which he handled an academic audience and academic subjects . . .

> A word or two about the cost involved and the sum of his achievement before we dedicate ourselves and his memorial. The cost of such self-giving, joyous as it was in the paying, freed from any sort of self-pity or I think of any thought of self-aggrandisement, nevertheless was inescapable. Every prophet, every minister of the Gospel must be both a challenge and an inspiration; and in his case the challenge was manifest. He met a certain amount of real malice, a good deal of misunderstanding and, of course, the immense difficulties which this city and our country had to confront at the time of the slump, just before I left Liverpool during the 'thirties, when the threat of war grew near, and supremely during those years of blitz and terror, when its first Dean lived night and day in this Cathedral and when it so narrowly escaped almost total destruction.
>
> Those years, though at the end of them, when he visited us in Cambridge, he seemed to have lost nothing of his vitality and his friendliness and his charm, nevertheless, those years had brought their inevitable collapse. Fullness of life leads to a Cross. That is the price which we have to pay if the fullness of our life here is to become life eternal. And of the Cross which he suffered in his last years, this is neither the time nor perhaps the place to speak. Some of us watched the paying of it and will not easily forget the pain that it involved. Yes, but let us think rather of the splendid loyalty of the band which he had gathered together of workers in this great Cathedral, of the staff, the Cross Guild, the Choir, the Sidesmen, the Vergers, and indeed of all those linked up with the direct service of the sanctuary, of Chris Wagstaffe and his own close friends among the clergy and laity, of the splendid service they rendered in maintaining the quality of life which he had seen and encouraged and indeed inspired, maintaining the quality of God manifest among us, taking new forms and gaining new resources, and employing new and splendid means. The cost was worth the pain.

Frederick Dwelly had first come to a partly-built Cathedral, and he did not live to see its completion. But what he had seen through to great strength was the sense of the Cathedral community and, as Raven summed it up so tightly, 'Community is what this Cathedral Church has always stood for and enabled'. Dean Dwelly would be a very, very hard man to follow.

The man called upon to follow Mr. Dwelly was already within the great Cathedral community. It is not surprising that Dr. Dillistone was not at first anxious to take over the post after the many years during which Dwelly had stamped his mark on the office; but Dean Dillistone was a great scholar and a man of great serenity of manner, and he soon established himself as a most approachable and effective Dean. One of his Cathedral colleagues commented:

> It needed a man of great humility to work with people who were themselves so attached to the Dwelly days. You didn't want a man who was going to make noisy pronouncements or antagonise. Dillistone was unobtrusive but firm and he made the Cathedral a diocesan home again.

At his installation, Bishop Martin had taken the image of keys as a central notion in his sermon. They had been formally presented to the new Dean, and later their significance was underlined:

> Keys are used to lock doors, but they are needed also to unlock doors and throw them open. I trust that in the Dean's hands the keys will be widely used and with the full intention to throw open the doors of this House of God to all who shall come.

He metaphorically did throw open the doors, and was always ready to use his precious time to go out and meet people. This writer vividly remembers his own temerity in inviting the new Dean to cross the road and talk to the prefects at the Liverpool Institute. Rarely had the prefects' room ever been so tidy, and rarely had that group of young men listened to a clergyman with such quiet concentration.

Building work was proceeding steadily, but very slowly, on the first bay of the Nave and on the Bridge which was to span the space. All the stone on the Bridge was prepared and fixed by John Rowbottom and four other masons. The architect was 21 years ahead of the builders, having worked on the plans for the Nave at the height of the war. He had decided that the Nave should be at a lower level than the main body of the building and, even more significantly, he decided to design a break between the two parts of the building in the form of a great bridge topped by a gallery and a

The partially completed Nave Bridge in 1960. By this time Scott had abandoned the idea of using the Bridge to house a section of the organ, but was keen to design a framing device so that someone entering at the west end did not have an entirely unbroken view of the Altar.

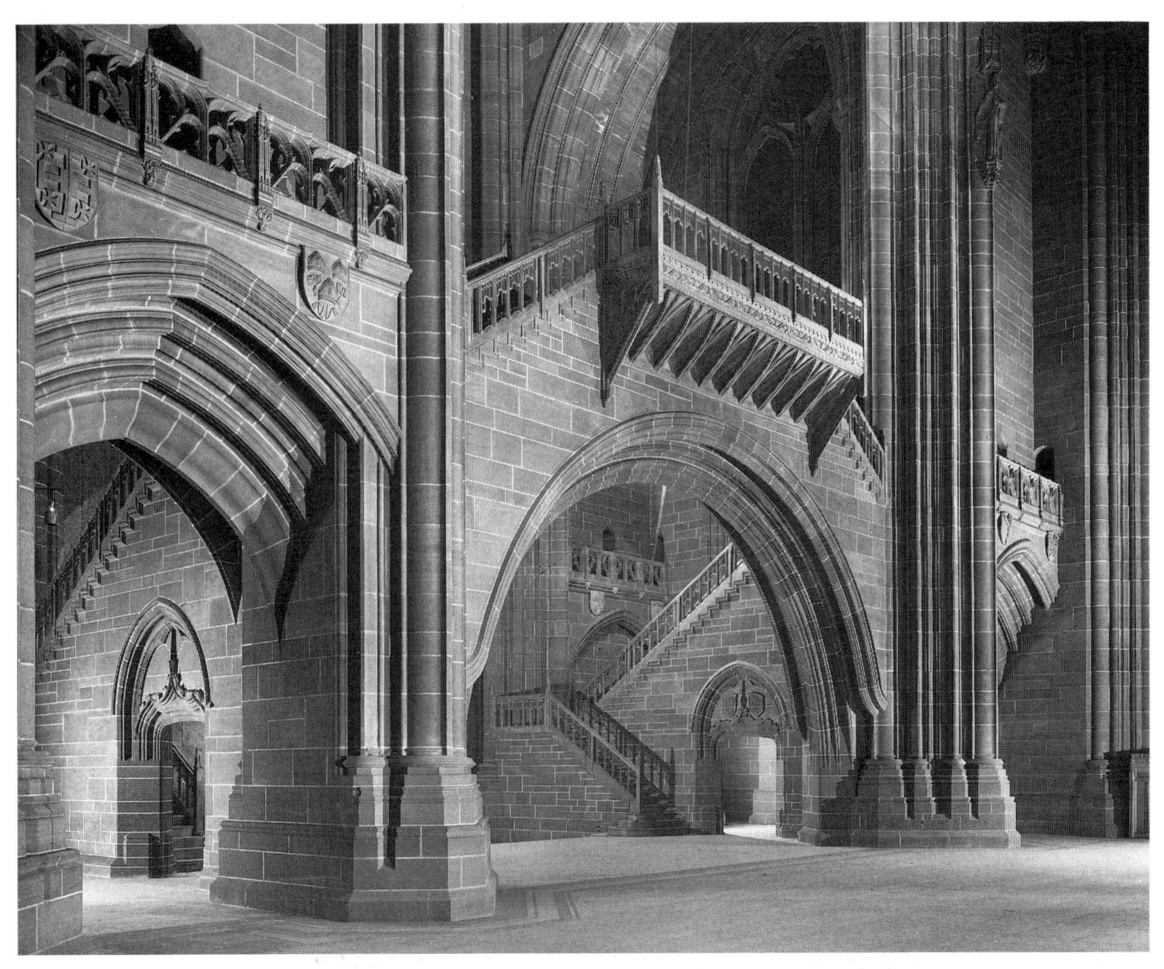

The newly completed Bridge provides a spectacular feature between the Nave and the rest of the Cathedral.

section of the organ. He believed it necessary in such a vast building to provide an architectural feature to draw the eye and prevent the viewer from trying to take in the whole building at a glance. If anything the Bridge would, by comparison, make the building appear even larger. Scott must have eagerly awaited the day when the temporary wall would be stripped down and he might stand at the west end to see Altar, Reredos and East Window framed by the rounded arch of the Bridge.

Though he saw the vision many times in his mind's eye, he was never to see it in reality. In February 1960, in his eightieth year, he died. It will remain for all time one of the great sadnesses that the mind which produced the great dream was not permitted to see the great reality: his hopes had been defeated by two world wars and the resulting inflation. A generation of Cathedral names was passing, but by this time the community, as well as the building which they had created, had sufficient strength of itself to carry the enterprise forward in spite of all the problems.

One of the problems was rather amusing, and must have caused several red faces. From the outset the members of the Stained Glass Committee had been meticulous in their consideration of the details of the windows. William Wilson had been commissioned to make the Bishops' Window on the south side of the new bay of the Nave, but the Committee had not seen the finished sections of the window in the studio in Edinburgh. Only when the window was completely installed did anyone notice the imperfections – Archbishop Temple did not look like Archbishop Temple, and Bishop Chavasse was incorrectly dressed. As Vere Cotton wrote to William Wilson:

> Bishop Chavasse is depicted in a cope, a vestment which he abhorred and regarded as popish. Anyone who knew him, and there are many still living, would, I am sure, be either horrified or amused at seeing him so depicted. I am afraid you will have to rerobe him in a chimere which I gather may be black (this could, I imagine, be modified to dark blue) or red, and a rochet.

Wilson had to seek clarification; he did not know what chimere and rochet were.

A splendid compromise was reached. The head of Chavasse was removed from the coped figure, and a new and better likeness of William Temple inserted; then a new body, properly attired, was made to take Chavasse's head. Fortunately, while all this was going on during 1960 and 1961, the first bay of the Nave remained hidden from public view.

On Saturday 22nd April 1961, the first bay of the Nave and the Dulverton Bridge (so-named because of the financial support of the Dulverton Trust) were handed over to the Dean and Chapter. It was twenty years since the last section had been taken into use, and twelve years had been spent on one relatively small section of the building. The address at the service was given by Sir Alan Tod, who underlined the changed financial circumstances under which the building was slowly progressing: 'Today every stone set in its appointed place in the building, costs approximately twelve times as much as an exactly similar stone similarly placed in 1904 when the building began'. Later in the year he expressed this in even more dramatic terms: 'The total expenditure on the present Nave of three bays would in 1904 have been sufficient to provide one of thirty-six bays, extending along Rodney Street as far as Maryland Street, on the far side of Leece Street'.

The Cathedral community were justifiably pleased with themselves that day, but Sir Alan put the Liverpool achievement into perspective:

> Have you ever looked at the soaring grandeur of Ely Cathedral on its few acres of high ground, and thought what it meant in sacrifice and labour to the sparse communities scattered among the waters of the Fens? Yet, twenty miles west, on the edge of the same Fens, rose a second great Cathedral, Peterborough, and less than fifty miles north, a third – Lincoln. What we are doing here in Liverpool, pales into insignificance compared with what Ely, Peterborough, Lincoln and a score of other English cities achieved six and seven hundred years ago, and I am fully

confident that what we have set out to do, we too, shall achieve, but only as I have said, if the effort be sustained.

What was being done in Liverpool may well have paled into insignificance when measured alongside some of the achievements of the Middle Ages, but nevertheless the Liverpool achievement was great. That achievement involved not only the slow and costly new building in the Nave, but the necessary repair and upkeep of the existing parts of the building. During Dr. Dillistone's time as Dean, major work was undertaken on the organ. The original pneumatic action, installed prior to 1926, was coming to the end of its efficient life, and between 1958 and 1960 the instrument underwent a major re-build – this time by Henry Willis IV. The action was completely electrified and a new humidifying system was installed. Further essential work was the re-pointing which had to be undertaken to the whole of the outside of the Chancel.

Economies had to be made in the running of the Cathedral itself, and shortage of money and manpower on the 'building site' side of the temporary wall were matched by similar shortages on the consecrated side. For much of the time Dean Dillistone ran his Cathedral with only one other full-time clergyman – the Chancellor, Basil Naylor – and the part-time services of three other men. Years later, in his happy retirement in Oxford, Dr. Dillistone spoke in glowing terms of all those who helped run the Cathedral during those difficult years. People such as Stanley

The new Bridge provides a superb setting for large musical occasions.

Henry Goss Custard stands at the Central Space console with his hand on the shoulder of his pupil, the young Noel Rawsthorne.

Williamson, the Cathedral Secretary; Ronald Woan, Director of Music; and Mrs. Betsy Brooks, who performed wonders in the Cathedral kitchen. These people had known and loved the old Dean, and willingly transferred their staunchest support to the new one. On occasion, clergy were in very short supply, and Dr. Dillistone remembers with amusement at least one Sunday when he was the only clergyman on duty and had to do everything in all the services.

One Sunday in 1959, what was described as 'the most ambitious religious broadcast ever handled, including the Coronation' took place, when ABC Television broadcast a Cathedral Eucharist. Millions of people were able to see the splendour, dignity and sincerity of worship in Liverpool Cathedral. The service impressed one young man watching at home in Flint, North Wales - Ken Riley - a young man destined later in his life to design many great services in the Cathedral, as Canon Precentor. Dean Dillistone was at the start of the movement in the Cathedral to place the Eucharist at the centre of Sunday worship and, not without some opposition, he foresightedly introduced a celebration of the Eucharist at 11 a.m. one Sunday in each month.

Whatever the difficulties, the Cathedral Committee were determined to see their task through, and they explored ways of saving money and manpower. One possible saving lay in using less expensive materials than cut stone in some of the upper parts of the Nave, and the inner walls of the Triforium Gallery were subsequently built of brick. Thought was given to the construction of the vault itself, and in the barrel vaulting of the aisles of the second bay, some reconstituted stone was used: a mix of Portland cement and Woolton Quarry sand. From ground level, the eye could not detect the change, and so more adventurous experiments were explored. When there were plans to use artificial materials for the second bay vaulting, the editor of the Bulletin felt it necessary to remind his readers of the exact nature of the vaulting:

> . . . consider the nature of gothic vaults. In spite of their apparent strength and solidity these splendid structures are essentially ceilings not roofs. Their principal purpose is to minimise draughts and conceal the unsightly underside of the outer wooden roofs, and their function is more aesthetic than structural.

Architects, quantity surveyors and consulting engineers came to recommend for the construction of vaulting, a material which they called 'Woolston'; an organic polyester resin reinforced with fibreglass and faced with a coating of resin and sand, which was 'chemically inert, fire resistant, and easily cleaned. It can be moulded to any desired shape, it is completely rigid, and it can be cut with a saw'. By the end of 1963, the decision had been taken to use Woolston in appropriate places in the upper parts of the second bay, and the dramatic decision was taken to make a start on the third and final bay.

Sadly, 1963 saw the departure of Dean Dillistone. The pressure of his work in running the great Cathedral had made the continuation of his academic work almost impossible, and though the community viewed his departure with regret, he was sent on his way to his new post as Chaplain and Fellow of Oriel College, Oxford, with the warmest affection and good wishes. He had given so much of himself to the growing Cathedral, finally relinquishing his work with:

> a feeling of deep thankfulness for being allowed a share in the development of Liverpool Cathedral, and with strong confidence that through the continued efforts of all who love this great building, it will increasingly fulfil its calling to be a noble witness to God in Diocese and City.

In the 'Stop Press' note at the end of the 1963 edition of the *Bulletin*, the following words appeared: 'Her Majesty has appointed the Rev. E. H. Patey, a residential Canon of Coventry Cathedral, as Dean of Liverpool Cathedral in succession to Dean Dillistone. Canon Patey is aged 48'.

'Not stones . . . but life'

CHAPTER
- *Fourteen* -

DEAN Dillistone had seen the first bay of the Nave, with its beautiful Bridge through to completion, and steady progress was being made on the second bay. After his departure for Oxford, the leadership of the Chapter was taken temporarily by Basil Naylor, the Canon Chancellor, and building work continued. The Chapter was in possession of a splendid but incomplete Cathedral, and significant decisions had to be made.

No one, then or now, would attempt to minimise the problems facing

The meeting of two Deans: Frederick Dillistone on the left and Edward Patey on the right. From left to right, the others are Canon Naylor, Canon Hopkins, 'Bunny' Hunter of the Cross Guild and Canon Ellis.

the builders of the final section of the Cathedral, or the problems facing those whose responsibility it was to carry forward the life of the Cathedral through the second half of the twentieth century. Liverpool was a changed city: a city in decline, with many financial, political and social problems. No-one in the 1960s would ever have set out to build such a Cathedral as had been planned in the early years of the century, but the building had been started, and could not simply be abandoned as some kind of grotesque ecclesiastical folly. Liverpool Cathedral has always attracted the right man at the right time, and the Cathedral Company eagerly awaited the arrival of Edward Patey.

This narrative has several times tried to read the thoughts of eminent Cathedral people: Chavasse, as he travelled home to the Palace before the Town Hall meeting; Scott, with the burning excitement of a young architect on the threshold of his career; John Rowbottom on his first day on the building site. Edward Patey was a prolific communicator, and we know from his own words some of the great questions which occupied his attention as he moved north from Coventry: What are cathedrals for? What useful purpose do they serve in the contemporary scene? Did not cathedrals epitomise in stone and glass the solidity of the ecclesiastical establishment? Were not Deans, from Trollope to *All Gas and Gaiters*, the personification of the institutional *status quo*? Should the Cathedral be finished at all, and if so, how? What kind of a setting should the Cathedral be given when the surrounding area, made derelict by slum clearance, came to be re-built? Where was the money to come from to complete the work which had been put in hand sixty years earlier? Was it not already large enough, with room for four thousand people on great occasions? With the worsening economic situation and the massive social problems facing the surrounding area, could more vast expenditure on stone and stained glass be justified? Did not people matter more than buildings? He even thought for a time that it might be his duty as third Dean to put an end to further building.

Probably the last of the archive photographs of the view up Washington Street. Over the years thousands of visitors to the Cathedral have been inspired by this view and regret its passing.

A view of the Cathedral showing progress on the second bay of the Nave in 1965. The general decay of the houses on the slope in front of the building is evident. Visitors were beginning to approach the Cathedral through a tangle of urban dereliction.

It is easy to imagine how many Cathedral feathers were ruffled by a Dean who asked so many, and such uncomfortable, questions; but those questions needed to be asked. There is a great danger that every magnificent building will tend to smother some of the perceptions of its custodians. Almost inevitably, such a building can focus all of its attention on the past to such an extent that it becomes a dinosaur. Dean Patey had to be able to rise above the jests and jibes of friends and critics alike. Brian Redhead, the broadcaster, once introduced him as the man 'who looks after the only unfinished ancient monument in the country'. Patey himself tells the story of the young secretary who worked in an office near to the Cathedral, and spent much time gazing at it. When asked why she was so interested, she replied, 'Because they are taking such an awful long time to pull that old church down'.

The temptation to call a halt to the building process, put up a brick wall and make do with what they already had, must have been great; but the new Dean soon realised how much Liverpool Cathedral meant to so many people, and he told a story which might be seen as a direct parallel with a story told by Chavasse in the Town Hall in 1901:

> This was not a simple matter of civic pride or ecclesiastical triumphalism. It was a genuine act of faith and devotion on the part of thousands of people. I was not thinking so much of the great industrial and commercial undertakings whose large cheques helped us forward. I know of an old lady, for example, a pensioner who came to the Cathedral at frequent intervals to hand over an envelope full of pound notes, sometimes fifty, on occasions one hundred, from her savings 'to help finish our Cathedral'. She would not give her name and address and she sought no publicity or even acknowledgement.

The new Dean understood that the Cathedral had to be completed.

Liverpool had installed as its new Dean a man with forward-looking imagination, with the courage to make controversial decisions, and a man who was a brilliant communicator. He was a tall, loose-limbed figure, frequently slightly dishevelled in appearance, with a constantly-moving face and a strong, memorable voice. Although some of the more conservative members of his community were frequently shocked by some of the Dean's experiments, they liked the man and readily acknowledged that Liverpool and its new Cathedral were regularly part of local, national and international news. In his first address to the Friends and Builders on 20th June 1964, Patey threw down the challenge to the community.

An interesting view of the final bay being built at the west end of the Cathedral in 1969. The timber is in position for the construction of the arch over the west doors. The photograph must have been taken from a crane.

Interior view showing the lower section of the west wall to the design of Frederick Thomas and Roger Pinkney.

Liverpool, unlike a medieval cathedral, was not 'imprisoned' by quaint traditions, and there was no good reason to 'ape the medieval':

> Nor is it for them to reproduce unquestioningly the old Cathedral pattern in a modern setting. For what Cathedrals have been in the past is not necessarily what they should be in the present, or what they ought to become in the future. Which means that to be a Cathedral Builder in the twentieth century is more than just to be concerned with construction of fabric and furnishing. For a new Cathedral is an empty shell until the builders have been able to create within it life, purpose and vision. And this is the hardest part of the task.

Even to finish the empty shell was to prove an extremely taxing operation. Morrison and Sons, the firm which for 63 years had been responsible for the construction of the building, went into liquidation in 1967. Many of the masons had spent a lifetime on the Cathedral, and such an experienced team was irreplaceable. If the site were closed and the team dispersed, all hope of finishing the building within a decade would have been dashed. Because the Cathedral had always been a profitable area of Morrison's work, however, it was possible for negotiations with the Receiver to guarantee unbroken work on the building, and not a single day was lost. The Cathedral Committee acted decisively and set up Liverpool Cathedral Contractors Ltd. with the intention of completing the work by direct labour.

Work was progressing steadily on the third bay of the Nave, with both north and south walls reaching over forty feet in height. The preparation of the foundations for the West Front was hampered by the presence underground of an old collapsed tunnel which had been excavated in the eighteenth century to give access to the quarry. Final details were being completed on the second bay, to be handed over to the Dean and Chapter on 4th May 1968.

The other major decision of 1967 related to plans for the west front itself. Throughout the history of the building, the Committee had become used to the architect's continual modifications to the plans, and it had caused them no concern that for many years they had not had detailed plans of the western elevation. The full scheme was only published in 1942: the walls to a height of 86 feet were to be plain and unadorned, apart from a string course, but above that the work became more and more elaborate, right up to the tracery of the parapets of the two low towers. A porte-cochere took the building to the very edge of the ravine, so giving the impression that the great mass of the west front rose up out of the rock of the old quarry itself.

When calculations were made in 1966, the estimated cost of the front itself, quite apart from the third bay, would be £1,300,000, and the Committee did not feel justified in attempting to raise such a massive sum for a part of the building which added nothing to its seating capacity, nor to its opportunities for worship.

The architectural responsibility for the final phase of the Cathedral building lay, after Scott's death, with Frederick Thomas, his partner and former office manager. His leadership was later to be recorded in an inscription at the west end of the building, and his ashes were to be placed beneath the marble floor of the south nave aisle. Only very recently has light been shed upon how the final design for the west front was prepared.

Readers of the *Daily Telegraph* on Tuesday 18th December 1990, read the obituary notice for Roger Arthur Philip Pinkney, which carried information apparently unknown to the present Cathedral community. Pinkney, like Scott, had been greatly influenced by church architecture while still a schoolboy, and in 1919 he had entered Scott's office and worked on such major projects as Ampleforth Abbey, Battersea Power Station and Liverpool Cathedral. He later went into partnership with another architect, Arthur Gott, but was approached by Frederick Thomas when a fresh, and cheaper, design was needed for the west front at Liverpool. It was believed that he had Scott's 'feel' for Gothic work, and was capable of producing a design wholly in keeping with Scott's spirit and intentions.

Though the east and west fronts differ markedly in their use of elaborate detail, there are elements common to both. At both ends, a high arch encloses a huge window flanked on both sides by twin buttresses. Both ends are finished with octagonal turrets, those at the west being larger and echoing the shape and line of the central tower. The most prominent feature of the west front is the way that the arch projects 15 feet 6 inches beyond the window, so enclosing the steps up to the west door, and the area between the gates and the wall itself. In Scott's original design there was a small rose window high up under the point of the arch; in the new design, three lancets seven feet wide, rise 52 feet 9 inches to a spectacular fanlight 31 feet wide and nineteen feet high: in all 1,600 square feet of glass. The East Window depicted *Te Deum, We praise thee, O God, we acknowledge thee to be the Lord*, and the subject chosen for the West Window was to be *Benedicte, O all ye works of the Lord, bless ye the Lord, praise him and magnify him for ever*. The editor of the *Bulletin* summed up the situation dispassionately:

> The new design closely follows what were undoubtedly Sir Giles Scott's intentions up to 1942, and preserves an important element in the 1942 design, in that the decorative features, apart from the window, are all confined to the zone above the 86 feet level. It is in complete harmony with the rest of the building, and the component parts are all pure Scott. Whatever view may be taken of the relative architectural merits of the 1942 and the 1967 designs, a question on which there are bound to be divergencies of opinion, on financial grounds, the case for making the change is unanswerable.

On 4th May 1968, the second bay of the Nave was opened and dedicated by the new Bishop, Stuart Yaworth Blanch. He had come to Liverpool from the post of Warden of Rochester Theological College, and prior to that Wycliffe Hall. He was later described by Edward Patey as 'the most 'unclerical' of parsons' and quickly established himself as a popular Liverpool figure.

Two days after the Cathedral ceremony, the Dean rose to speak – not in the Cathedral, but in the Town Hall – at the launch of the Finish the Cathedral Appeal, 67 years after Francis James Chavasse had risen to speak in the same building at the very start of the great Cathedral enterprise. Chavasse had known that the completion of the work would be at the hands of later generations. He had not been able to see the effects of the two World Wars and the effects of crippling inflation, but Edward Patey must on that day have felt himself to be part of that challenge-to-build launched by Chavasse. Patey's appeal was not looking backwards with nostalgia into a world long gone, but into a vibrant future. His actual words deserve to stand alongside the words of his predecessor, as he led his charge into the challenge of the world ahead:

> What of the task to which we have set ourselves today of finishing the Cathedral, and raising the money necessary to do it?
>
> That the building is a masterpiece, I have no doubt. It is sometimes described as Gothic or neo-Gothic. But I dislike these labels. For Sir Giles Gilbert Scott, and Mr. Fred Thomas, his close associate, have given us a building which is timeless. It cannot be labelled or put into any category. With its marvellous use of height and line – 'the art of

enclosing space,' as John Betjeman has called it – it belongs to every generation. Architectural fashions may come and go. But I believe that in every century men and women of taste and sensitivity will look at our building high above the Mersey and say, 'this really is a Cathedral!' And it is already abundantly clear that only when it is completed to the last stone, will its full glory be revealed. By 1975 the people of Liverpool will have given not only to the city and diocese, but to the world; not only to this century, but for a thousand years to come, one of the world's great buildings. On these grounds alone we need feel no hesitation or reluctance in launching our £500,000 Finish the Cathedral Appeal.

But a Dean is neither the director of a building operation, nor the curator of an ecclesiastical museum, nor the promoter of a tourist attraction. He is the servant of the Church of God. My job (in collaboration with my colleagues) is to use the Cathedral as an instrument for the Kingdom of God. This is our yard-stick.

However noble and beautiful the building, I could not in conscience support the raising of this great sum for which we ask if I did not deep in my heart believe that what we have set in hand today can with honesty be said to promote and not hinder the glory of God and the mission of Jesus Christ in His Church.

Two things seem to be happening in the Church just now. One is that we are learning all over again that people matter more than buildings. That the Church is human beings, not bricks, mortar and stones. We know that we must never become slaves to plant and machinery. We know that we are called to be the pilgrim people of God, and pilgrims must travel light. Furthermore, since the Church exists primarily for others and not for itself, it must be more concerned with the service it renders to the world than with its own well-being and survival. And this is why some people are sincerely opposed to building appeals in particular. Does not all this, they say, divert our attention and energy from the real mission of the Gospel in the world today?

I have great sympathy with this view. It has much truth in it. And certainly if I believed for a moment that this final effort of ours were in any way to divert the Church either of our own day or of the future from its true purpose of evangelism and service, I would not be standing here in support of this appeal.

But there is something else happening in the Christian world today which is relevant to our concern. What are the future needs of the Church? The parish ministry must go on. In many ways this is the front line of the Church and always will be. Furthermore, we are beginning to discover the need for ever smaller groups, Christian meetings in homes, in factories, in schools, in offices, for prayer, Bible-study, and for the planning of common action and witness in society.

But also, particularly in urban and industrial areas, we are beginning to see increasingly the need for great centres of worship, evangelism, and experiment. And this is why, not only in our own country, but in many parts of the world, Cathedrals are beginning to find a new and dynamic role within the life of the Church.

I said that Cathedrals are finding a new role. In some ways it is the old role seen in a new light. Excellence in the ordering of worship had always been the Cathedral's job; and thanks to the brilliant and exacting leadership of our first Dean, Dr. Dwelly, we can claim that Liverpool has remained true to the best traditions of Cathedral life. Furthermore, our distinguished Organist and Director of Music enable us to continue the high standard of choral music which people from all over the world have come to expect of the great English Cathedrals.

But today, more than ever before, easy transport (particularly in a heavily populated diocese such as ours) makes it possible many times in the year for great congregations to assemble in the Cathedral for acts of worship and witness involving either the diocese or various sections of the community in which we live. Even now, there are several times in the year when – for all the space of our great building – we have to ration places and restrict numbers for some of our services and events. The need for a great central building where several thousand people can come together for worship will, I confidently believe be even more essential for the good working of the church in the future than it is today. Furthermore, with the completion of the Cathedral, we shall not only have the total building capable of holding three thousand or more, but the Central Space, the completed Nave, and the Lady Chapel will provide us with separate units capable of holding greater or lesser congregations according to need.

And this kind of flexibility is the key. For a Cathedral must above all things be a workshop for the Kingdom of God in which worship is offered, and the Gospel proclaimed through the greatest possible number of media, and within a wide variety of cultural patterns. Indeed, I believe that our Cathedrals will only survive into the future if they become dynamic centres of experiment.

Not all experiments will succeed. Certainly not all experiments will meet with universal approval. But without experiment we die. For in a world of rapid change there is still so much more yet to be discovered about the worship of Eternal God, and about the proclamation of the Gospel of Jesus Christ. Cathedrals are the places, above all else, where such discoveries can and must be made.

Both for traditional worship and for experiment, Giles Scott and those who have turned his great vision into reality, have given us an instrument for the Kingdom of God second to none in the world. Our building has dignity, it has space, it has flexibility. If we are able – as surely we will – to raise the money we seek, and finish the job we have planned, future generations of Christians of Merseyside, and far beyond, will surely thank God for us, and for the marvellous gift we have been able to pass on to them.

Dean Patey's enthusiastic words were backed up with action, and many years after some of the Patey experiments, the experiences of those events are alive amongst the people who were present.

In December 1966, I boiled a kettle and made two cups of coffee right under the vaulting of the Central Space. This was not part of a Patey 'happening': I just happened to be assisting one of my colleagues who was installing and operating the lighting for the very first dance performance to take place within the context of worship in the Cathedral. I was teaching at that time at the I. M. Marsh College of Physical Education when third-year students were invited to present a suite of dances for Christmas as the centre of an act of worship. Certain members of the Cathedral congregation were disturbed at the thoughts of dance of any kind within the building but, for those students who performed and the people who came to watch, those dances were a richly memorable experience.

Light was the central symbol in the three dances. The first had as its focus a spot of light high up on the Chancel arch. The dancers were at first earth-bound, clad in sombre greens and browns – costumes dyed personally by the choreographer in the staff laundry in the college. Prophetic figures mobilised the other dancers who were drawn with yearning towards the light beyond their reach. In the second, the Nativity dance, the tiny focus of white light was upon a Madonna constantly supported by strong, gentle Joseph. During the rehearsals for this piece, clusters of children from a neighbouring school used to wander in, and on one occasion the dance group was joined by an elderly Chinese gentleman in pumps, who waved his arms about on the edge of the dance. The music of Aaron Copeland's *Appalachian Spring* accompanied the third dance, which showed the spreading of the light from complete darkness and stillness to a rich, circling, swirling flow of movement. Dance, making use

Mary, Joseph, angels, shepherds and wise men in one of the three dances presented by the students of the I. M. Marsh College. The floor was cold on the feet, but the students found the Cathedral an inspiring setting for their work.

as it does of light, movement, colour, texture, rhythm, gesture, and music, can be a deeply moving spiritual experience – but not everyone saw it this way. 'I have decided that I can no longer be a member of the Friends of Liverpool Cathedral as I do not agree with the Cathedral being used for ballet dancing,' wrote one protestor. Had the lady been present at the performance, she might not have taken such a hard and closed line.

An even greater outcry accompanied one of the Cathedral Christmas events of 1967 when it was shown on television. The Dean was aware that the Cathedral Christmas services did not necessarily make any strong appeal to many young people, and the event was conceived in order to present the message of Christmas to a much wider audience:

> We attempted to present the truths of the meaning behind the Christmas story, and the consequences of man's rejection of those truths evident in world hunger, oppression and the nuclear threat. The medium we used was rock music [the Bee Gees], folk music, traditional church music [by the Cathedral Choir], the Bible [passages read in 'scouse' by Kenny Everett], film and drama [the Shepherds' Play from the Wakefield Cycle, played by the Liverpool Everyman Theatre].

The Dean's watching of the programme at home was punctuated by telephone calls, one demanding that he 'get this blasphemy stopped'. There were also positive reviews and encouraging letters: 'It is the only Church service we will attend this Christmas, but thanks to the combined efforts of you and your young artistes, it has helped to create a bridge which will make it easier for me and my children to find our way back'.

Many people for whom dance and pop music were unpalatable, might have felt more at home among the forty thousand visitors who attended the Festival of Flowers in 1970. For the Dean, the idea of such a festival was not immediately appealing: 'I wondered whether flower arrangements might not suggest that the religion we preached was an escape from reality into some cloud cuckoo land. But in the end I decided to take the risk.' The Dean later admitted that his misgivings were groundless because, 'It encouraged thousands of people to come to the Cathedral for the first time and helped others to see it again with new eyes'.

The more traditional features of Cathedral life and worship also flourished. Despite there being no choir school at Liverpool, the quality of the choral services was high under the direction of Ronnie Woan. Noel Rawsthorne's brilliance as an organist was revealed in recitals, on record and on tour. Yehudi Menuhin gave a recital of unaccompanied Bach in 1969 and wrote afterwards, 'It was a great experience to play in your magnificent Cathedral'. Under the direction of Basil Naylor, there were important developments in the performance of the liturgy at the Eucharist and the service became central to the worshipping life of the community. The Cathedral's own folk group, the Crofters, so called because they rehearsed in the undercroft, was founded in 1965 and became extremely popular. Somehow, the great building attracted and nurtured human talent in the service of the worship of God.

'Until it be thoroughly finished'

CHAPTER
- *Fifteen* -

RESOURCES for the Finish the Cathedral Appeal flowed into the fund at an encouraging rate, though the work was held up by delays other than financial ones. There was a strike by masons on the site in the late summer of 1968 which was not settled until the following February. In the spring of 1970, the production of good stone from Woolton was halted because of geological faults which necessitated the removal of thousands of tons of poor grade stone in order to uncover new beds of good stone. Time was used to overhaul plant and make changes on the site to speed the building progress once it started again.

Sadly, two of the Committee's most important and long-serving members died in the autumn of the same year: Sir Alan Tod and Colonel Vere Cotton. As the chronicler of the building of the Cathedral, Vere Cotton produced a set of records which might well be seen as unique in the whole history of Christian building.

No-one was to blame when the Committee gots its sums wrong over the Finish the Cathedral Appeal. All that could be done was to take the problem to the people of the diocese and beyond, and ask for their further assistance. From Chavasse onwards, the Bishops of Liverpool have been active in their support for the Cathedral enterprise, and one of the first tasks facing the new Bishop, David Sheppard, was the need to appeal for a further £460,000. Sheppard was known by many people inside and outside the Church: his career as an England cricketer had originally brought him into the headlines, and his social concerns as Warden of the Mayflower Centre, and then as Bishop of Woolwich, were widely known. The Dean wondered secretly how the Bishop would react when asked to speak on behalf of yet another Cathedral appeal.

The problem did cause him much self-questioning: he had always placed the heart of his Christian ministry in the people rather than the buildings. But he recognised that the Cathedral was a very special project and the responsibility of each generation:

> . . . the issue facing us is not whether we should decide to build a great Cathedral. The issue we face is whether to keep faith with other generations who have carried the great dream for seventy years. In this sense, it is the same issue people face when an ancient Cathedral needs expensive work. When it is a matter not of very ordinary buildings, but of the great buildings of history, I believe we should. And Liverpool Cathedral is one of the great buildings of our century. This is 'our' Cathedral to a great many people. It reflects something very special of the character of God in the City . . . We believe we are right to want to see our Cathedral finished and keep faith as one generation with this great enterprise which previous generations began.

When Chavasse spoke to his people, he had stressed that they were to start building in faith for the future, and Dean Patey was able to make the same claim when the end of the project was nearly in sight: 'We are not just building this Cathedral for our own time, but for the enjoyment and inspiration of people a thousand years hence'.

Within four months, £230,000 had been received. The end was indeed in sight but, as can so often be the case, the 'last mile' proved to be one of extraordinary difficulty.

Early in 1976, the last of the Committee's investments in the stock market were sold, and from then on revenue had to come entirely from direct giving. Though covenants guaranteed money over a number of years, cash-flow problems became acute. By July, financial resources were so low that the Committee had only enough money to undertake a further two months of work. The future of sixty men and the speedy completion of the Cathedral were in jeopardy.

For the first time in the history of the Cathedral project, government help was sought, and given through employment subsidy and the Manpower Services Commission. The Committee was responsible for all materials and all overhead costs, but the wage bill was underwritten by the government scheme. The great arch over the West Window was rising steadily, and tentative plans were being made ready for a service of completion in the spring of 1978.

At the end of 1976, 130 timber packing cases were stored in the undercroft, most of them labelled 'Glass With Care'. Of these, 96 contained the new Benedicite Window. Here were over two hundred thousand pieces of glass which would eventually be installed as one of the greatest stained glass windows of the twentieth century, covering an area of 1,600 square feet.

Amongst those people who had seen the design for the window, the excitement was high because they realised it was to be the most powerful window in the whole building. 'Space and stone' had been central to Scott's design: in the Nave, the colours in the windows had intensified from east to west. The F. G. Thomas/Roger Pinkney designs for the west front were an exciting challenge to Carl Edwards, the stained glass artist, even though he had understood Scott's intentions:

> Glass and colour has become important. His original idea was that there should be a great wall of stone without glass and one's attention would be forced back to the east end but instead there will be a huge area of rich colour . . . It is not like painting with solid colours, for the light spreads and mixes as it streams through. This is where the craftsman's skill adds the touch of magic.
>
> Each sliver of glass not only transmits its own coloured light, but is chosen to change and blend the light from surrounding pieces. It is certainly the last such great window to be built in this country. Apart from lack of demand, the materials are irreplaceable. The kind of glass used – with its hundreds of tints and imperfections – is not being made any more.

To the frustration of the stained glass artist, the separate panels of glass had to remain in their packing cases until the work of the masons was further advanced.

It had been hoped that 1977 would be a year of excitement and growing satisfaction; instead it was, in the words of Dean Patey, 'amongst the most traumatic in the whole story'. One catastrophe after another meant that the proposed date for the Queen's visit, Ascension Day 1978, had to be postponed. The remaining exterior stonework was all well over one hundred feet high, and at such a dangerous height, the masons were constantly hampered by bad weather. St. James's Mount can be breezy even in high summer, but spring 1977 produced a succession of gale-force winds which made fixing impossibly dangerous, and work targets fell behind by many weeks.

The workforce knew that the Liverpool enterprise which had given employment for three quarters of a century was now almost at an end and, inevitably, skilled masons were leaving the site for new projects which offered long-term employment prospects. Because of their age, some of the most experienced men were no longer able to work a full day and became part-time, and conditions were not appropriate for the recruitment of apprentices. Alongside the packing cases of stained glass were twelve

Tom Murphy, one of the last of the Cathedral craftsmen, with the model of the royal coat of arms he was to carve in stone to go over the west doors on the inside on the building.

In comparison with the earlier days, a small handful of men was still there to see the building through to completion. Tom and John Rowbottom are at the right side of the front row.

crates containing costly, specially-made bronze fixing bars for the window. The crates were stolen – the contents were never recovered, and the production of replacement fittings caused an agonising delay of nearly five months.

Apologetic communications went to Buckingham Palace. Even during the winter of 1978-9, the *Newsletter* had to admit, 'It is not yet possible to give a precise date for the completion of the Cathedral, but we can say with confidence that it will be sometime this year'. Eventually, with more than a little uncertainty, 25th October was settled as the date for the service.

As the early months of 1978 sped away, panic set into the Cathedral community. The Lord Lieutenant, the Queen's representative on Merseyside, wrote anxiously to the Dean only two months before the date of the proposed ceremony, 'For heaven's sake, try to get some pep into the thing . . . It would be quite improper for us to invite Her Majesty the Queen to Merseyside to celebrate the completion of a great Cathedral only for her to find the building still clad in scaffolding'.

For those with a discerning eye, some of the final work at the west end will for all time be a reminder of that time of unseemly haste. High winds in 1990 brought down finials from the turrets and revealed what can only be described as shoddy workmanship. Some of the stone used would, in the early phases of building, have been rejected as being fit only for rockeries and garden walls, and in places the pointing of some of the complicated stonework is a disgrace, with spaces plugged with crumpled newspaper and pointed over. Not long before his death in 1991, John Rowbottom said, 'I think some of it will fall down'. He was right.

Despite feverish activity at the west end, the Dean and Chapter were, over many months, calmly planning the great service of Dedication and Thanksgiving. Dean Patey was determined that the service should be in no sense an anachronism:

> We have . . . to ask very seriously what kind of celebration is appropriate to mark the completion of a twentieth-century cathedral in a modern industrial diocese. It would be a significant step if we could find a way of making this a joyful, celebratory, popular and contemporary event, without sacrificing necessary dignity, and without blurring basic theological insights about the role of the Church in the world. We need particularly to emphasise that although the Cathedral was planned in a world which was passing, it is designed to be used by a world which is coming into being. The service must look to the future as much as to the past, and this must be reflected in the style employed.

The man who had created such a meaningful and memorable Consecration service in 1924 was Frederick Dwelly. In 1978, the liturgical genius who pulled all the ideas together was the Cathedral Chancellor, Canon Basil Naylor. He had joined the Chapter in 1956, to replace Frederick Dillistone when he became Dean. The two men had worked closely together and Basil Naylor's choreographic skills had much to do with the success of Cathedral services. His choreography for the Cathedral

Eucharist remains largely unaltered to this day. He was a musician with a particular interest in Bach, whose works he enjoyed playing on the Lady Chapel organ, and he is remembered still as a lively, hospitable, good humoured, cultured man. There would be nothing shoddy or rushed about the service he was to design.

The shape and underlying theme of the service was made known in the autumn edition of the *Newsletter.* The clue to the form of the service lies in the Prayer of Sir Francis Drake, composed during the reign of the first Elizabeth:

> O Lord God, when thou givest to thy servants to endeavour any great matter, grant us also to know that it is not the beginning, but the continuing of the same, until it be thoroughly finished, which yieldeth the true glory; through him who for the finishing of thy work laid down his life for us, our Redeemer, Jesus Christ.

Beginning, continuing and finishing are the concepts which shaped the service, the focus of which was to move gradually from the east – the first section to be completed – to the west. The climax of the service would be at the west end below the great Benedicite window. In Basil Naylor's own words:

> A climax because the *Benedicite* window represents all God's creation and all that stems from it – races, nations, industry, commerce, social relations and family life. At the far East end, facing it across the whole length of the Cathedral, is the *Te Deum* window, which represents the Church, the Reredos its faith, the Chancel its structure. And that Church (*Te Deum*) has been commanded and commissioned to bring to all creation (*Benedicite*) the gospel of service, love, salvation. This continous challenge is the second and the greater theme running through the service and is symbolised by the movement of the choir and Cathedral processions throughout the service from East to West. So that when the Queen leads the congregation out of the Cathedral at the end, she will be leading them to face the city, the community and the world, where alone what is professed in the Cathedral can become real, positive and meaningful.

As the day of the service approached, it became clear that not everything would be ready. The Queen would not be able to lead the procession out through the west doors – the west doors were not in position and parts of the exterior were still shrouded in scaffolding. During the week leading up to 25th October, there were days of torrential rain, followed by panic as torrents of water spouted in unexpected places. The vergers had the task of arranging four thousand chairs, as the television crew set up their rig.

Despite all the problems, frustrations and delays, the Cathedral Church of Christ in Liverpool was ready to celebrate the achievements of 74 years. At 10.30 a.m. the clergy of the diocese entered in procession from the east and took their positions on the north side below the Chancel steps to face the seat in which Her Majesty would sit. Five minutes after they set off, visiting senior clergy of the Northern Province and representatives of other denominations entered from the west. From the east, the choir procession made its entrance, followed by the Chapter members. All eyes were watching at 10.50 as the Dean, Stuart Blanch, Archbishop of York and Malcolm Harrison, Chairman of the Executive Committee, proceeded to the Rankin Porch to join the Lord Leiutenant and the Lord Mayor to await the arrival of Her Majesty. All this movement was accompanied by Noel Rawsthorne as he played Charpentier's *Te Deum Prelude* and Karg-Elert's *Nun Danket*.

At 11.00 there was a moment of silence until a fanfare played by a section of the Merseyside Police Band announced the arrival of the Queen. She was wearing a coat of striking royal blue, with a small round brooch on her lapel, and the softer and lighter shades of her blue hat were matched exactly by a small scarf. Once seated in the body of the Cathedral, she was flanked by the Archbishop in gold cope and mitre to her right, and the Dean in the rust-coloured Cathedral cloak on her left.

After the singing of the national anthem, Mr. Philip Radcliffe Evans, grandson of Sir Frederick Radcliffe, read the words of Bishop Chavasse from beside the foundation stone, and the congregation were taken back in thought to the very start of the Cathedral project:

> It is my earnest desire that the new Cathedral of Liverpool shall be built by all and for all, that it shall be the church of the people, where rich and poor meet together to worship God, and where the Gospel of our Lord Jesus Christ is fully preached. It must be the best that we can give, and its walls and towers rising high above our city must be a silent but majestic witness to God and the Unseen.

This Prologue section of the service was completed with the Prayer of Sir Francis Drake.

The 'Beginning' featured Bishop David, sixth Bishop of Liverpool, standing at the consecration cross way up in the Chancel, as he read the prayer used by Albert Augustus David on Consecration Day in 1924. Immediately after this, the clear, confident voice of the Precentor, Canon Gordon Bates, rang out through the Cathedral as he chanted the words of *The Rejoicings*, composed by Martin Shaw for performance by the choir in 1924, and concluding: 'Alleluia! The Lord is in his holy temple: Alleluia, the Lord is here to bless: Alleluia! Amen'.

In 1924, *All people that on earth do dwell* had been sung, but during the singing of the hymn in 1978 there was an act of great symbolic significance, as Archbishop Dereck Worlock, Roman Catholic Archbishop of Liverpool, presented a copy of the Jerusalem Bible to Dean Patey, 'as a token of our friendship, and of the commitment we share to the Word of God'. In reply, Dean Patey spoke of the 'growing friendship between our two Cathedrals, at either end of Hope Street'. In the light of Roman Catholic and Protestant tensions in the early days of the Cathedral, the meeting of Dean and Archbishop indicated the progress in ecumenism which had been made in three quarters of a century.

After the lesson and a second singing of *The Rejoicings*, the Most

The Cathedral, complete at last, except for the west doors, packed with 3,000 people for the service of thanksgiving and dedication. The Queen is seated below the Chancel steps on the right. This photograph gives a good view of the two organ cases which face into the Central Space, as well as of the East Window.

Reverend Stuart Blanch, Archbishop of York, Primate of England, was maced to the pulpit for the sermon. Considering the number of people present in the Cathedral, and the live television coverage, the former Bishop of Liverpool looked and sounded remarkably relaxed, but very dignified and confident. Bishop Chavasse in 1901 had called for a great Cathedral on the Liverpool skyline to proclaim the importance of God in the lives of the people of Liverpool. As his text, Archbishop Blanch chose words from St. Luke's Gospel: 'Some of the Pharisees in the crowd spoke to Jesus, 'Teacher,' they said, 'Tell your disciples to keep quiet.' Jesus answered, 'I tell you, if they keep quiet these stones themselves will start shouting'.' The Archbishop put his congregation at their ease by telling them a wartime story concerning Mussolini and his inability to draw crowds as large as those drawn by the Pope. After the laughter, the congregation listened intently to his words, and the heart of what he had to say was an emphatic endorsement of the words and labours of Chavasse, Scott, Radcliffe, Raven, Dwelly, Dillistone – all the great members of the Cathedral company:

> The stones of this great Cathedral from the quarry in Woolton have been shouting since 1910, shouting about the high and lofty One who inhabits eternity, but who is near to those who are of a humble and contrite spirit. This is one of the great buildings of the world, not simply performing a function, but reminding us of the greatness and majesty of God. In this temple we see the Lord high and lifted up. I have never been able to enter this Cathedral without a revived sense of the majesty of God and a revived sense of my own unimportance in the scheme of things. But strangely enough this has managed to combine a testimony to the high and lofty One who inhabits eternity with a testimony to the God who is near to those who are of a humble and contrite spirit . . . The days for dogmatic utterance and thunderings from the pulpit are over – and I do not regret that – but that is no reason for keeping quiet. In music and art, and speech and literature, in reasoned discussion and in poetry, in service to society and in sacrifice on behalf of it, we need to proclaim our faith in Christ as One who is near to suffering humanity and yet remains the high and lofty One. If we, as disciples of the Lord keep on keeping quiet, these stones will shout aloud to succeeding generations as long as this nation remains a nation, and this city remains a city.

The sermon over, the service moved into the second sequence, 'The Continuing', as choir and Cathedral processions moved down from the Chancel into the Central Space for the act of thanksgiving, led appropriately by Dr. Dillistone. His final prayer, the words of his predecessor Frederick Dwelly, had been composed in 1941 for the service of Solemn Entry:

> O God, the Father of our Holy Risen master, Builder of Souls, Lord of the Universe, whom no place containeth yet who dost abide with us always; Receive our remembrance of all souls who with their hands and minds or treasures have laboured to place thy name here; Bless them

> and the work of their hands, and cause their whole life to be made glorious after thy disposal, O thou who in love aboundest unto all by the mercy of the Father, the Grace of the Son, and the Gifts of the Holy Spirit.

During the singing of what has been called the 'Builder's Anthem' - *Hail, Sovereign Lord*, with words by Sir Frederick Radcliffe and music by Gustav Holst - many minds in the Cathedral were taken back into many great occasions of the past, and remembered the spirit that, in the face of all odds, was determined to keep faith with the past. Thoughts went, rightly, into the past; but the impetus of the service was forward, drawn towards the splendour of the newly-completed west end of the building which was to be the setting for the final sequence, 'The Finishing and the Future'.

During the singing of the hymn *Tell out, my soul, the greatness of the Lord*, the choir led the procession westwards to the Nave and took up their positions on raised stalls below the West Window. Without the firm lead from the choir during their movement, some of the congregation made a false start to the hymn, but the combined forces of Willis and Rawsthorne soon brought everything under control. The Queen, the Archbishop, the Dean and the diocesan and Cathedral processions all moved westwards and took up their places below the Nave Bridge where Mr. Malcolm Harrison, Chairman of the Cathedral Executive, formally handed over the final phase of the building into the care of the Dean and Chapter. At the request of the Dean, the Bishop of Liverpool dedicated the final bay, the choir sang *The Rejoicings* for the third time, and Archdeacon, Treasurer, Chancellor and Dean led the final sequence of prayers.

Her Majesty was seated below the Bridge with an uninterrupted view of the choir and the torrents of blue and gold of the Benedicite Window above. John Madden, a former chorister, had been commissioned to compose a work for the occasion, and his *Song of Creation* was performed by choir, soloist, brass ensemble, Willis organ, and Ian Tracey on an electronic organ imported for the service.

The 1978 service must rightly be seen as the greatest service since the consecration in 1924. It was broadcast live on television, and widely reported in the press, including *The Times*.:

> The completion of Liverpool Cathedral has inevitably occasioned less public excitement than would have been expected when it was begun. Yet it would be unwise to conclude from this that yesterday's celebrations were out of place. On the contrary, they reflect in the first place a sense of justifiable pride in a symbolic achievement. Every Cathedral built in this or any other country, for the Church of England or any other denomination, is an expression of religious faith. It is a material reflection, always requiring the devoted work of generations, of the spiritual urge. Its accomplishment is always a triumph of technical application and of determination. So it is in this case. There will always be those who will say that the money and energy should have been

> devoted to worthier purposes, and those in poverty and distress will not benefit from the erection of a building. But it would be foolish to regard these as alternatives. It is not the case that money which would otherwise have been given to the poor has been diverted to the Cathedral.
>
> Even if it had, it would still have been serving a valuable purpose. The life of the church may be dispersed these days, but nonetheless it needs its centres of worship and activity. This is what Cathedrals provide, and if the church is to be relevant to the present age, these centres must not be only in pleasant cities away from large conurbations. A living church needs its new Cathedrals, and the celebrations over Liverpool Cathedral commemorate not only the completion of the dreams of three quarters of a century ago but also the continued vitality of the Church of England.

The Telegraph leader writer wondered whether some people might have viewed the day with some cynicism:

> In such a setting, does not her Anglican Cathedral look like a huge anachronism? Even some of the devout seem inclined to apologise for it, on the grounds that money (all of it raised by private subscription let it be noted) might have been better spent on works of mercy or on some more utilitarian places of worship.
>
> Such sentiments are wholly out of place. The Church proclaims her message by striving, as the architects of Liverpool Cathedral did, to build for as near to eternity as is humanly possible. We should surely by now have learned the error of supposing that Christian virtues will continue to flourish in a society which fails to nourish the faith from which they spring, and great ecclesiastical architecture is one of the most fertile sources of such nourishment. This Cathedral will stand, even to the eyes of the unbelieving, as a symbol of what patience and devotion can achieve in the face of endless difficulties and some catastrophes. It is a triumphant proclamation of hope.

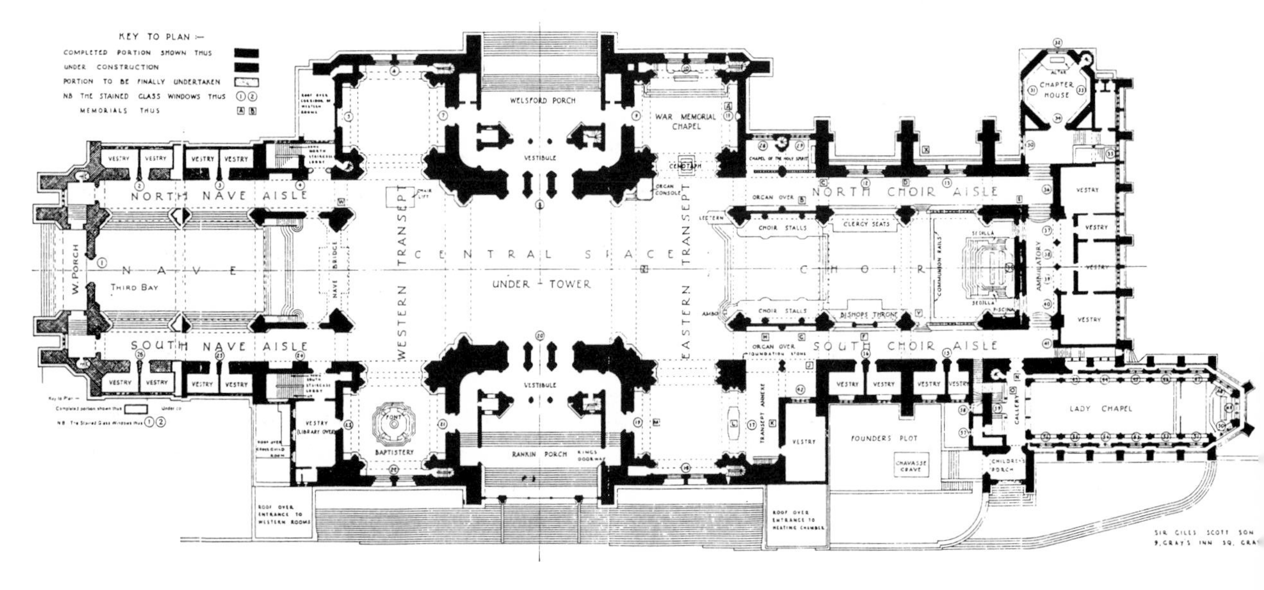

The final floor plan of Liverpool Cathedral.

CHAPTER
- Sixteen -

Comings and goings

IVERPOOL Cathedral has had many examples of famous people whose lives for a time were woven into the fabric of the Cathedral community. One group of people enters that community as unknown names at a very early age: voice trials are held regularly in order to ensure a steady supply of boys to sing in the choir. After their treble days of musical glory, Christmas tree processions and soaring descants, many choristers are lost to the world of Church music, although Liverpool boasts such notable exceptions as Ronald Woan and Noel Rawsthorne.

Choristors at Liverpool Cathedral in the autumn of 1989.

In the same year as the Service of Thanksgiving and Dedication, one little boy joined the choir of his parish church, Holy Trinity Wavertree, and began to learn to sing under the direction of the organist Alan Topping, himself a former Cathedral chorister. Peter Lynan was intelligent, musically talented and already playing the piano, serious-minded, and fascinated by the organ. The organ console at Holy Trinity was not hidden away up a winding staircase, and Alan Topping became more and more aware of the inate musicality of the little boy who was so frequently to be found standing near the organ, listening and watching. The parish organist recognised that such musical talent might not be tapped fully in a parish church, and suggested to Sheila and Malcolm Lynan that they arrange for their son to audition for the Cathedral choir.

Father and son set out early one Sunday afternoon in December, to attend a Cathedral carol service, arriving in time to secure seats on the front row of the congregation, where they could see and hear the choir well, and watch the conductor. After the service, when most of the congregation had left, they wandered around the building, and although Peter found it 'too big', he decided that he wanted to be a part of the music-making in that immense and beautiful building. 'I had to sing *Once in Royal David's City* for my audition piece,' Peter said later. 'Then I was accepted as a probationer. You spend a lot of time just picking up the atmosphere of the place, listening and watching.' Peter felt a very small part of the great building, and he remembers being lifted up by Ian Tracey, who was showing the boys around, and held alongside the cross on the High Altar to demonstrate the large size of the cross and the small size of

Ian Tracey, shortly after his appointment at the age of twenty-six.

the new probationer.

Much of Peter's training as a probationer was with Ian Tracey, destined to be a very strong influence on his whole musical development; and it was with Ian that he shared one of the most influential experiences of his life. One Saturday afternoon the probationers were being sent home as they arrived, because they were not needed for the Mothers' Union service. Sheila Lynan was staying for the service, and so asked Ian whether he would mind letting Peter sit with him in the organ loft. That first sight of the console, that first service sitting alongside Ian, convinced nine-year-old Peter that he wanted to play the organ and opened the door to a career in music.

There were very significant musical 'goings' early in the decade, as both Ronald Woan and Noel Rawsthorne decided to retire from their positions, having made enormous contributions to the musical development of Liverpool Cathedral. They were themselves products of the Goss Custard/Edgar Robinson years, and they handed on cathedral music in a very healthy state when Ian Tracey, at the age of 26, was made Organist and Master of the Choristers.

Ian had been in full control for only a short time when there was one of the most significant 'comings' in the history of the Cathedral. Throughout his time at Liverpool, Dean Patey had been an active figure in creating new working relationships with the Roman Catholic Church but, when he first came to Liverpool, he did not even dream that he might one day receive the Pope as an honoured guest in the Cathedral. For so long, Liverpool had been the setting of violent animosity between Roman Catholics and Protestants, that some people feared that a Papal visit might not pass without some unfortunate incidents.

The gloriously sunny day in May 1982 was a memorable day for Peter Lynan, who wrote about his memories for his school magazine:

> As I got out of the car at Mount Pleasant Car Park it was hard to believe that in about five hours time my brother and I would be singing on television in front of the Pope. My mum was in the Cathedral Singers so she came as well. We had to have a special pass to get into the Cathedral and we had to have a pass for the car park. We came out of the car park and stood at the corner of Brownlow Hill. We started to cross the road. It is not very often that you can cross a main road without looking. There were no cars on the road at all. In Rodney Street all the St. John's Ambulance Brigade were ready waiting for the people to faint.

Security was intense, and to a young chorister, the sight of Special Branch men and sniffer dogs at work round the Cathedral was intriguing and amusing. The service started some time before the Pope arrived, but

Peter was within sight of a television monitor, and was able to glimpse odd shots of the Papal progress through the roads of the city. Tension was high when the fanfare sounded for the beginning of Parry's anthem, *I was glad when they said unto me* and the congregation rose, thinking that the Pope had arrived. The next fanfare did herald the arrival, and the start of the processional hymn:

> Everyone started clapping so you could hardly hear the hymn we had started singing. The only time when the congregation could hear the organ was when Mr. Tracey used the Tuba Magna, the second loudest organ stop in the world.

For everyone present the visit was, in Dean Patey's words, 'a triumph'. The warmth of the welcome for the Pope was tremendous, and marked such an important step forward in the progress of ecumenism in Liverpool. For those people who, in the early days of the Cathedral, had worried about a Roman Catholic architect, a Lady Chapel and a crucifix, a Papal visit would have been inconceivable. The Pope was to be driven along Hope Street to celebrate the Papal Mass at the Metropolitan Cathedral, and his words indicated that he was aware of the significance of that road: 'I have been told that as I travel through Liverpool our motorcade will be passing along Hope Street. The name struck me immediately as an expression of the aspiration of the people who live here, and expression of their hope in the future.'

The Pope flanked by Bishop David Sheppard and Dean Edward Patey. The visit by the Pope to both Cathedrals was one of the most significant ecumenical events of all time. The cooperation of the Cathedrals led the way towards better understanding between Roman Catholic and Protestant in the city.

The Roman Catholic Cathedral at the other end of Hope Street viewed, appropriately, from the top of Liverpool Cathedral.

The future of Liverpool Cathedral was to be without the leadership of Dean Patey, who retired in 1982, as did the other members of the Chapter. The development of the life and worship of the Cathedral in the last quarter of the twentieth century was to be in the hands of new leaders, and the community waited with anticipation.

Nine years later, Edward Patey and his wife Margaret called into the Cathedral, and were delighted to find the nave given over to a Language Festival of work produced in Liverpool schools. The Cathedral was awash with children, some of them involved in interactive drama built around central characters from *The Hunch-back of Notre Dame*. The Dean Emeritus thought and spoke about his time in Liverpool; firstly of how part of him had wanted to turn down the Deanery and stay in Coventry, 'because it was new and starting from scratch – a twentieth-century cathedral with no tradition'. He had not been part of the Liverpool community for long before he realised that some of his thoughts about the two cathedrals were wrong: 'A great many of the things which we thought new and exciting and dynamic and innovative in Coventry, Dwelly had already done', because he was 'an absolute genius'. Although the 'gentle, persuading, loving' ways of Dean Dillistone had done much to smooth some of the Cathedral problems, there was still the legacy of a divided Cathedral. Dwelly had 'divided to rule', and left a Cathedral made up of separate sections with little 'sense of Cathedral community'.

Patey was able to look back with great satisfaction at the way in which the two Cathedrals and the friendly relations established between the two had prepared the way for the Roman Catholic/Anglican spirit of co-operation. He remembered with delight the little Irish lady he had met through his work with the Race Relations Council. She so wanted to see the Pope, but knew that she had no way of obtaining a ticket to admit her to the Metropolitan Cathedral. The generous Dean gave her means of access to the Anglican Cathedral, where she even managed to secure a seat right at the front. She was so overcome with the excitement of the occasion that she dropped her Rosary, which was retrieved, blessed and returned to her by the Holy Father himself.

Dean Patey approached retirement certain that he had held 'the best job the Church of England can give anyone', and intensely aware of 'the sheer privilege of using this place as a workshop for nineteen years'. Before the end of my conversation with him, we could hear Ian Tracey at the organ.

'The best thing I did here as Dean was to appoint Ian Tracey,' he said, and strode off down the Cathedral to see again the young man to whom he had given the great responsibility of Cathedral music.

Before his actual retirement, he had been visited by the Prime Minister's Appointments Secretary, who had asked him what kind of a man ought to succeed him, and the retiring Dean had advised that it be someone 'strong on my weak points' – a good administrator. Sad though the Cathedral community was to see the departure of its vigorous, imaginative, brave Dean, one of the Cathedral Committee was reported to have said, on the arrival of the new man, 'At last we've got a Dean who understands finance'. And the old Dean was delighted because, 'I had such a good innings'.

The Papal visit to Liverpool Cathedral was watched on television by Derrick Walters, Canon Treasurer of Salisbury Cathedral. He had only one experience of Liverpool: driving out of the Mersey Tunnel into a welter of traffic and never managing to meet up with one of his college contemporaries. That same year, the Treasurer was walking through the Close at Salisbury when he was approached by a stranger seeking directions. The tall, spirited young man with an engaging smile, bright eyes and large hands, turned out to be Ian Tracey, making his way to his first Cathedral Organists' Conference. That meeting marked the beginning of an extremely fruitful relationship which was destined to carry music at Liverpool Cathedral into a firm, guaranteed future. The Crown Appointments Secretary had done his work well, and Derrick Walters was to become the fourth Dean of Liverpool.

The Very Reverend Derrick Walters, fourth Dean of Liverpool.

As Canon Treasurer at Salisbury he was used to a small, ancient Cathedral with a pattern of daily worship stretching back through the centuries and, mainly because of its famous spire, the building was a major tourist attraction. When he was offered the Deanery of Liverpool, he knew that he and his family were moving into a very different world, a world in which particular expertise would be called upon. He had grown up in South Wales before going to the London School of Economics and then to theological training at Ripon Hall. He had been engaged in a varied ministry in Swansea, Sheffield and Derby before he had moved with his wife Joan and sons David and Michael, to the Close in Salisbury.

He remembers an early visit to Liverpool

before his installation, when he found himself walking through a deserted Cathedral, until he heard the sound of voices on the other side of a door and introduced himself to the vergers as their new Dean. He felt just how much energy his predecessor and his Chapter colleagues had put into the drive to finish the building, and he realised that his energies and skills must be directed towards bringing life and people and new jobs into the Cathedral and its surroundings: 'I walked into this marvellous Cathedral and it was absolutely empty and it did seem we had an important role to play.' Anyone who watches the Dean as he processes out after Choral Evensong each day will discover two interests and qualities not frequently found together in the same person: he is deeply committed to the continuing life of the worshipping community within the tradition of the Church of England and, at the same time, he has economic vision and unwavering determination to bring schemes to fruition. As he told a *Guardian* reporter:

> While our primary role is to let the Cathedral help people in their encounter with God, you can't ignore the context in which we're working. It is desperately important that we create new jobs in the city because that's what gives people a sense of pride and meaning.

When Derrick Walters moved to Liverpool, the Deanery was five miles away, and none of the Canons lived near to the Cathedral. The building developments over the road from the Cathedral became a priority with him, and without his sound economic vision, faith, and dogged hard work, the developments might well have foundered on the rocks of Liverpool politics.

Throughout the exciting Patey years, there had been intense concentration on finishing the building, and on imaginative and exciting great services and events, which many times a year filled the Cathedral. But the new Dean and Chapter were keenly aware that between great events the building was too often unhealthily quiet and empty, and they must have seen it as a priority to ensure that they were leading a seven-days-a-week Cathedral. Despite the absence of a choir school to ensure the availability of choristers, Choral Evensong came to be celebrated on six days in the week during term time. The youthful enthusiasm of the young Organist and Master of Choristers and his assistant, Ian Wells, was an important factor in the success of this development.

The tourist season in the summer months had always brought people in, but the Cathedral needed a constant flow of people daily throughout the year. A special service on Thursday 13th September 1984 heralded a new era in Cathedral community life. The service entitled 'Heritage 84' was a triple thanksgiving:

> It is an act of Thanksgiving in this Heritage Year for the rich inheritance into which we have entered as members of this Nation, this Country, this City. It is an act of Thanksgiving for the completion of our new Visitor Centre and Refectory, which will be a great asset to us in the future work

in the Cathedral. It is an act of Thanksgiving that the Cathedral Appeal for £450,000, launched three years ago, has not only been reached, but also surpassed this summer.

The refectory and visitor centre had been created with great flair out of the two least-used parts of the building – the Welsford Porch (which did not actually lead anywhere), and the North West Transept (an area usually blocked from public view). The refectory, one of the great successes of the completed Cathedral, was established with faith, good will and lots of voluntary help, welded together by the unflappable determination of Margaret Riley. It was not unknown for the Canon Treasurer, as he was then, to spend a busy Saturday afternoon up to his elbows in washing up. Plate glass windows through into the Cathedral and out across Gambier Terrace provided superb vistas for the visitors enjoying coffee and hot scones, lunch or afternoon tea with sticky chocolate cake, below Scott's discreetly illuminated vaulting. The venture was so successful that a second dining area was established down in the Western Rooms to cater for larger organised groups during the day, or in the evening. Increasingly, groups are coming to the Cathedral for conference or lecture, celebratory meal or a simple supper and a guided tour of the Cathedral in the quiet of a summer evening. The venture is beginning to be financially beneficial to the Cathedral but, equally important, is the fact that it draws many people in who might not otherwise have come near the building. The facilities are now an integral part of the Cathedral's ministry of welcome.

Many people like to be able to buy some souvenir in the visitor centre, which has developed in several directions by providing postcards and guidebooks, photographs, prints, pottery and glass, and also by stocking a good selection of books and church supplies.

One afternoon early in May 1989, I was conscious of a procession of footsteps passing my office door, and when I went to investigate, I discovered a group of men assembling what appeared to be the heavy frame for a large oak box. Subsequent conversations revealed that the oak frame was the beginning of a new mobile organ console which was going to be built in the Cathedral by David Wells and his team. Many years earlier, a young man from Dublin called Victor Hutson had heard Goss playing the organ from the gallery console, and regretted that it was not possible to see the hands and feet of the recitalist. That young man's energy and initiative brought him financial success, while his passion for the organ at Liverpool Cathedral increased. His passion was so great that he thought nothing of travelling from Kuala Lumpur just for the Easter Monday recital. It became his wish that he should provide the money for a mobile console, but rather than leaving the money in his will, he wisely made the funds available during his lifetime, so that he and thousands of other organ enthusiasts could enjoy the fruits of his generosity.

For weeks David Wells and his team worked painstakingly in cramped conditions off the south choir aisle, aware that they were making history within the Cathedral by building the largest mobile console in the world.

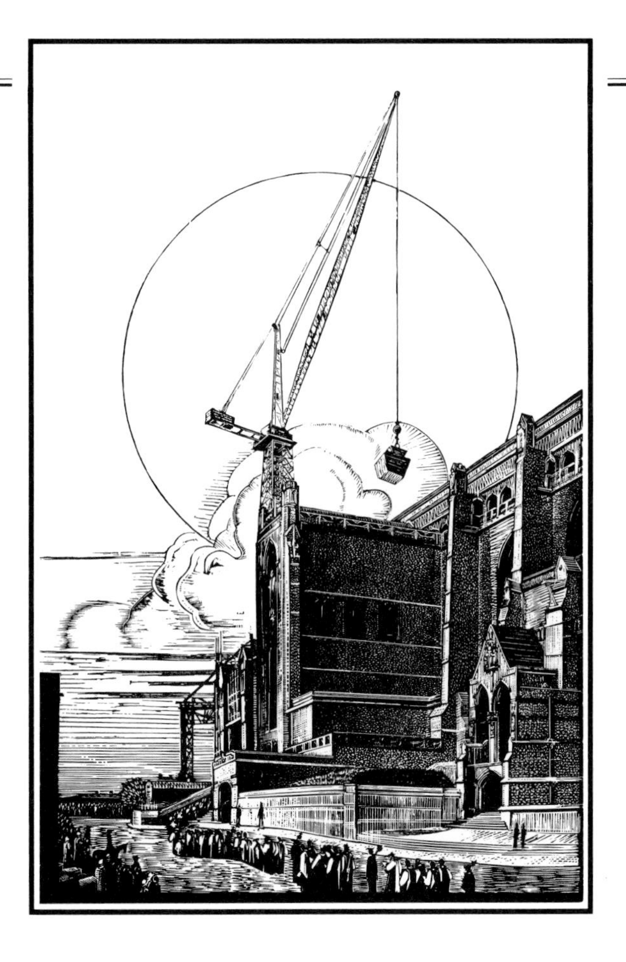

CHAPTER
- Seventeen -

Over the road

THE finished Cathedral viewed from Hope Street and Gambier Terrace rose majestically from the romantic gorge formed by the gardens created from the cemetery which had once been quarry. Viewed, as it was by most visitors, from the riverside, however, the result was incongruous in the extreme. This splendid new, yet somehow timeless building, rose out of a squalor of dereliction and neglect. Even before the Second World War the land in front of the Cathedral was showing harsh signs of urban decay. By 1980 the landscape was a disgrace to any city, and prompted more than one Cathedral visitor to remark, 'Your building is

One of Scott's plans for the land in front of the Cathedral, drawn in 1948. The open view up to the Rankin Porch and the Vestey Tower has much to recommend it.

magnificent, but why can't the city give it an appropriate setting?'

The question was not new, and even when Liverpool was under nightly wartime attack, Scott was already thinking about the nature of the landscape from Great George Street up towards the Rankin Porch and the Cathedral; thinking and producing intriguing little pen and ink sketches of his ideas, which he included in friendly letters to Dean Dwelly. The oldest surviving written account of his ideas appeared in a letter dated October 25th 1941:

> I have been playing about with ideas for the 'lay out' immediately around the Cathedral, it is good fun. Of course the picturesque jumble is not convincing if artifically produced and it is bad for the outlook of the buildings themselves, but I want to get an open treatment with little houses brought in front of the huge mass of the Cathedral, giving some striking views as you come round corners . . .
>
> There would be a number of pleasant residential squares probably two storied buildings, if flats they could be entered from opposite sides so as to avoid a common entrance, each flat would have its own front door

away from other doors. The diagonal views of the tower indicated above would appear to come by chance across the squares.

Some of these ideas were carried further after the war, and published in the December 1948 edition of the *Architectural Review*:

> The slope on the ground on the quasi-South side of the Cathedral is considered too steep to allow of the direct frontal approach to the Great Porch for vehicular traffic. This fact suggested the diagonal approach roads which are a predominating motif of the lay-out. I also feel that, for a building of this character, it is desirable to bring the small adjoining buildings in front of the Cathedral, so that they appear to be clustering around the base of the Cathedral which towers above their roofs. For a Gothic building this treatment seems preferable to a vast empty space such as might be suitable for a building in a classic or other monumental style. The combination of a romantic lay-out with a certain formality of treatment provides an interesting problem. The plan has been prepared to give fine vistas to those walking in the streets, rather than to make a formal pattern as viewed from an aeroplane . . .

The city authorities had for many years been giving their attentions to the sloping site. The *News Chronicle* for 24th October 1936 carried an architect's impression of a scheme being prepared by the City Engineer's Department. Even from this early stage, strong disagreements surrounded most of the proposals. Early in the following year, two different city committees produced very different proposals for the area in an attempt to provide the most striking vista of the whole building. The Health Committee's plan involved cutting a wide new road at right angles to Great George Street and carrying this through up to the Rankin Porch. This plan would have destroyed Great George Square and a Pugin church. The Housing Committee's plan also had a wide road up to the porch, but without such a degree of demolition. Disagreement rumbled on, the plans were forgotten, and further ideas were put forward in 1948 by Mr. H. T. Hough, the City Engineer. His scheme had a dignified formality. A choir school and houses for the clergy were planned at the top of the slope on the east and west sides of the site. The central section included four flights of steps up from Great George Street with trees and formal lawns on either side. Though the city planners may have been able to agree on a single scheme, the politicians certainly could not.

In 1966 a plan was published that was so ill-conceived as to arouse vocal and legal opposition from the Cathedral authorities. Traffic problems in the city were becoming acute, and the scheme proposed the construction of an inner ring road six lanes wide, cutting around the Cathedral in an arc that would in some places be sixty feet above ground level. To compound the difficulties, the land between the new road and the Cathedral was scheduled for high-density building of council flats and houses. Some in the city wished to counter this scheme with one which surrounded the Cathedral with picturesque parkland. Dean and Chapter were not in favour of either of these extremes. They did not want a beautiful cathedral stuck up in isolation on a hill; neither did they want to be cut off from the rest of the city by urban motorway and high-rise flats.

The ideas produced by Scott years earlier were far more in keeping with what was needed, and can now be read as powerfully prophetic:

> I would like to see this area developed as a beautiful residential area, for our cities should not be merely places to work in, but charming places to live in as well. It can be done, but people will only be tempted back if the transformation is effective over a large area. A tinkering policy will not get them back.

Throughout the 1970s the violent disagreements rumbled on, to the pain and frustration of the Cathedral community, whose feelings were admirably summed up in the words of the Dean:

> Although these were matters entirely outside the control of myself and my colleagues, the continuing wrangling, bitter arguments and accusations and counter-accusations of double dealing and behind the scene bargaining inevitably became associated in the public mind with the Cathedral itself, and it cannot be said that it helped us in our task of proclaiming the gospel of neighbourly love entrusted to us by Jesus Christ.

An unusual view which shows both the Lady Chapel and the Chapter House.

Wrangling and frustration might have festered for a decade on this matter, had it not been engulfed in a wider and far more violent uprising – the Toxteth Riots of 1981. In the wake of the destruction, Michael Heseltine was sent to Liverpool with wide powers to listen to what people had to say, and to make far-reaching recommendations. For the good of Liverpool as a whole, and the Cathedral in particular, he was able to put forward practical suggestions and had government support to see them to fruition:

> A major site surrounds the magnificent Anglican Cathedral. It is a city site of world importance. I have discussed with the City and the County Councils, who own the site, the way in which it may be developed, in keeping with its location. I have agreed with the County and City leaders that the following procedure will be recommended to their councils.
>
> First a planning brief will be drawn up which will suggest the use of the site for public open space, housing to rent, housing for sale, and a primary school. I have asked the Housing Corporation to explore with the local authorities, ways of acquiring the land, and to consider how the development can then be managed. Once the planning brief has been approved an open competition will be established, the results of which will be widely displayed. They will be subject to proper public scrutiny and consultation with all parties, including, of course, the local communities.

In a letter to the Dean, Michael Heseltine showed the strength of his feelings on the matter, and the hope that the years of frustration and delay were nearly at an end:

> I share wholeheartedly your reaction to the history of neglect of this site and your hopes for the future. I hope that the open competition which the Housing Corporation are now preparing to mount will indeed result in a design for the site worthy of the setting and with the necessary backing to see it carried through to completion. I am most pleased that you support the action now being taken.

Considerable interest was generated in building and architectural circles by the news of the competition, and by April of 1982 eighteen entries had been submitted, six of which were chosen to go through to the second round. Plans and statements were put on public display in the Cathedral, including those of three men who had particular confidence in their scheme: David Humphries, quantity surveyor with Tweeds; Martyn Coppin, architect with Brock Carmichael Associates; and Alan Smith of Cruden Construction. The aims of their scheme were outlined in their statement:

> The objective has been to establish a clear character and unit which reconciles the national, religious and architectural significance of a Cathedral, its attendant requirements and attraction for visitors, with the important needs of the community living within the site.
>
> To achieve this a major element is the large landscaped area which

expands diagonally from the square formed at the Duke Street/Great George Street junction to culminate in a paved Plaza in front of the Rankin Porch. Pedestrians entering the site from the Duke Street square progress through a formal landscaped park, the broad sweep of houses framing the magnificent view of the Cathedral. Progressively wider flights of steps and changes in landscape from soft to hard, heighten the dynamic sense of approach with the Cathedral's full scale and richness becoming apparent on arrival in the Plaza.

The Plaza is the climax of all pedestrian approaches including the tightly framed, intimate route from the centre of Great George Street. In addition to meeting the Cathedral's ceremonial and service requirements, the Plaza would be a natural focus for community activities (open air plays, markets, meetings, concerts, etc.).

To establish clear boundaries to the residential areas and discourage casual entry by the public, the houses have been grouped in a series of

Aerial view of the development of the land in 1990. The oval courts give a very comfortable sense of community and there are interesting views of the Cathedral and of the city from many windows. One resident whose bedroom looked over to the Cathedral Tower felt that conditions reminded him of the bottom of a brick kiln!

Interesting angles and levels provide a pleasant setting for the finished Cathedral. Though not to Scott's design, he would surely have approved – though many people do regret the passing of the grassy slope down to Great George Street.

clearly defined private mews courts. All related car parking and private rear gardens are screened from general view. Three storey in height, the scale, detail and form of the family houses extends the established character of the area.

The scheme has a broad scale of overall form and consistency of character reflecting the civic scale of the setting and approaches to this national monument, variety being achieved through changes of level and angle.

In August 1982 this scheme was selected, and the formal start to the building operation was performed in October 1983 by Patrick Jenkin, the Secretary of State.

Francis James Chavasse had not planned that the Cathedral should be cut off and remote from the city it was to serve; Giles Gilbert Scott had not wanted his great building to be in isolation, high up on the Mount and away from the homes and daily lives of the people. The houses that began to rise on the site, throughout the difficulties of the 1980s, represented a tangible symbol of the Cathedral's involvement with, and concern for, the life of the people of Liverpool. Editions of *Dean's Journal* in 1985 revealed how passionately Dean and Chapter felt about the role of the Christian Church at a time of painful social and economic difficulty in the city. The Dean's anguish at the state of affairs was fearlessly stated in editorial after editorial, and Ken Riley's brilliance as a preacher cut deeply into people's consciences in his civic sermon in 1984:

Exactly ten years ago, passing the Cathedral late one Saturday evening, I came across a man crawling up the steps on his hands and knees. Going up to him I saw that his wrists were cut and there was blood all over the steps. The ambulance came within three minutes and he was whisked off into the night, blue light flashing and bell clanging. I don't know the end of his story: I don't know whether we got to him in time or not. Some would say he was a representative of Liverpool: hurt, desperate, hopeless - and they would stop there.

Dean Dillistone and Mrs Joan Walters, wife of the present Dean, after the opening of Dillistone Court.

Yet he was on the steps of Liverpool Cathedral - built by the people of Liverpool in our time; begun in 1904 and enshrining the hopes and aspirations of Liverpool through bad times as well as good; through the 'thirties Depression and two World Wars. Perhaps the total scene that night more truly represents our city. Yes, there are those who are hurting and hurting badly - as there are in every other city - what the poet H. D. Carberry calls 'hurt creatures, sobbing out their sorrow to the rhythm of the blues'. Yet that is not the whole story. There is also what he calls a 'magnificent reaching out,' a yearning for something beyond all that is sham and shoddy, part of that divine discontent with things as they are, a reaching out for things as they might be, even things which seem beyond ourselves, of which this building is a sign. That too is part of Liverpool.

Before he was assassinated, Robert Kennedy wrote, 'Some men see things as they are and say Why? I dream of things that never were and say Why not'. And Cardinal Suenens of Belgium warns us that such sentiments are not optional but necessary if we are to survive the future: 'To hope is a duty, not a luxury'. To hope is not to dream but to turn dreams into reality. Happy are those who have the courage to dream dreams, who are ready to pay the price, so that their dreams take shape in the lives of men.

Our dream is that spelt out by Her Majesty the Queen at the Garden Festival - the renewal of Liverpool. But as the good Cardinal reminds us, there is a price to be paid and it is not merely an economic matter. Poverty may indeed imprison the spirit, but is it not the eclipse of the spirit itself which has so led to the impoverishment of our national life? If in those halcyon days when 'we never had it so good' in the 'sixties and 'seventies, the motto of enough of us was 'Take care of number one and to hell with everyone else,' we should not be too surprised that at least some of our citizens have actually arrived in hell in the 'eighties!

Many of you, like me, grew up in what is now referred to as 'relative poverty': back-to-back housing; outside loo; a square meal of bread and jam; cricket up the entry and the odd smashed window when the drive to the covers went wrong. The strange thing is that many people look back to those days and say, 'We were poor but happy'. What has changed, that such poverty as we now have so threatens the fabric of society?

Is it not precisely in the realm of the spirit that the change has come?

> With the wholesale destruction of the old communities has come the collapse of that web of community values which bound us together. There is now no common loyalty to anything and anyone beyond ourselves, and there is no common compassion which can heal our wounds. 'Do not talk to me of reconciliation,' said an inner city priest, 'that is too bland; first, we must all get on our knees and ask forgiveness for our communal folly.'
>
> 'For evil to succeed it is only necessary that good men do nothing.'
>
> As we talk of many problems in Liverpool, and as our politicians, councillors, churchmen and officers embark on tackling them, there is an issue to be faced which we evade at our peril, pinpointed by the American playwright Arthur Miller: 'There is a spirit gone. I do not know how we are to reach for the spirit again, but I know that without it we flounder'.

At every point in its history, the Liverpool Cathedral community has reached forward with hope and their achievement has become a visible symbol of hope for the wider community. In the dreariest days of the depressed 'eighties, the slow developments 'over the road' were at least helping to regenerate a broken city.

The site proved even more difficult to work than had been expected. The land was derelict and had to undergo a major reclamation programme. Tests indicated serious irregularities below ground, partly as a result of an old quarry on part of the site, and partly because the cellars of demolished houses had not been carefully filled: and the structural consultant, Roger Hetherington, and his engineers had to solve some interesting problems on such a steeply sloping site.

Political wranglings within the city caused even greater problems than the poor ground. By June 1986, the clergy housing was complete, and the opening ceremony was performed by Sir Douglas Lovelock, K.C.B., First Church Estates Commissioner. Even this part of the project proved problematic, as Sir Douglas's train was considerably delayed, and the organist had to improvise for far longer than he had expected.

Good buildings were rising on the site for Housing Corporation and Cathedral, but confidence in Liverpool was at a low ebb and buyers were not in evidence for the houses to be built in the remaining courts. The whole project was saved from ruin when the Dean and Chapter took on the responsibility for the rest of the housing, which they were eventually able to lease to Liverpool Polytechnic for the student residential accommodation it so badly needed.

A Living Cathedral

CHAPTER
- Eighteen -

UR Cathedral story has been pieced together from the perceptions of a wide range of people – from stonemason to Bishop, from chorister to Dean, from historic photograph to letters from the famous. Today's Cathedral is not bereft of great figures whose contribution to the life and growth of the Cathedral community will emerge clearly in the future; but I cannot view the Cathedral through their eyes, because the impressions of the living Cathedral which I perceive through my own senses are so vivid that they dominate my vision of today.

In the summer term of 1988, I spent half of my time as a principal lecturer in Liverpool Polytechnic, and the other half working with teachers and children visiting the Cathedral. It was an intimidating community in which to operate in those early weeks, but a community towards which I was strongly drawn. An unfinished cathedral with cranes and scaffolding on the tower was one of my early memories as a child; the Cathedral as a worshipping community was my daily experience as a middle-aged man.

The offer of early retirement from my Polytechnic teaching career arrived with the cards on Christmas Eve. Liverpool Cathedral did not have an education officer: I believed one was needed, and I had the audacity to ask the Dean and Chapter to appoint me. The spring term of 1989 ended without my knowing whether retirement had been granted, but All Fools Day saw me installed in my new position, knowing that I had become a teacher in the biggest and most exciting educational resource in the North West.

I had been in post for only a fortnight, when 95 Liverpool football supporters were killed at Hillsborough, and Liverpool Cathedral was needed as the setting for a memorial service. Chavasse's words about the proposed cathedral could not have been more clear or more right: the Cathedral stood as 'a visible witness for God in the midst of this great city'. The Cathedral community, like any other community, is going to be subject to tensions and disagreements, but that awful loss of innocent life focused the Cathedral community upon its duty at that time. A service was needed at which the individual, the Church, the city, the nation, could express sorrow and support; in which the grief of the bereaved could be acknowledged and channelled. Here would be some who had never been in the Cathedral before, who had no links with the Church, but whose need for spiritual support had never been greater.

Every single department in the Cathedral was working at full stretch for the week leading up to the service on Saturday 29th April. Helen, Jenny and Sharon in the office never stopped answering the telephone and coping with requests for tickets for the service from people in great distress. Maintenance team, security staff, vergers, refectory employees and volunteers, cleaners, choir and clergy gave of their time unstintingly.

The creative energy of Precentor and Organist quickly devised a service that was simple yet memorable, significant and dignified. Here was a service which would remain in the memories of the bereaved for ever. They had been through the harrowing hours of the funeral; the memorial service would be painful for all those present; and yet, through the architecture of the great building, and through the sensitivity and imagination of music and liturgy, personal grief might be faced, shared, controlled.

Security on such occasions has to be high yet discreet. The leaders of the main political parties were to be present, along with the Duke and Duchess of Kent, the Archbishop of York, Cardinal Basil Hulme, and a wide range of Church and civic figures. For days before, the building was being prepared for radio and television coverage of the service. The entire building had to be searched and checked overnight, and searched again with sniffer dogs early in the morning. It was a strange sight to see eager, highly-trained labradors and spaniels at work behind the High Altar and around the Bishop's Throne.

The whole Cathedral from Sanctuary to the west end of the Nave was filled with people, and great processions entered from east and west. After the singing of *Abide with Me*, 95 candles were lit as the choir sang 'Thou knowest, Lord the secrets of our hearts: shut not thy merciful ears unto our prayers' to the music Henry Purcell had composed for the funeral of a queen. The Book of Remembrance containing the names and ages of those who had lost their lives, was carried from the west and placed on the High Altar as the choir sang *Pie Jesu* from Andrew Lloyd Webber's *Requiem*: 'O Holy Jesus, who takes away the sins of the world, grant them rest eternal'. After the readings and sermon, symbols of sympathy were also taken to the altar. The Books of Condolence carried messages and expressions of sympathy. This procession was accompanied by the choir singing Edgar Bainton's setting of the words from *Revelation*: 'And I saw a new heaven and a new earth'.

The processions through the building by members of the Cross Guild were deeply moving. Many of the young men and boys were obviously distressed, but they had their parts to play in the service, and they carried them through with simple dignity.

The profound silence after the Blessing was eventually broken by the solo voice of Martin Polglase, Head Chorister, as he sang the opening words of what has become the Liverpool Football Club 'anthem':

When you walk through the storm
Hold your head up high
And don't be afraid of the dark.

The tension in the Cathedral as he sang was almost unendurable, until he was joined triumphantly by organ, choir and congregation. Though the pain and distress could not be drained away, the Cathedral had united individual griefs and pointed the way beyond temporal sorrow. The Dean hallowed the Hillsborough Memorial Stone with the words: 'In the faith of Jesus Christ, Who died and rose again, we hallow this stone as a perpetual memorial to those who died at Hillsborough'.

Anglican, Roman Catholic and Free Church leaders all played their parts in the service, and together they spoke the words of blessing over the city:

God bless Liverpool
  and make her people
  strong in faith,
  steadfast in hope,
  and generous in charity
through Jesus Christ our Lord, Amen.

Such unity was undreamed of at the start of the century when the Cathedral itself was no more than a dream.

The eyes of the world had been on Liverpool Cathedral on that Saturday morning, but by 3 p.m. the building was re-ordered as the choir procession entered to sing the daily service of Choral Evensong. In some ways, that Hillsborough day will always sum up for me one of the essential features of the Cathedral: it stands ready for the Cathedral community to celebrate their daily services, and it also stands ready to answer the needs of many other groups and organisations who come in, maybe once a year, maybe only once in a lifetime.

The yearly cycle reflects the great festivals of the Christian Church whose year begins four Sundays before Christmas, at Advent. At this time the Church uses the symbol of light in darkness to prepare for the birth of Christ at Christmas. Advent processional services have always been memorable preparations for the coming of Christ. Liverpool Cathedral celebrates its great procession of light at 3 p.m. on Advent Sunday, in a darkened building. The procession of choir and clergy assembles at the west end, and as the service progresses, candlelight is brought through, right up to the High Altar, until for the final hymn every candle and bulb in the building is ablaze. Here is a service at which the imaginative precentor can use the architectural features of the building to the full, without the dangers of empty theatricality. In recent years most of the chairs have been removed from the Central Space for this service, the congregation being seated in the Chancel and below the Chancel steps. The impact of the slow approach of the candlelit procession through the vast space is very powerful.

The next scene in the Cathedral Advent is the annual performance of

Members of the Cross Guild, former Cathedral Choristers, wait in the darkened Cathedral before the start of the Advent Procession.

Handel's *Messiah* by the Cathedral choir, singers and orchestra. The singers are a voluntary group of about a hundred men and women who rehearse regularly through the year under the direction of Ian Tracey. They perform sometimes with the Cathedral choir and sometimes alone, so constituting a choral society within the Cathedral which is able to perform big works to a high standard. For the right work, the Cathedral makes an inspiring concert hall, and the singers feel themselves to be a small yet significant part of the Cathedral's musical life.

About a week after the performance of *Messiah*, excitement grows within the Maintenance Department as they await the arrival of the Christmas tree – each year taller than the year before. The 1990 tree was so big that it was towed into the Cathedral by a tractor. Faith, hope, ingenuity and muscle-power are all needed before eighty feet of tree stand proudly ready to be decorated with hundreds of coloured lights. The same team of men that copes with all the varied maintenance work of the vast and complex building, from blocked drains to loose finial, from fine carving to storm damage on the roof, sets to decorating the tree and wrapping hundreds of chocolate bars to hide under the branches for the many very young Christmas visitors.

The run-up to Christmas is always extraordinarily busy because so many organisations come to the Cathedral to hold their own carol services. In 1989 a group of very young children from St. Vincent's School for the Blind celebrated their service in the Lady Chapel. For them the 'light' of Advent was provided by the playing of an excellent brass instrumental group. These children brought the message of Christmas up to the main Cathedral and walked in procession right to the west doors to the accompaniment of a mighty organ voluntary. They were able to hear the building they could not see, and feel its length. The same year an infant school, with parents and friends, held their Christingle Service in the Nave, and then carried their lighted Christingles with the greatest care right up to the High Altar.

Every year the three church secondary schools celebrate their carol services in the Cathedral with choirs and bands and orchestras. Toxteth primary schools, the Area Health Authority, the Towns-womens' Guild, Liverpool representatives of the legal profession are amongst some of the Cathedral's regular Christmas visitors.

All this is quite apart from the Cathedral's 'own' services, which every year attract vast crowds of people. Two Sundays before Christmas, the crib is blessed and the lights of the tree are switched on at a service to which many handicapped people are invited. On the Sunday immediately before Christmas, the lighted holly bough is carried through the Cathedral and placed up in the Sanctuary. It is not unusual for the Cathedral to run completely out of chairs on these occasions. And the recital of all the Christmas music on the Saturday before Christmas is very well attended, particularly by people from parishes all over the diocese who are unable to attend the Cathedral Sunday services because of their own parish commitments.

A celebration of the Eucharist at midnight on Christmas Eve was instituted mainly for the Cathedral community itself, but the popularity of the service is spreading, and certainly not reducing the congregation which gathers at 10.30 a.m. on Christmas Day.

January is one of the quieter months in the building, and the cleaners are able to have all the chairs moved from the Central Space so that they can scrub and buff the floor until the lights are reflected in the black marble. The small team of cleaners take great pride in their work, and their energies never seem to flag despite the area of stonework to be kept

The Holly Bough Procession moves through the congregation at the carol service on the Sunday before Christmas.

free from dust and dirt.

The first Saturday of Lent is the time for the annual performance of J. S. Bach's *St. Matthew Passion* by the Cathedral choir, singers and orchestra. On the Saturday before Palm Sunday, the same musical forces perform the *St. John Passion*. Every year performers and audience alike experience the power of these profound works performed in such an appropriate setting. Five minutes after the end of a performance, a willing band of security men and tired singers have to move the staging, re-order all the chairs and make the Cathedral ready for the following day's services, ever grateful that Scott had not thought of installing pews, but had provided a building which could be used with such flexibility. Scott must have been well ahead of his time when he thought to install a large chairlift in the floor of the Cathedral so that hundreds of pieces of furniture could be moved efficiently.

The procession with palms on Palm Sunday leads the community into the services of Holy Week. The service on Good Friday morning is called 'The Way of the Cross' – a Good Friday procession. The congregation is seated up in the Chancel as the choir enters from the west singing the Litany, but from this point onward choir, clergy and congregation stand and move round the Cathedral, as the service follows the Passion story. The first move is to a simple wooden altar below the Chancel steps, where are placed a chalice and patten, while thoughts centre upon the Upper Room and the Last Supper. Gethsemane is remembered in the War Memorial Chapel, the Judgement Hall in the Derby Transept, and Golgotha at the foot of a great rough wooden cross near the Nave Bridge, where the choir sings *Crucifixus* by Antonio Lotti. To the singing of *When I survey the Wondrous Cross* the whole company moves down into the Nave for the singing of the great final chorale from the *St. John Passion*. Many members of the congregation would have been present just a week before at the full performance, and the one chorale brings back the total experience of the Passion story:

> Ah! Lord when my last hour is come
> Bid angels bear my spirit home
> To Abraham's bosom going;
> My flesh, laid in the quiet tomb,
> Shall sleep until the day of doom,
> Nor pain nor sorrow knowing.
> Then, waking from the dark abode,
> Mine eyes shall see thee face to face
> In boundless joy, O Son of God,
> My Saviour and my throne of grace
> Lord Jesu Christ give me ear to me
> Who brings unending praise to thee.

In a move of sheer liturgical genius, we travel beyond the tomb as the whole company walks in silence through the great west doors, beckoning us to the life beyond, and reminding us that the gates of hell shall not prevail against us.

In 1924 Sir Frederick Radcliffe had challenged the Cathedral clergy in these words: 'The laymen of Liverpool are giving you this great gift: I sometimes ask myself if you will be able to use it'. The answer is beyond doubt.

A service of meditation in the Lady Chapel in the afternoon, is followed by 'Love so amazing, so divine . . .', a sequence of words and music held in the main Cathedral in the evening. Year by year the numbers attending this service increase, attesting to the appreciation of the congregation for the inspiration brought to all the services by the choir and music staff.

A simple vigil service in the early evening of Holy Saturday is a quiet preparation for the flowers, the music, the rich ceremonial of the Eucharist for Easter Day. The following day, the bank holiday, sees the Cathedral packed yet again, this time for the Easter organ recital by Ian Tracey. At the end of Easter Monday, a very tired Cathedral company takes its leave of the building, ready for some rest, but also ready for a massive Boys' Brigade service on Low Sunday afternoon.

Whitsunday afternoon has become the traditional time for the communities of Anglican and Roman Catholic Cathedrals to come together through the medium of an ecumenical procession along Hope Street from one Cathedral to the other. Ecumenical progress is heartening, particularly when one remembers the animosity between Catholic and Protestant which had been so marked during the early years of the Cathedral story.

Throughout the summer tourist season, thousands of visitors, intent on 'doing' both Cathedrals, take the same short walk. A team of guides, or Interpreters as they are called, is on hand to meet visitors and answer their casual questions, or to work with the groups of teachers and children for whom the Cathedral has become a part of their study programme.

During the summer months, a series of special services is held which over the years have become part of the Liverpool liturgical cycle: Battle of the Atlantic Service, Civic Service, Judges' Service – for an hour or so, different organisations come to worship in their Cathedral. Many of those attending may not be regular attenders in their parish or any other church, but in the Cathedral they are made welcome and the sheer majesty of the great building is in itself an assurance to people that though they may wander from the Church, the Cathedral Church of Christ will always be there to receive them: 'something to speak for God in this great city'.

One of the main features of a Cathedral summer is now the annual festival. In the words of the Dean: 'The Liverpool Cathedral Festival each July commemorates the laying of the Foundation stone in 1904 and the vision and generosity of our founders and benefactors. They were determined that the Cathedal should be a centre of excellence in architecture and art and craftsmanship.' As well as being Organist and Master of the Choristers, Ian Tracey is the Chorus Master of the Royal Liverpool Philharmonic Choir, and the co-operation between the two

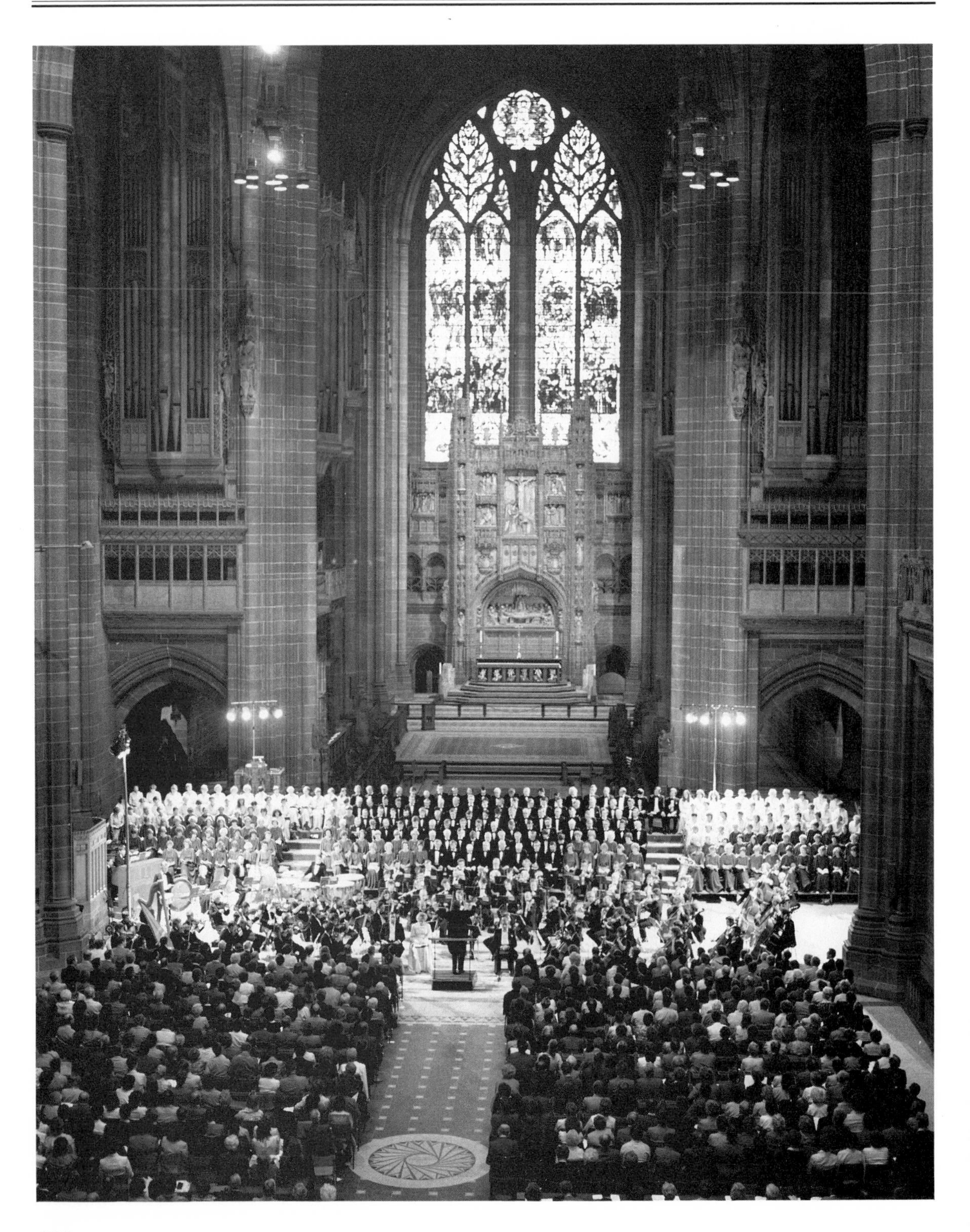

institutions has made possible many exciting performances including, in 1990, Mahler's Eighth Symphony, the *Symphony of a Thousand.*

Some of the elements in the weekly cycle of Cathedral affairs may seem rather mundane and worldly, but without them the worshipping life of the community could easily founder. Monday morning sees the heads of departments and the clergy together in the Dean's office for the weekly staff meeting. Many of the items are predictable: a local Mothers' Union group wishing to come for afternoon tea in the Western Rooms and a tour; arrangements for a recital by a visiting music group; fixing of the dates of ordination and confirmation services eighteen months in the future; possible dates for a memorial service; problems of car parking; and of visitors falling down the steps into the Nave because they are so enthralled by the West Window that they do not see the danger.

By lunchtime, the Sunday arrangement of furniture may have been radically altered – to enable the cleaners to scrub a large section of the floor or to accommodate a special service. A thousand chairs may well have to be shifted just for a single service and then put back in other positions 24 hours later. The verger who the day before might have led a bishop through a packed Cathedral, today shifts five bags of refuse from the refectory after lunch. The cleaner seen in the morning mopping acres of marble might be seen in the afternoon down in the undercroft ironing surplices as she works her way through the choir laundry. Later on the same day, the same cleaner might be seen in different garb as a waitress at an evening function in the Western Rooms.

Despite there being no choir school at Liverpool, there are choral services six days out of seven during term time. Boys alone sing on Monday, full choir on Tuesday, men alone on Thursday, and full choir Friday, Saturday and Sunday. The commitment by the choir members and their families is considerable, but they seem all to recognise the significance of their role in leading much of the worship in their Cathedral. Boys fortunate enough to win a place in a cathedral choir school may well have sung at their auditions as accomplished young musicians of eight or nine. The youngest probationers at Liverpool will be six, or even younger. They arrive with no previous training, but able to show brightness and intelligence, and a good ear. They will manage a hymn tune at audition rather than a Handel aria. The music staff at Liverpool undertakes the whole training. Not every probationer makes the journey through to the choir, though most do and have much reason to be grateful for the skill and patience of Ian Wells, from whom they learn to sing and read music. The Cathedral is having no problems of recruitment, and in 1991 they may well have sixty applications for only four vacant places. They are young professionals who are expected to work extremely hard, though they make the most of their free moments as they hurtle round playing football, often shrieking and yelling and quite unconcerned at the thought of top A on the first page of the anthem. The boys thoroughly enjoy the social aspects of being a chorister. As Andrew Kay

A great musical occasion in the Cathedral: a performance of Mahler's Eighth Symphony by the Royal Liverpool Philharmonic Orchestra and Choir, the Cathedral Singers and the Three Choirs Festival Chorus.

reported:

> The most favourite choir day is Sunday because we get two hours play. The worst day is Friday because we have a practice then a service then another practice with no break in between at all. I've never had a solo but I've sung a duet in *In Dulci Jubilo* with Robin Panter. I was terrified, but I just opened my mouth and luckily a sound came out. After a few bars I began to cool down and got used to it. Talking of brilliant music I have made a list of music which I think is 'mega'. *Let all the World* – Ralph Vaughan Williams, *Insanae et Vanae Curae* – Haydn, *Spatzenmasse* – Mozart, *Missa Sanctae Nicolae* – Haydn, Kelly in C, *Wash me Thoroughly* – Wesley, *O Be Joyful* – Britten, Leighton No. 2, and ALL Christmas carols! I don't know what direction my life would have been going now if I hadn't joined the choir, but I know it wouldn't have been as good as it is now!

Even the most unmusical member of the Cathedral community cannot ignore the recurring cycle of èvery second Friday: the days when David Wells and one of his assistants are at work tuning the organ. With use and variations in temperature, such constant attention to the instrument is essential. It is probably imagination which leads me to think that the quiet, gentle stops seem to stay in tune and need little attention, while the big reeds are attended to with painful regularity.

The Cathedral doors open at 8 a.m. every single day of the year. There are many fixed points and activities which happen every day, but no two days are ever the same. The passage of time will sieve the significant events of today for the future historian. My choice of incidents is wholly subjective, though the experiences will stay with me for ever. Though the great services with eye-catching ceremonial, fanfares of trumpets and congregation of two thousand are stirring occasions, for me one of the most musically impressive moments took place one Thursday evening when Evensong was sung by men's voices in the War Memorial Chapel. There were no more than six in the congregation when the choir sang Orlando Gibbons's setting of *Jesu, grant me this I pray*: not many people to see the tears streaming down my face because of the profound Christian truths of the words and the excellence of the performance. At the other extreme, I shall always remember the sight of the procession of the smallest of the choirboys in cassocks and surplices trying to climb decorously over a rope across the Sanctuary steps, inadvertently left in place by a verger and two canons who had been trying to catch a fly-away gas-filled balloon which was hovering ominously above the High Altar.

For me the Cathedral is full of memories of sounds: of Canon Ken Riley exhorting nearly a thousand children to shout 'Alleluia' as loudly as they could; of Ian Tracey playing Langlais in almost total darkness at the end of an Easter Vigil on Holy Saturday; of being part of the Mahler Eighth Symphony, the *Symphony of a Thousand* – brass on the under-tower galleries, soloist in the organ loft, massive orchestra and choir and the collosal sound of Henry Willis's masterpiece; the final phrases of the soloists just before the last chorus in the *Matthew Passion*, and the incomparable last chorale in the *John*; being on the floor of the bell chamber as one of the experienced ringers 'rang down' the tenor bell; almost shaking high up in a chamber of the organ as David Wells tuned the Tuba Magna only feet below me; Batten Fourth Evening Service, Maurice Green's *Lord, let me know mine end, Past the o'clock*, Ian playing at the Anniversary Recital.

I remember special visitors of course: discovering that Prime Minister Margaret Thatcher, even in a brief conversation, showed considerable knowledge of the archive resources of our twentieth-century Cathedral. There was great excitement when the news broke that Her Majesty the Queen was formally to open Queen's Walk, the area formerly referred to as the plaza. It was entrusted to Custos and Education Officer to organise the arrival, deployment and departure of two thousand Liverpool schoolchildren who thronged excitedly into the Cathedral, anxious for a good view of the Queen. It was also my duty to help to keep the two thousand spectators entertained during the half-hour wait before Her Majesty's arrival. To the intense embarrassment of one of my daughters, my voice, with the aid of a radio microphone, boomed out through the Cathedral. 'Bloody Hell,' said a surprised young man standing near her, 'Is that God?' 'No,' replied his neighbour, 'it's her father.'

It was a special privilege to bring John Rowbottom, on his final visit, into the Cathedral through the great west doors he helped to build. He was very frail, but his eyes twinkled with pride and delight as the Dean led him in as an honoured guest. It was very hard, but a great honour, to speak at

David Wells, the man responsible for the upkeep of one of the finest pipe organs in the world, on one of his fortnightly tuning sessions.

Terry McDonald, sculptor and carver, carving the inscriptions on the gateposts of Queen's Walk in 1991. He learned his craft from Herbert Tyson Smith, who carved the foundation stone in 1904.

The Queen being welcomed to the Cathedral in 1991. Left to right are Dean Derrick Walters; Mrs Joan Walters; Bishop David Sheppard, Mrs Grace Sheppard and Bishop Michael Henstall.

his funeral six months later; to stop by the Bridge of which he was so proud; to follow his coffin up to the High Altar where he was remembered and honoured by his family and friends in the building in which he exercised his craft for 49 years. His ashes are interred in Founder's Plot, close to the grave of Bishop Chavasse: both men could justifiably claim, 'We built a Cathedral'. For the 49 years of their marriage, John's wife Evelyn had wanted him to carve a bird bath to put in her garden: he was too busy building a Cathedral. But the sense of community and continuity at the Cathedral is so great that Tony Baker, the stonemason currently at work on the building, carved a bird bath for her. Tony met John only once, but he now works with many of John's tools – tools which had belonged to Owen Pittaway – and after his relatively short time working on the building, Tony is proudly part of that company who built a Cathedral. Craftsmanship goes on and is fostered in the place; everywhere there is evidence of the woodworking skills of Maurice Bray, and Maurice is now helping to train Paul, one of the first apprentices for many years to serve his time at the Cathedral.

For many of us who work there, the Cathedral is far more than just a building. It helps me to make sense of life. Only a few hours after the death of my father, I said Morning Prayer in the Chapter House with Ken Joplin, the Dean's Verger. My mother had died only six months before. To say that service was hard, but the experience of saying those words within the walls of my Cathedral was important. They were the words used by the worshipping community throughout its history: 'O come let us sing unto the Lord, let us heartily rejoice in the strength of our salvation'. In the prayers at Choral Evensong early in December 1989, I heard the news that Peter and Malcolm Lynan were in hospital after a motorway accident in fog, in which Malcolm's mother had been killed. It was very important to me, seven months later, to be the member of the staff who welcomed and introduced Peter when he came to give one of the Saturday organ recitals. He and his father were fully recovered from the accident, he had good results from his first year at Oxford, and he had returned to play the organ again in his Cathedral.

The Christmas services in 1990 were as well attended as ever, and for the Carol Recital on the Saturday before Christmas there was not a single empty seat. One young lady slept through the whole recital. At three months old this was not surprising, and she snuggled comfortably in her father's arms, having only weeks before been baptised in the Lady Chapel. The Canon Treasurer and the family had both felt that the Lady Chapel rather than the Baptistry was the appropriate setting for the ceremony. At a quiet service one Sunday in November, a little child was welcomed into the Christian Church and into the community of the Cathedral Church of Christ in Liverpool. She was the youngest member of a very famous family; her great-great-grandfather had inspired his diocese to build a Cathedral. His name was Francis James Chavasse.

Postscript

by the Very Reverend Derrick Walters, Dean of Liverpool

Peter Kennerley has done a splendid job in searching through the archives and writing this fascinating account of the building of Liverpool Cathedral. As a twentieth-century foundation we are fortunate that we have such a detailed archive of the construction of the building and the great moments of our history.

Mr Kennerley has told his story with immense skill. He has included some delightful anecdotes to enlighten the tale and solved some major mysteries.

I have no doubt that those who love the Cathedral will see the book as an essential companion to Vere Cotton's account of Liverpool Cathedral

In generations to come those researching Liverpool Cathedral will say, 'Look it up in Cotton and if it's not in Cotton, try Kennerley.' We are indebted to Peter Kennerley for allowing us to share in his research that deepens our understanding of Giles Gilbert Scott's masterpiece.

Acknowledgements

I shall always be indebted to the Dean and Chapter of Liverpool Cathedral for responding so positively when I asked them to appoint me to the Cathedral staff. Without their confidence in me and their constant support this book could not have been written. All the Cathedral staff and the wider community of volunteers, worshippers and visitors have been most supportive, and their interest has kept me going whenever my energy has been flagging.

No student of the Cathedral - past, present or future - can ever give adequate thanks for the labours of Vere and Elfreda Cotton, who recorded the development of the Cathedral in the one hundred editions of *The Liverpool Cathedral Bulletin*. The lady referred to by all the Cathedral community as Granny Cotton is one of the most remarkable people I have ever met. In her hundredth year, she has the longest and richest store of Cathedral memories of anyone in the world.

I am grateful to Professor G. E. Aylmer, Master of St. Peter's Hall, Oxford, for allowing me to quote from the Chavasse Papers in the Bodleian Library, and to Steven Tomlinson and Colin Harris of the Department of Western Manuscripts for making access to those papers so easy. In Liverpool John Vaughan, Honorary Senior Fellow in the School of Education, Liverpool University, Anne Clayton of Liverpool Polytechnic and Janet Smith of Liverpool Public Libraries have been of considerable help over the whereabouts of archive materials. John Chavasse, grandson of Bishop Chavasse, has allowed me access to the family photographs. Sir Giles Scott's neice, Mrs Elizabeth Hoare, and daughter-in-law, Mrs Richard Scott, allowed me to use family photographs.

Over the final production of this book I am extremely grateful to the Friends of Liverpool Cathedral for their financial support, and to Canon Huw Thomas and Gordon Nixon, Cathedral Finance Officer, and David Stewart of Charles Wilson Booksellers for their steady interest and practical guidance. I shall always remain indebted to Alistair Hodge and the staff of Carnegie Publishing Ltd for the excellence of the personal and professional skills which they have brought to every stage of this project.

On a more personal level, I am indeed grateful to my wife, Hilary, and daughters, Rachel and Elizabeth, for putting up with a fanatical husband and father and being 'widowed' and 'orphaned' by a Cathedral. My friends George Allcock and Ian Gattis have been supportive over the whole enterprise. To Peter Lynan, Organ Scholar of St. Edmund Hall, Oxford, fell the painstaking task of dating the illustrations. His friendship and hospitality on my research trips to Oxford were greatly appreciated.

Bibliographical note

A great number and variety of primary and secondary sources have been consulted during the research for this book.

The single most important source for a detailed study of the history of Liverpool Cathedral is the Cathedral's own archive, to which I have been privileged to have had access. Though not open to the public, serious students may apply to search through its many treasures. Among the Cathedral papers are Building Contracts (1904, 1906, 1925, 1950); the Minute Books of the Cathedral Executive Committee; huge numbers of unsorted manuscript letters of Scott, Pittaway and others; and literally hundreds of photographs, among them the Morrison family collection donated by Mr and Mrs Derrick Morrison.

Among the secondary, printed material also held in the Cathedral archive are the following, some of which may also be found in other local and regional libraries:

Liverpool Cathedral: Public Meeting at the Town Hall (Diocese of Liverpool, 1901).

Proposed Cathedral for Liverpool (1903).

Liverpool Cathedral: The Story of the Past, the Need of the Present, the Dream of the Future (Cathedral Committee, 1904).

Liverpool Cathedral: Souvenir of the Laying of the Foundation Stone (Cathedral Committee, 1904).

'The Cathedral Souvenir: Royal Visit to Liverpool' (newspaper supplement, *Liverpool Daily Post and Echo*, published by authority of the Cathedral Committee, 1904).

Rev. Charles Harris, *The Building of the new Liverpool Cathedral* (Cathedral Committee, 1911).

J. B. Lancelot, *Francis James Chavasse* (Basil Blackwell, 1929).

H. Goss Custard, *The Organ of Liverpool Cathedral* (c.1940).

Vere E. Cotton, *The Book of Liverpool Cathedral* (Liverpool University Press, 1964).

F. W. Dillistone, *Charles Raven* (Hodder & Stoughton, 1975).

Joe Riley, *Today's Cathedral* (SPCK, 1978).

Edward H. Patey, *My Liverpool Life* (Mowbray, 1983).

Canon Ken Riley, *Liverpool Cathedral*, pictorial guidebook (1987).

Ian Tracey, *The Organs in Liverpool Cathedral*, (4th edn., 1991).

The Liverpool Cathedral Committee's Bulletin (1925–1978).

Liverpool Cathedral Newsletters (Nos. 1-85).

Liverpool Cathedral Service Sheets, 1904–1991.

Liverpool Cathedral Dean's Journals.

Also important for a study of the Cathedral story are the Chavasse Papers, which include letters, Cathedral papers, newspaper cuttings and sermon notes. They are the property of St. Peter's College and are lodged with the Bodleian Library, Oxford.

The Cotton Papers, consisting of letters and Cathedral papers, are lodged with the Liverpool Record Office.

The Radcliffe Papers, consisting of letters and Cathedral papers, are lodged with the Liverpool Record Office.

In private hands are the following collections: Chavasse family photographs; Scott family photographs; photographs and 16mm film shot by Dr. William Eldridge.

In any historical study concentrated in our own century the memories, recollections and perspectives of individuals are of immense value. I am grateful to the following people whom I have interviewed during the research for this book:

The Very Rev. F. W. Dillistone;
The Very Rev. E. H. Patey;
The Very Rev. D. R. Walters;
The Rev. Canon K. J. Riley;
The late John Rowbottom;
Tom Murphy;
Terry McDonald;
Derrick Morrison;
John Greene;
Geoffrey Rimmer;
Mervyn Roberts;
Noel Rawsthorne;
Ian Tracey;
David Wells;
and Peter Lynan.

Note on the illustrations

Front cover: A pre-war photograph showing the half-complete Cathedral soaring above the Liverpool skyline [Cathedral collection].
Back cover (from top): the Cathedral under construction [Cathedral collection]; John Rowbottom, stonemason, at work [by permission of Studio Photographers, New Ferry]; Liverpool Cathedral at night [P. Kennerley].

The superb line drawings and the illustrated letters at the heads of chapters are the work of Edward Carter Preston – many were used to illustrate service sheets and other Cathedral publications but as far as we know this is the first time so many have been published together. The cartoons for the stained-glass used in the margins have been reproduced from the originals by Peter Kennerley.

The vast majority of the photographs in this book have come from the Cathedral archive. Most were commissioned by the Cathedral authorities during the various stages of construction, and many are the work of the highly talented Stewart Bale. The author and publisher are grateful for the permission of the Dean and Chapter to reproduce so many of these superb illustrations. The following photographs came from private family collections, and are reproduced by permission of the owners: page 15; page 19; page 55; page 93; page 128. The photograph of Bishop Chavasse on page 13 is reproduced by permission of the Bodleian Library, Oxford. The photographs of the consecration service on pages 76 and 77, and the photograph on page 87, are reproduced by permission of *The Times.* The photograph on page 78 is reproduced by permission of Central News. The photograph of the fixing of the final pinnacle on page 149 is reproduced by permission of Joe Marsh. The aerial view on page 177 is reproduced by permission of Airviews (M/cr) Ltd. The photographs on pages 200, 202, 210 and 226 are reproduced by permission of Carl Fox Photography. The photograph on page 219 is reproduced by permission of George Allcock. The photograph on page 222 is reproduced by permission of John Mills, with thanks to the R.L.P.O. The photograph on page 199 is reproduced by permission of *The Liverpool Daily Post and Echo*. Most of the colour plates were commissioned for the Cathedral *Guide* from J. Whitaker and C. Wood. The colour photographs of the High Altar Reredos; the choir stall Liver Bird; the effect of light on stone; the modern stained-glass detail; and the Cathedral by day are by the author. The colour plate of the 1978 Service is by Thomas-Photos, Oxford.

Some of the photographs in the Cathedral collection are of uncertain provenance. Wherever possible we have attempted to trace the copyright owners but, especially in the case of some of the older photographs, this has not always been possible.